The World Explorer Series

# Exploring Church History

## 20 Centuries of Christ's People

# Perry Thomas

PUBLISHING
SINCE 1928

The author gratefully acknowledges permission to reproduce illustrations from the following sources:

Joe Maniscalco, Dos Rios, California (Page 2)

Copyright by David Hugg, Sr. (Page 8)

Courtesy of the Billy Graham Center Museum (BGCM), Wheaton, Illinois (Pages 26, 62, 82, 100, 116, 146, 166, 176, 184, 200, 208, 209, 215, 222, 242, 244, 272)

www,clipart.com (Page 46)

Ginger Duzet, Elgin, Illinois (Page 62)

www,clipart.com (Page134)

Engraved by J.C. Butre. Used with permission from Particular Baptist Press. (Page 186)

Luis Palau Evangelistic Association (Page 263)

Church Growth International (Page 267)


Unless otherwise marked, all Scripture quotations are from *God's Word®*, Copyright ©1995 God's Word to the Nations, Published by Green Key Books. Used by permission.

Scripture quotations marked (NASB) are taken from the *NEW AMERICAN STANDARD BIBLE®*, Copyright © 1960, 1962, 1963, 1968, 1971, 1972, 1973, 1975, 1977, 1995 by The Lockman Foundation. Used by permission. www.Lockman.org

Scripture quotations identified as CEV are taken from the *Contemporary English Version*, Copyright ©1991, 1992, 1995 by American Bible Society. Used by permission.

Acknowledgements and other ancillary copyrights:
World Publishing
Nashville, TN 37214
www.worldpublishing.com


Editor: Terri Hibbard, South Elgin, IL
Cover: Design Corps, Batavia, IL
Text design, layout and illustrations: Linda Eckel, Little River, SC


Printed in the United States of America
ISBN 0-529-11697-9
1 2 3 4 5 6 7 8 9 10/08 07 06 05

# Contents

# JUST HOW LONG IS A CENTURY?

A century—100 years—sounds like a very long time. But is it really?

You are reading this book in the twenty-first century or the 2000s. I started writing it in the twentieth century or the 1900s. My father was born in the 1800s and so was my grandfather (who knew Abraham Lincoln). My grandfather's parents, my own great-grandmother and great-grandfather, were born in the 1700s, when John Adams was second President of the United States of America. That makes four centuries already: the 1700s, the 1800s, the 1900s, and our own 2000s. Multiply that amount of time by five and you have 20 centuries, the amount of time Christ's People have been living on planet earth.

The expression most often used for the story of Christ's People is *church history* or Christian history. Retelling that story year by year, decade by decade, would fill a large library. Even describing Christ's People century by century would make a thick volume. This book starts out exploring church history by looking at the two-thousand-year story of Christ's People in two big blocks of four centuries each. Chapter 1 considers the question: What were Christ's People like at their beginning, 20 centuries ago? Chapter 2 looks at the first 400 years of church history—from A.D. 29 to A.D. 400—while chapter 3 covers the next block of 400 years.

When we get closer to the current day, the rate of change becomes so great that we will need to divide the centuries into smaller segments: For the time period of A.D. 800 to A.D. 1400, each chapter will include two centuries. Then we will halve the block again to only one century per chapter for the 1400s, 1600s, and 1700s. Two pivotal periods in church history—the 1500s and 1800s—are so full of important events that it takes two chapters each to tell their story. The most recent century will be covered in three chapters: one for 1900-1950 and two for the period of 1950 to the present.

## CHRIST'S PEOPLE? CHRISTIANITY? CHURCH?

Why the term *Christ's People* rather than the Church or Christians or some other similar phrase?

Because that is what the book is all about—or rather, that is who it is all about. In the great Syrian metropolis of Antioch 20 centuries ago, people first started using the nickname *"Christ*-ians" for followers of Jesus the Christ. That word means "Christ's people," or "members of Christ's party."

When people speak of the Christian religion in general, or of areas where many Christians live, they sometimes use the word "Christianity" or even the broader word "Christendom". This book makes little use of such terms. Its focus is on *people*—people of every race and place and time, people for whom following Jesus the Christ is the most important thing in life.

Another expression often used to describe all Christians everywhere is *the Church*. Sometimes, for instance, all Christians with European roots are referred to as *the Western Church*. Although this is a book of church history, it makes little use of such expressions, for two good reasons:

- When people see the word *church*, they sometimes think only of a building, a place where Christians gather.

- When people see the word *Church* (with a capital C), they may think of one particular group of Christ's People, such as the Methodist Church or the Roman Catholic Church or the Church of God.

This book is about Christ's People—*all* of Christ's People.

Our experience drives our perspective and expectation. Someone who knew all about Christ's People in the early 1800s would find it hard to recognize them in the 1900s. And someone who knew all about Christ's People in the early 1900s would find it hard to recognize them in 1950. Likewise someone who knew all about Christ's People in 1950 would be utterly amazed at who they are and what they are becoming in the century of the 2000s.

# CHANGES? OR STILL THE SAME?

Yes, the 20-century-long story of Christ's People is full of surprising changes. Highlights of the many twists and turns in church history are reflected in the list of key events at the end of each chapter. Because much of world history has been driven by what Christ's People have done, it seems fitting that the dating system most used throughout the world is A.D. for *Anno Domini* or "the Lord's Year." Since the dates in this book are all after the time of Christ, this abbreviation is used only with dates from A.D. 1 through A.D. 99. (See the adjacent box.)

There is also a different way of looking at the story of these 2000 years. Rather than emphasizing what has changed, one might say that Christ's People have always stayed the same—ever since that time 20 centuries ago when Jesus the Christ said, " . . . I will build my church. And the gates of hell will not overpower it" (Matthew 16:18, *God's Word*™).

Christ's words have been proven true, over and over again. Many times during these past 20 centuries church history has seemed about to come an end and Christ's People have seemed to be fading away. They have forgotten the words and ways of Jesus the Christ. They have acted like ordinary people or even worse. They have been pressured by their enemies, pushed out of their homes, and even persecuted to the point of death.

Many people have predicted that future centuries would find no more Christians anywhere. During the 1900s more enemies tried harder to wipe out more of Christ's People than ever. Yet what actually happened was just the opposite: In the current century more people in more parts of the world are following Jesus the Christ than ever before.

## How We Count Years and Centuries

For at least 15 centuries, most people have been dating events by using the term *Anno Domini*, usually abbreviated A.D. These Latin words mean, "the Lord's Year." Our years and centuries are marked by how long it has been (approximately) since the birth of Jesus the Christ. (People who do not recognize Christ as Lord sometimes use the term *Common Era* or C.E.)

It was five and a half centuries after Jesus' birth when Christ's People first tried to estimate exactly when he had lived on planet earth. While opinions vary, it is generally accepted that their guesses were about four years off. Jesus was about 30 years old when he began his public ministry; this was probably around A.D. 26. It was about three years later when Jesus died on the cross and rose from death. That is why the date of A.D. 29 has been used in this book as the beginning of Christ's People in history.

"Who has determined the course of history from the beginning? I, the Lord, was there first, and I will be there at the end. I am the one!" (Isaiah 41:4).

How is it that a movement starting 20 centuries ago in a tiny corner of the Middle East has now become a worldwide community of faith?

How have Christ's People survived at all, considering all the troubles caused by their enemies and their own failures?

How does it happen that today there are more of Christ's People—many, many more—than there are followers of any other religion?

Possible answers to these questions and many more will be revealed throughout this book. Because of the brevity of this volume some questions will remain unanswered. However *Exploring Church History* approaches this comprehensive topic somewhat differently than other similar books as shown in the chart below.

| Other Books | Exploring Church History |
|---|---|
| • Focus on Christ's People of European origins or backgrounds. | • Expands focus on Christ's People beyond Europe to Asia, Africa, and other continents. |
| • Focus only on Roman Catholic Christians, or Protestant and evangelical Christians, or both. | • Includes Eastern Orthodox Christians and other believers (such as those nicknamed "Nestorians") as well. |
| • Include unrelated dates of events and names of people, groups, and movements. | • Limited to only those names and dates really needed to tell the story. |
| • Emphasize noted men in the history of Christ's People. | • Includes noted women in the history of Christ's People. |
| • Include long, hard-to-understand theological terms (even though titles say "brief," "made easy," or "plain language"). | • Uses everyday words, so that ordinary men and women can easily read and understand the 20-century story of Christ's People. |

You may be surprised by some of the events included in these pages. Or you may wonder how you would have added to the history of Christ's People at various times. Perhaps you'll even help write the sequel to this book. Remember, Christ's People have now been living out His story for 20 centuries . . . and still counting!

# Exploring Church History

## Jesus the Christ

"I am the Alpha and the Omega . . .
who is and who was and who is to come"
(Revelation 1:8 NASB).

# 1. A Tiny Beginning
## (A.D. 29)

Christ's People got their start 20 centuries ago in the Middle East, a small, troubled part of Asia now claimed by Israel, Palestine, and Jordan. No impartial observer of their beginnings could have guessed that they would someday spread all over the world.

When Jesus Christ himself lived on planet earth, he was not a famous person—except for a few short years in that one small geographical area. Actually his name was *Jesus*, a Greek version of the old Hebrew name Joshua, meaning "the LORD Saves" or "Savior." *Christ* is not so much a name as a title that was given to Jesus; it means "Messiah" or "the Anointed One", the great Savior-King that God had been promising for ages past to send to his people on earth. Thus it is more accurate to call him Jesus the Christ.

## HEBREW ROOTS

The Hebrew or Jewish people of the Middle East have played a unique role in world history. In long past centuries most nations worshiped many gods; the Hebrews insisted that God is One. More than that: The Hebrews believed they themselves had a special relationship with God. Led by Moses the Lawgiver, the Hebrews agreed to a special *covenant* or promise: The Lord Almighty would be their God, and they would be God's obedient people. Through many centuries, under the leadership of judges and kings, prophets and priests, the Hebrew people held fast to their ancient beliefs.

Yet the way was not smooth for these special people of God. Again and again they disobeyed God's commandments. Sometimes they began to worship the love goddesses and harvest gods of the other peoples living all around them. When that happened, often they were conquered by their enemies and even carried off to foreign lands as captives. Prophets kept on reminding them: *Worship only the Lord God Almighty!* Written teachings of the prophets, along with stories of earlier centuries and ancient songs of praise to God, were all gradually collected to make up the Hebrew Scriptures that we call the Old Testament.

Many of the Hebrew prophets predicted that God would someday send a *Messiah*, the Anointed One, a great Savior-King. Some of the Hebrew prophets added another prediction: that the Hebrew people themselves would somehow become a blessing, a source of strength and guidance for all other people.

# JESUS THE CHRIST

It was just 20 centuries ago when Jesus, one of the Hebrew people, left his boyhood home in Nazareth to become a traveling teacher. Those who followed him found that he healed their diseases, helped them in their troubles, forgave their sins, and showed them what God is like. These followers came to believe that Jesus was not only the Messiah, the Christ: In some unexplainable way Jesus was God himself, come to earth to lift his followers' heavy burdens and point them toward heaven. One way they described Jesus was "the Word of God"; another more common expression was "the Son of God."

Many people looked at what Jesus did and listened to what he said; not as many followed him. He had only 12 special disciples; their names are now given to boys all over the world: Peter and Andrew, James and John, Matthew and Thomas and all the rest. Jesus the Christ called these 12 his *apostles*, meaning "sent-out ones." And he did send them out: to heal and to help, to tell others how to know and worship God. Later he commissioned 70 people and sent them out with much the same responsibilities. Women such as Mary Magdalene, Joanna, and Susanna were also numbered among Jesus' first followers.

But Jesus himself ran into trouble with two important power structures of his time and place in history: religious leaders and government officials. Leaders of the ancient Hebrew religion accused Jesus of teaching that traditions and rituals were not really important as long as you love God with all your heart and treat other people right. Officials of the Roman Empire became uneasy when people in the streets of old Jerusalem shouted for Jesus as if he were a conquering king. After a rigged trial and a nighttime session of police brutality, Jesus was nailed to two crossed pieces of wood and left to die in agony.

That was on a Friday. Jesus' followers saw his broken body placed in a rocky tomb. Then on the following Sunday the most amazing news began to spread among Christ's People: *Jesus is alive!* Mary Magdalene and several other women were the first to get the word, then Peter and John and Jesus' other disciples. Death could not destroy the power of God that lived in Jesus.

Over a period of six wonderful weeks the resurrected Jesus appeared to his followers again and again— once in the presence of more than 500 people. He helped them understand that his death on the cross was a sacrifice for the forgiveness of sins, like the animals their Hebrew ancestors had been sacrificing on altars for centuries past. He told them to spread the Good News of salvation to all people every- where, thus fulfilling the ancient prophecy that blessing would come to the whole world through the Hebrew people. Then Jesus the Christ went back to his heavenly home with God.

# HOW CHRIST'S PEOPLE BEGAN

Not long after that, Christ's People gathered in an upstairs room in Jerusalem. Some 120 men and women had stayed faithful during all the fearful ups and downs they had experienced since Jesus' trial, death, and resurrec- tion. Then God's Holy Spirit came upon them, as Jesus had promised. They put their fears aside. They found new words and new languages to speak. Rushing out into the narrow, crowded streets they began to share the Good News about Jesus the Christ with everyone they met. Before that day was over their number had increased to 3,000. Not long after that the total topped 5,000.

## Jesus the Christ Teaches About Love

An expert in Moses' Teachings stood up to test Jesus. He asked, "Teacher, what must I do to inherit eternal life?"

Jesus answered him, "What is written in Moses' Teachings? What do you read there?"

He answered, "Love the Lord your God with all your heart, with all your soul, with all your strength, and with all your mind. And love your neighbor as you love yourself."

Jesus told him, "You're right! Do this, and life will be yours."

"But I tell everyone who is listening: Love your enemies. Be kind to those who hate you. Bless those who curse you. Pray for those who insult you."

"Do for other people everything you want them to do for you. If you love those who love you, do you deserve any thanks for that? Even sinners love those who love them."

"Rather, love your enemies, help them, and lend to them without expecting to get anything back. Then you will have a great reward. You will be the children of the Most High God. After all, he is kind to unthankful and evil people. Be merciful as your Father is merciful."

*—Luke 10: 25–28; 6:27–28, 31–32, 35–36.*

Even among those first few thousand believers, there were hints that Christ's followers might someday spread all over the world. Those who heard the Good News on that special day in Jerusalem had come as religious pilgrims from many different places. Many of them became Christ's People. They traveled back to their homes on three continents: Egypt and Libya in Africa, the deserts of Arabia and the valleys of the Tigris and Euphrates rivers in Asia, the Mediterranean island of Crete, and the great city of Rome in Europe.

Now God's Holy Spirit was living in the lives of Christ's People. Yet the future seemed full of dark questions for Christians of 20 centuries ago. In past centuries God's people, the Hebrews, had made many mistakes; they had disobeyed God many times. After all the Jewish people were human beings like everybody else. In much the same way Christ's People might fail to be and to do what Jesus the Christ had taught them by example and command. How could mere weak men and women ever hope to become Christ's People here on earth?

That was not the only question facing Christ's People at that time. Nearly all of them were Jewish, in a world where most people were not. They were a very small group following a brand-new religion (although it had close ties with Judaism, the time-honored religion of the Hebrews). Other religions—most of them far older—commanded the allegiance of far greater numbers of followers.

Their leader, Jesus the Christ himself, had been killed because he had gone against the power structures of his time; officers of the Roman Empire had nailed him to a cross. That same mighty empire ruled the Middle East, most of Europe, and large sections of Asia and Africa. Roman emperors were beginning to be worshiped as if they were gods. What would happen to people who insisted, "There is only one Lord God Almighty, and Jesus the Christ is Son of God and Savior"?

Still more questions: The Roman Empire was only one of the world's great centers of power and civilization 20 centuries ago. To the east stretched the Persian Empire, including what are now Iran, Iraq, Kuwait, and more. Still farther east were India, Japan, China . . . and the great Chinese Empire included as much land and as many people as the Roman Empire did. An ancient religion called Zoroastrianism was the official way of worshiping in Persia. Both Hinduism and Buddhism were strong in India. The emperors of China supported Confucianism. Shintoism was woven into the whole fabric of culture in Japan.

How could Christ's People ever hope to make a dent in the hearts and minds of these great nations in Asia, Africa, and Europe? Who would believe that all people everywhere could trust in Jesus the Christ and in so doing could be saved from their sinful lives and given a home in heaven?

Only the coming centuries would provide the answers to these perplexing questions that faced Jesus' followers at the beginning of their journey.

## The Appian Way

The Apostle Paul walked Roman roads of stone like this
on his missionary journeys.

# 2. Amazing Growth
## (A.D. 29–400)

Suppose some of the early followers of Jesus—Mary Magdalene or Joanna, for instance, or the apostles Peter and John—had fallen into an enchanted sleep early in the first century after his death. Suppose they did not wake up until nearly four centuries later in 400. How would these earliest Christians have described their feelings when they looked at Christ's People 16 centuries ago?

Amazement. Utter amazement.

They would have remembered the believers as a little group of 120 men and women. True, that little group had rapidly grown to more than 5000 believers, . . . but now, Christ's People seemed to be everywhere!

Even more amazing: They would have remembered watching in horror as officers of the Roman Empire killed Jesus the Christ by nailing him to a cross. Now, the cross was a sign of victory waving over Roman armies. And the Christian faith was now the official religion of that great empire!

How did it happen? Why did it happen?

## HOW?

First consider the *how* question. During their first four centuries Christ's People found some advantages to living in the Roman Empire. At sea Roman sailors had done a good job of chasing off pirates. On land Roman soldiers had done a good job of smashing enemy armies—and common bandits. Roman engineers had successfully built harbors and highways; some of those Roman roads such as the Appian Way are still in use even now. Travel by land or sea within the Roman Empire was reasonably safe and relatively easy. Christ's People used those land and sea routes to spread the Good News about Jesus the Christ.

Another answer to the *how* question: Almost anywhere in the Roman Empire many people spoke Greek, the language of learning and culture. When Christians told the story of Jesus in new places, they did not usually need to learn a new language or find a translator, as most Christian missionaries through other centuries have had to do.

Peace and safety, Roman highways and sea routes, a language known almost everywhere—these are some answers to the *how* question.

# WHY?

But *why* did Christ's People increase so quickly over the Roman Empire?

For one thing, the older Roman religions were on the way out. Many people no longer believed in fantastic (and immoral) stories about quarreling gods and goddesses. Many were looking for something better; they were ready to give any new religion a hearing.

A surprising number of non-Jewish people in the Roman Empire had been strongly attracted to the religion of the Jews that featured one God instead of many and also called for clean living. Jewish meeting-places dotted maps throughout the Roman Empire, offering ready-made starting points for telling the Good News about Jesus the Jewish Messiah. Yet, many of the people who came to those synagogues were Jewish sympathizers only; they held back from following all the Jewish customs (such as being circumcised in a religious ritual).

On the other hand, anybody could become a Christian—anyone who turned his or her life over to Jesus the Christ. You did not need to belong to a certain ethnic group or class in society. In the early days some religious people thought that only those who followed Jewish customs could become true Christians, but this idea was quickly dropped. Jew or non-Jew, rich or poor, woman or man, child or adult— anybody could become one of Christ's followers through faith in him.

Not that it was easy to live as a Christian: This new faith held high expectations for its members. They were expected to be kinder and gentler, more honest and stronger, more generous and more loving than anybody else. It was for this very reason that many men and women were attracted to them. As if a better life here on earth were not enough, believers also had the promise of a home in heaven after death.

That was something worth talking about. Everywhere they went, Christians told other people about their Savior. We know well the names of some of those who first shared the Good News such as Peter and Paul and Priscilla and Aquila.

Perhaps no one else had as much to do with the increase of Christianity all over the Roman Empire as a highly educated man named *Paul*. At first he was known as Saul, an enemy of Christ's People. Nothing he learned during his many years of higher education led him to believe that a crucified teacher could be the Messiah, God's great Savior-King. Then he had a miraculous meeting with the risen Christ and everything about him changed including his name. After that nothing could stop Paul—being beaten, stoned, shipwrecked, or threatened with imminent death. When locked in jail, Paul told the jailers the Good News. When he was put on trial before kings and governors, Paul tried to get them to join Christ's People, too.

In Syria, Cyprus, Turkey, Greece, Malta, and Italy (perhaps also in Spain and in present-day Serbia and Croatia), Paul preached the truth of Jesus the Christ. Everywhere he went he left behind groups of new believers. He wrote many letters, telling these new believers who Christ is and what they should become as Christ's People. We know these letters as books in the New Testament.

## Two Testaments, Many Books

Christ's People never stopped using the Hebrew Scriptures. They sang the Psalms; they read ancient accounts of the Hebrews who had a covenant, a special promise-relationship with the Lord God. But they soon realized that there was now a new covenant, available to anyone Jewish or non-Jewish who followed Jesus the Christ.

The first specifically Christian writings were letters sent to new believers. The Apostle Paul wrote thirteen of them; John wrote three, Peter two. Some of these early Christian letters have names on them; others do not. Those who had personally met Jesus also began to put his story into written form. The Apostle Peter told Mark what to write. Matthew and John, like Peter, had been among Jesus' first 12 followers; they wrote what they remembered. Luke, a Greek physician, interviewed many of those who had known Jesus. Tradition and inference suggest he wrote not only the story of Jesus the Christ but also a second volume telling about the first generation of Christ's followers called *The Acts of the Apostles.*

There were many other Christian writings. Some were used by believers in one area but not by believers in another. Little by little Christ's People felt the Holy Spirit telling them which writings were trustworthy, which ones told the Good News in the best possible way.

Gradually they began to call the Hebrew Scriptures *The Old Testament,* meaning the old covenant. The collected Christian writings were called *The New Testament.* And both together were called *The Bible* which means *many books.* To show that these are no ordinary books Christians sometimes use a fuller title, *The Holy Bible.*

Along with Paul we need to remember a man of little education named Peter. He was one of Jesus' first 12 disciples or apostles. He was working as a commercial fisherman when Jesus called him. Warmhearted and quick to speak out, Peter sometimes wished he had known when to keep his mouth shut. He especially remembered with burning shame that dark night when Jesus had been captured by his enemies and Peter had denied him three times, each time stammering something like, "I'm not one of his people. I don't even know who you're talking about!"

After Jesus died and rose from death, he forgave Peter and again commissioned him. Peter became the main speaker on that day known as Pentecost when Christ's People grew in number from 120 to 3,000. In the power of God's Holy Spirit, Peter worked miracles, endured beatings, and bravely spoke out in the presence of those who had killed Jesus. He even took the Good News to a Roman army captain.

The end of life for both Paul and Peter came in Rome, the great capital of the Roman Empire. Ancient traditions say they both died there for their faith. Paul was beheaded—a death with dignity, befitting his honored status as a Roman citizen. Peter, so the story goes, was about to be crucified when he blurted out that he was not worthy to die as Jesus had died. So at his own request he was nailed to the cross with his head downward.

From the very beginning women have played a major role among Christ's People. And they have done so in many different ways.

Dorcas worked quietly. She sewed clothing and then gave it away in Jesus' name to widows and orphans in Joppa (now a part of Tel Aviv), the busy Mediterranean seaport where she lived (Acts 9:36-42).

Lydia was a businesswoman in Greece; she sold the expensive purple-dyed cloth that the rich and famous of her times liked to wear. When she heard the Good News about Jesus the Christ, she offered her large house as a center of activities for Christ's People in her city, Thyatira (Acts 16:13-15).

Priscilla was married to Aquila. They worked together making tents. They opened their home to Paul when he was a traveling Christian teacher and offered him a job in their shop. When another traveling teacher—Apollos—seemed to have heard only a part of the Good News, they took him home with them and tactfully taught him what he needed to know about Christ. As a way of helping to share the gospel among their customers, Priscilla and her husband even closed their business at Corinth in Greece and crossed the sea to set up shop at Ephesus in Turkey (Acts 18:18-26).

But many of those who spread Christ's story never made it into the history books; some people call them *the Nameless Ones*. For instance: We do not know the names of Christ's People who first took the Good

News to such great Syrian cities as Damascus and Antioch or to the areas around Naples and Rome in Italy. (By 300 Antioch was the third largest city in the Roman Empire, with a population of 500 thousand— and half of those were Christians.)

One clever person has remarked that writing church history is like a sports reporter trying to describe a ball game when half the players are invisible.[1] We are not able to see those Nameless Ones, nor can we see all the ways God was at work in human history. But their contribution is evidenced in the growth of Christianity.

The Roman Empire did not know what to do with Christ's People. Because Christians would not worship the emperor as a god, sometimes they were thrown in prison, beaten up, even killed. Because Christians often held their meetings in secret, wild tales about them began to spread. Following the command of their Lord Jesus, believers often ate the Lord's Supper together—broken bread to remind them of his body broken on the cross, red wine to remind them of his blood poured out to forgive sins.

"Aha!" cried their enemies. "In their secret meetings those wicked Christians are eating human flesh and drinking human blood!"

Many of Christ's followers met death bravely; we call them *martyrs*, meaning faithful witnesses. Starting around the year 150, about every 50 years the persecution of Christians in the Roman Empire grew especially fierce. By the early 300s there were more than 18 million Christians in the world, but Roman emperors and lesser government officials may have wiped out as many as 300,000 of them.[2]

Yet, persecution itself helped answer the *why* question about the multiplying of Christ's People. Tertullian (c.150–c.230), a sharp-tongued Christian leader in North Africa, once said, "The blood of the martyrs is seed." Many spectators crowded into Roman arenas to watch Christians being thrown to hungry lions or killed with fire and sword. Many of those same spectators began to ask themselves: *What is this new way of life, that people are even willing to die for it?* So the blood of the martyrs fell to the ground like seed, to bring a bountiful harvest of new believers.

Christ's People in the Roman Empire—like minority groups in societies anywhere—were often blamed for things that were not their fault. In A.D. 64 a terrible fire raged through Rome for six days, destroying 70 percent of the city. Many Romans thought that the Emperor Nero himself had kindled the blaze to make way for his building projects. Nero tried to avoid further criticism by blaming and persecuting the Christians.

Regarding such matters, Tertullian said: "If the River Tiber reaches to the walls, if the River Nile does not rise to the fields, if the sky does not move or the earth does, if there is famine, if there is

## Martyrs—Young and Old, Female and Male

**Perpetua:** As a young mother in North Africa, Perpetua became one of Christ's People. Almost immediately she was thrown into prison.

The Roman governor was actually a kindhearted man. "Have pity on your baby," he urged Perpetua. "Have pity on your old gray-headed father. Honor the emperor as a god."

"I will not," she calmly replied.

After nursing her baby in prison, Perpetua joined other believers in singing a psalm as they walked into the Roman arena. First she was gored on the horns of a wild cow while leopards attacked other Christians. Then when a young, trembling Roman warrior was sent to kill her, Perpetua herself took his sword hand and guided it to her throat.[3]

**Polycarp:** For many years Polycarp had been a Christian leader in western Turkey. In his old age he too was hauled into the arena. Romans accused Christians of being atheists because Christians would not worship the old Roman gods and goddesses. So the Roman governor ordered Bishop Polycarp to say, "Away with the atheists!"

The old man did so ... but not as the governor intended. Instead, Polycarp waved his wrinkled hand toward the thousands gathered in the stadium and groaned, "Away with the atheists!"

The governor tried again. "Curse the Christ, and I'll set you free."

Polycarp shook his white head. "Eighty-six years I have served him, and he has done me no wrong; how, then, can I curse my King who saved me?"

The governor threatened him first with lions, then with fire.

"Your fire will burn but for an hour," said Polycarp. "You do not know about the fires of hell that never go out."

And so old Polycarp died in the fire for the sake of the Christ.[4]

---

plague, the cry is at once: 'The Christians to the lion!' What, all of them to one lion?"[5]

Sometimes Christ's People went out as missionaries, not particularly because they wanted to, but because they were forced to do so. Even in Bible times, when fierce persecution broke out in Jerusalem, Dr. Luke recorded: "The believers who were scattered went from place to place, where they spread the word" (Acts 8:4). And again: "Some of the believers who were scattered by the trouble that broke out following Stephen's death went as far as Phoenicia, Cyprus, and the city of Antioch. They spoke God's Word only to Jewish people." (Acts 11:19).

When Jewish freedom fighters rebelled against the Roman Empire and Jerusalem fell to invading armies in A.D. 70, even more Christians had to flee. And as they scattered, they took with them the Good News about Jesus the Christ.

Persecution in Persia caused Christian refugees to start carrying the gospel across the Arabian desert into areas now known as Yemen, Bahrain, and Qatar. Others sailed to India and strengthened the churches that were already there.

A young Christian from Syria made a long ocean voyage with a friend and the friend's uncle. They were shipwrecked off the coast of Ethiopia; the only survivors were the two young men, who were captured and enslaved. The slaves began to tell their masters the Good News about Jesus the Christ. Soon they were set free, and churches began to spring up in Ethiopia.[6] (In spite of Muslim pressures through the centuries, two-thirds of all Ethiopians are still Christians today.[7])

Above all, the main reason why Christ's People increased all over the Roman Empire and beyond was not because of anything they could be or do in their own strength. "Christ is risen!" the Christians reminded one another when they would meet for worship on the first day of every week. "Christ is alive! Through God's Holy Spirit, Christ lives in each one of us."

A Christian writer once summed it up this way: Christ's People in those early centuries "out-thought, out-lived, and out-died" their enemies in the Roman Empire.[8] A great deal more than just the continent of Europe was included in that vast empire, too. Nowadays it is a little hard to remember that in those early centuries, Christ's People were especially numerous all the way across North Africa, from Egypt in the east to Morocco in the west. They were strong in the Middle East, too; by the year 300 there were Christians in every province of the Roman Empire.

# WHERE?

Where beyond the Roman Empire did the gospel reach?

Strong ancient traditions say that Thomas, one of the original 12 apostles, got all the way to India with the Good News about Jesus the Christ (and perhaps he traveled to Afghanistan as well). Certainly many sailors were following sea routes through the Red Sea and the Indian Ocean in those days, for they had learned how to ride the monsoon winds. About the year 180 a noted Christian scholar and teacher also traveled from Alexandria in Egypt to somewhere in distant India.

The strongest population center of Christ's People outside the Roman Empire was a cluster of cities and villages near the border areas where present-day Turkey, Iran, Iraq, Syria, and Armenia meet. Two small kingdoms in that region became officially Christian even before Rome did. One of those kingdoms—often referred to by the name of its capital city Edessa—is said to have heard the Good News from one of the 70 messengers sent out by Jesus himself. The other country, Armenia in the Caucasus Mountains, still has a strong Christian majority today, even after enduring centuries of Muslim pressure followed by 70 years of Communist rule.

Christians outside the Roman Empire were among the first to translate the New Testament into another language. They were also among the first to set up spiritual retreat centers housing communities of monks and nuns (see box below). And they were the first to worship in a church building rather than in a private home. All over the Middle East, tourists today can still see how Christ's People cleverly built churches into the ruins left by Egyptians, Romans, or whoever: Those early Christians were great recyclers!

One reason why the Christian faith multiplied so quickly in the Persian Empire was that the rulers of Persia at that time were nomads, outsiders without a strong religious tradition of their own. For many Persians, the Good News about Jesus the Christ filled a spiritual vacuum. This idea was expressed in an early hymn (see page 17).

As long as the Roman Empire was persecuting Christ's People, the Persian Empire often served as a safe haven. But when Christianity became the official religion of Rome, things turned around dramatically. At about that same time, new rulers arose in Persia—great shahs who wanted to bring back the ancient glories of Iran . . . including its religion of fire-worshiping Zoroastrianism.

## Founding Mothers and Fathers of the Monastic Movement

**Martin:** One day Martin (c.316-397), a soldier in France, saw a beggar shivering with cold, so he split his cloak with a sword and gave half of it to the beggar. That night in a dream Martin saw the Lord Jesus himself wearing the half-cloak. Soon after that Martin left the army and became a monk. Ultimately he became a famous bishop in Tours, France.

**Antony:** One of the most famous of the early monks was Antony (c.250-356), who lived alone in the Egyptian desert to the great age of 106. But just being alone was no surefire remedy for spiritual slackness.

**Matrona:** An early nun (or female monk) attested to this when she said:

"Many people living secluded lives on the mountain have perished by living like people in the world. It is better to live in a crowd and want to live a solitary life than to live a solitary life but all the time be longing for company."[9]

**Macrina:** As the oldest sister of a large, wealthy family in what is now Turkey, Macrina (c.327-380) cared for her little brothers after their mother died. When her fiancé died, she determined not to marry. Instead, she used her grandmother's estate to support a large charity hospital and to set up one of the first spiritual retreat centers for women.

**Basil:** One of Macrina's brothers, known as Basil the Great (c.330-379), was inspired by her example to start a monastery near his sister's convent. Eventually three of Macrina's brothers became bishops. 🍇

Between the years 340 and 380, some 190,000 Persian Christians died as martyrs. Fires of persecution blazed even hotter in Iran and Iraq than in Rome a few years earlier. Yet, fewer Christians denied their faith in Persia than in Rome. Even a favorite wife of one of the shahs did not escape: When she boldly proclaimed her faith, she was whipped and publicly humiliated. Yet, says the ancient chronicle, "her mouth filled with laughter" as she went to her death.[11]

Acceptance of the Christian message expanded not only in Africa and Asia but also in Europe. Ulfilas (c.311–383), a man nicknamed Little Wolf, told the gospel to the Goths, those warlike European tribal peoples who were threatening to break down the borders of the Empire. (When Ulfilas translated the Bible, he left out all those Old Testament stories about warring kings, lest bloodthirsty Goths get the wrong idea!)

Even with all those bold missionaries and faithful martyrs, Christ's People of 16 centuries ago still had not increased very evenly around the globe. They were relatively strong across southern and central Europe, around the Mediterranean Sea, across northern and northeastern Africa, all across the Middle East (perhaps even as far as Afghanistan), and also in certain parts of India. However there were no Christians in the great empires of China and Japan, in central and southern Africa, in most of northern Europe, and . . . none in other continents yet to be discovered.

# WHAT?

In those early centuries, did all of Christ's People live in peace and harmony with one another? Jesus himself had told them, "Everyone will know that you are my disciples because of your love for each other" (John 13:35). But after all, Christ's People were ordinary men and women, not angels. Almost from the beginning they disagreed with one another.

Many of their disagreements arose over *what* to believe and *what* to do as Christians. Some said that Jesus the Christ was a great teacher but he was not really God in human form; how could God suffer and die? Others said that Jesus was God, all right, but not a real human being. Still others argued over exactly *how* Jesus could be human and God at the same time. And some said that the God described in the ancient Hebrew Scriptures was not the same God who came to this planet in the person of Jesus.

Some said that this whole world is evil—that the only way to follow Christ truly is to turn your back on all the things of everyday life. Some even said that only those who rejected sexual relationships, inside or outside of marriage, could reach the highest standards for Christ's People. These ideas, of course, had a lot to do with the rise of the monastic movement (see pages 16 and 20). The same ideas caused many pastors and church leaders to decide not to get married.

Everybody agreed that Jesus had taught his followers to be baptized and to take the Lord's Supper together. But what did those special ceremonies really mean?

## Symbols of the Christ

Through the years Christ's People have used many symbols. Here are some based on Greek, the language spoken by many of Jesus' first followers.

 These three letters look like the first three letters of the name *Jesus* in Greek. They also stand for three Latin words, *In Hoc Signo,* from the command that the Emperor Constantine said he received while looking at a vision of the cross: *In Hoc Signo Vinces!* or *In This Sign, Conquer!*

 These letters are actually the first two letters of **Christ** in Greek although they look like *X* and *P.*

Christ's People initially used this familiar sign as a somewhat secret code. The Greek word for fish, *ichthus,* has only five letters—as shown in this symbol. These same five letters are also the first letters of five important words: *Iesous* (Jesus) *CHristos* (Christ), *THeou* (God's) *Uios* (Son), *Soter* (Savior).

Baptism involves being dipped into water and coming out again—a dramatic picture of Christ's death and resurrection, as well as a symbol of the Christian's own new life with Christ. But sometimes it was hard for a new believer to be dipped into water. Why not just pour water over the believer's head instead? And if baptism is good for grownups, why not baptize babies?

On the other hand, some people began to believe that baptism washed away their sins. Then what about the bad things you do after you are baptized? Many believers waited to be baptized till they were about to die; one of these was the Emperor Constantine (274-337), the ruler who started the process of making Christianity the official religion of the Roman Empire.

Christ's People in different places held different ideas. Christian customs and ways of worshiping began to develop in varying ways. Yet, most of Christ's People still wanted to stick together. They wanted to follow the true teachings of Jesus the Christ. They wanted to stay on good terms with all of their fellow believers. How could they do this, as they spread over wide areas and their numbers grew into the millions?

Christ's followers of those early centuries tried to remain together in three main ways:

1. They wrote *a clear statement of what they believed.* This brief statement came to be called *The Apostles' Creed,* although it did not really go back to the time of Jesus' 12 apostles. This creed is shown on page 20 along with some explanations and some thoughts that it was intended to correct. Later the Emperor Constantine sponsored a special meeting of Christian leaders at Nicea; a longer statement of belief that came out of that conference is called *The Nicene Creed.* (A brave Christian leader named Athanasius went into exile no less than five times, all because he stood firm for the divinity of Christ as stated in the Nicene Creed.)

2. They also made *a list of holy books* that became known as *The New Testament* (see the box on page 11).

3. They set up *a system of managers or overseers* called *bishops,* with spiritual ties going back to the times of Jesus and his first 12 followers.

Bishops were the pastors of Christ's People, but gradually they became more than pastors. Because most of them were wise and good leaders, other Christians were willing to let their bishops make many important decisions for them. An increasing number of the bishops decided to stay single, so that they could give their full attention to their work without the pull of family ties.

Some bishops felt they should be listened to more than others. The

## What Christ's People Believe (The Apostles' Creed)

I believe in God the Father Almighty, Creator of heaven and earth.

*Some thought that planet earth was evil, and therefore a good God could not have created it.*

I believe in Jesus Christ, his only Son, our Lord.

*Some thought Jesus was not God's Son.*

He was conceived by the power of the Holy Spirit and born of the Virgin Mary.

*Some thought Jesus was not a human.*

He suffered under Pontius Pilate,

*Pilate was the Roman governor when Jesus was killed.*

was crucified, died, and was buried.

*Some thought God's Son could not die.*

He descended to the dead.

On the third day he rose again.

He ascended into heaven, and is seated at the right hand of God the Father.

He will come again to judge the living and the dead.

I believe in the Holy Spirit, the holy catholic church,

*"Catholic" means general or universal, not split up into different parts.*

the communion of saints,

*"Saints" means all of Christ's People, who ought to stay in "communion," or in the same worldwide community.*

the forgiveness of sins, the resurrection of the body, and the life everlasting. Amen.

*[Explanation in italics added]*

bishop of Rome, for instance, wanted everyone to remember that the famous apostles Peter and Paul had been involved with the beginnings of Christianity in his city. In much the same way bishops in the capital of the Persian Empire, a large twin city on both banks of the Tigris a few miles from present-day Baghdad, felt that they should be considered the most important leaders of Christ's People all across Iraq and Iran.

Here's a popular saying from 16 centuries ago: *When the world became Christians, then the Christians became monks.*

The word *monk* means one or alone, like many other words beginning with the letters *mon-* or *mono-*. When being a Christian became the popular thing to do, many serious Christians felt they needed to get away from the world so they could concentrate on Jesus the Christ.

## LIGHTS OR SHADOWS?

When the Emperor Constantine began to stop the Roman persecution of Christ's People in 313, he also began to give special privileges to them. Sunday, the first day of the week, became a legal holiday. Many churches were built with government funds. Bishops became even more important than before; now they could wear rich robes and ride in government-owned chariots.

The Emperor Constantine also made an important change that impacted the future of Christianity: He moved his capital eastward from Rome in Italy to a place near what is now the border between Turkey and Greece. There beside a narrow strait between the Black Sea and the Mediterranean, he built a shining new city and named it Constantinople after himself. (We still call it by the Arabic form of that name: Istanbul.)

Constantine felt it would be easier to rule from his new capital because it was nearer the center of his empire. He left an assistant emperor to help him rule from Rome. But as you might expect, the two centers of the old Roman Empire began to drift apart. Likewise Christians who lived in the two sections began to move apart.

Breaking into two halves was not the only problem facing the Roman Empire. The Goths in Europe, the Persians in Asia, and other fierce tribes all around the borders kept on trying to break through the ring of forts and walls manned by Roman soldiers. Christ's People were now part of the power structure of the Roman Empire; what would happen to them if that empire's defenses broke down?

The stories of two bishops who lived around 16 centuries ago reveal some of the lights and shadows that began to pass over Christians as they became the most favored group in the Roman Empire. Ambrose (c.339–397) was the bishop of Milan, a city in northern Italy. John (c.347–407) was bishop of the new eastern capital city, Constantinople; people called him John Goldenmouth or Chrysostom because he was such a good preacher. Each of these bishops ran on collision course with an empress, the wife of a Roman emperor, with varying results.

At one point the Empress Justina wanted to use a certain church in Milan for a splinter group of Christians who had broken away from other believers. Bishop Ambrose quickly filled the building with Christ's People he could depend on for support; then he led them in singing hymns he had written. The empress decided not to attack a hymn-singing sit-in and recalled the troops she had sent to surround the church.

Another time the Emperor Theodosius ordered his soldiers to murder 7,000 people. When he arrived in Milan, Bishop Ambrose blocked his way at the church door. "You cannot come in here with blood on your hands!" he thundered. The emperor then backed down and tried to make things right.

In the east, Bishop John Goldenmouth had a harder time of it. First he was bishop of Antioch in Syria; then against his will he was made bishop of Constantinople. This was considered to be a highly important position like the bishop of Rome. Just as he had been preaching in

Antioch, John spoke out against Christ's People who wore fancy clothes and fine jewels and cared little for the poor. In this case the Empress Eudoxia did not like to hear such thoughts. She banded together with some of John Chrysostom's enemies and drove him away from Constantinople.

In the western part of the Roman Empire, leaders of the growing Christian movement seemed to be gaining more importance than governmental leaders. Questions arose: *Did Jesus ever teach that his followers should become part of the power structure? Wasn't he himself captured and killed by those who sat in the seats of power?*

In the eastern part of the Roman Empire, government authorities were telling leaders of Christ's People what they could and could not do. *Was this really any better than the situation had been before the Emperor Constantine had started doing away with laws that limited Christians?*

Outside the Roman Empire, such as in Iraq and Iran, believers were learning to their sorrow that changes in kings and kingdoms could make all sorts of trouble for their future.

Looking at Christ's People 16 centuries ago, an observer might see more lights than shadows. From a tiny group in one small area they had become the most powerful group over a large area. They had grown from 120 men and women to many millions.

Yet on the other hand that observer might see more of the shadows. *Were Christ's People really better off because they had become part of the power structure of the Roman Empire? What about other people who hated that power structure and fought against it? What would happen when that power structure finally collapsed?*

There were other shadows too. As Christ's People dispersed, they began to adopt local customs that had little or nothing to do with Jesus the Christ. For example, no one knows for certain what time of year Jesus was born, let alone the exact day or month. For centuries pagan people in Europe had been worshiping the sun god, especially on that day in late December each year when the days gradually began to get longer again. Christ's People selected that same day, December 25, and began to celebrate it as the birthday of Jesus.

In contrast, Christian believers did know that Christ's resurrection should be celebrated on a Sunday in the spring of the year. But the name they began to call that day, Easter, came from the name of a German goddess of springtime and light.

Other ideas also began to cast a shadow over what Christ's People believed and what they did. If a believer feels that he must wait to be baptized until he is about to die (as the Emperor Constantine did), then baptism becomes a kind of magic—a method of washing away all sin through enchantment, rather than a method of remembering Jesus the

Christ who died for our sins. In similar fashion many believers began to feel that there must be something almost magical about the bread and the wine used when observing the Lord's Supper.

Lights and shadows! Both were flickering over the followers of Jesus the Christ in 400. Which would win as Christ's People moved on through the coming centuries?

# KEY EVENTS
ॐ

## A.D. 29 TO 100

Jesus the Christ dies on the cross, rises from death, and commissions his followers to go everywhere, sharing the Good News of salvation.

Christ's People rapidly grow in number from 120 to 3,000 to 5,000 to many more.

Peter, Paul, and many others carry the Good News to all parts of the Roman Empire and even beyond into Asia and Africa.

Paul and others write many letters to help Christ's People follow true Christian beliefs and practices while turning away from false teachings.

Matthew, Mark, Luke, and John write the story of Jesus the Christ; Luke also writes the story of the first generation of Christ's People.

Paul and Peter are executed in Rome; many other Christians also die as martyrs.

Jewish freedom fighters rebel against the Roman Empire; when Jerusalem falls to Roman armies, even more of Christ's People scatter to other areas.

Christ's People completely break away from those who follow the ancient religion of Judaism; Roman persecution increases.

## 100 TO 200

The aged Apostle John dies—the only one of the original 12 who did not become a martyr.

Disagreements increase among Christ's People as to who Jesus really is and how best to follow him; Christian leaders write books and letters to explain and defend their beliefs.

To help maintain their unity, Christ's People begin to set up a system of managers or overseers called bishops.

Christ's followers begin lists of their special holy books, the new ones they are reading and the books of the Old Testament.

The aged Bishop Polycarp and many other Christians die as martyrs.

A noted Christian teacher from Egypt visits Christ's People in India.

Christ's People begin to state their basic beliefs in an early form of the Apostles' Creed.

Tertullian, a North African bishop, says: "The blood of the martyrs is seed."

Christianity spreads throughout most of the Roman Empire.

## 200 TO 300

Christ's People have now translated the Scriptures into seven different languages.

Christians are fiercely persecuted in Egypt and across northern Africa; Perpetua and many others die as martyrs.

Christianity is now in Asia from Syria in the West to India in the East, and from Armenia in the North to the Persian Gulf in the South.

In Rome, the imperial capital city, there are now 30,000 Christians.

Roman rulers again fiercely persecute Christ's People all over the Roman Empire; many die as martyrs.

Christ's People begin to worship in buildings other than homes; many of these churches are recycled from older structures.

Antony and others begin the monastic movement, especially among Christ's People in Egypt and throughout the Middle East.

Antioch in Syria is the third largest city in the Roman Empire; half of its 500,000 inhabitants are now Christians.

Armenia becomes one of the first officially Christian nations in the world.

## 300 TO 400

Christ's People may have numbered 18 million; Roman persecution wipes out perhaps 300,000 of them.

Shipwrecked travelers take the Good News to Ethiopia in Africa.

Christ's People are now in every province of the Roman Empire.

Emperor Constantine stops the persecution of Christians.

Constantine moves his capital from Rome to Constantinople; he presides at a council that adopts the Nicene Creed, clearly stating that Christ is divine.

In the Persian Empire 190,000 Christians die as martyrs.

Ulfilas takes the Good News to the Goths.

Bishop Athanasius goes into exile five times for defending the divinity of Christ.

The monastic movement is strengthened by Basil, Macrina, and others (including Martin, a French soldier turned monk).

Christ's People agree on an official list of books included in the New Testament.

Christianity becomes the official religion of the Roman Empire.

Bishop Ambrose in Italy resists imperial pressures; Bishop John Goldenmouth is driven out of Constantinople by imperial pressures.

**CHARLEMAGNE**

He was crowned Emperor on Christmas Day, 800, by Pope Leo III.
This was a new beginning for Christ's People in Europe.

# 3. LIGHTS AND SHADOWS
## (400-800)

On Christmas Day 800, a stately man kneels in prayer at St. Peter's church in Rome (not the great church that stands there today but an older building on the same spot). The middle-aged man, tall enough to be a modern-day pro basketball center, looks like who he really is: a king. He is Charles (742–814), King of the Franks, known in history books as *Charlemagne*, a word that means "Charles the Great."

As King Charles is about to arise from his prayers, a shorter man walks toward him. He is Leo, bishop of Rome, and in his hands he holds a golden crown. To the tall man's surprise, Leo places the crown on Charles's head.

Probably Bishop Leo signals in some way, for all the other worshipers in St. Peter's Church on that Christmas Day have been coached in advance. Like a well-trained cheering section they shout three times in unison: "To Charles, crowned Augustus by God, to the great peace-making emperor, be long life and victory!"

Who was Charlemagne?

He was the most powerful person in all Europe—ruler not only of the Franks who gave their name to France, but also of areas now known as Germany, Austria, Belgium, the Netherlands, and parts of Spain and Italy. Perhaps no other ruler has ever tried harder to use his power in ways that helped Christ's People.

But why was King Charles attending a Christmas service in Rome? His own capital city lay hundreds of miles to the north, near the border between Germany and Belgium. What was the great King of the Franks doing so far away from home?

Also, why did the bishop of Rome place a crown on Charles's

head? Was he not already a king in his own right? Who gave Bishop Leo the right to arrange another coronation service for the King of the Franks?

The words used by Bishop Leo's cheering section that Christmas Day indicated that Charlemagne was now the new Roman emperor. Why was a ruler from northern Europe being given this ancient title? There was still a Roman emperor reigning over Constantinople in the East, as well as an assistant emperor in Rome itself . . . or was there?

To find the answers to these (and other) questions we need to go back a few centuries in church history.

## NO ROMAN EMPEROR IN ROME?

Was there an emperor in Rome? Or an assistant Roman emperor? Not any more—not really.

The western half of the old Roman Empire had weakened through the centuries. In 410 fierce tribes from the North had stormed into the great imperial city. For three days they sacked nearly everything they saw—everything except the churches of Rome. Why? Because those warlike invaders considered themselves to be Christ's People too!

Men and women all across the empire were in a state of shock. How could it be that the greatest seat of power the world had ever known, that imperial city of shining palaces and temples and stadiums, had been brutally attacked by such uncultured barbarians?

In what is now Algeria, a North African bishop named Augustine (354–430) was one of those most shocked by the bad news about the plundering of Rome. Born to Roman parents, Augustine was rather dark-skinned and probably (like the Basques of Spain or the Berbers of North Africa) descended from some of Europe's earliest settlers.

His mother was a Christian who never stopped praying for him. Augustine made great strides in his studies but looked for pleasure wherever he could find it. By the age of 17 he was keeping a mistress who bore him a son. Disgusted with his own loose lifestyle, Augustine tried to find the meaning of existence in various religions and philosophies. After moving to Northern Italy, he came to know Ambrose the bishop of Milan.

Finally Augustine became a devout follower of Jesus and served for many years as a bishop in Algeria. He also became one of the greatest writers in church history, penning no less than 242 books plus many letters.

Augustine had already done more than anyone before him (some would also say more than anyone who came after him) to explain in detail who Jesus the Christ really is and what it really means to be a Christian. Now in response to such a wrenching crisis in world affairs caused by the sack of Rome, Bishop Augustine took up his pen once again.

He wrote about Rome and a city even greater than Rome. He wrote about God's rule among humankind and ways Christ's People could help make the Lord's Prayer a reality: "Thy kingdom come. Thy will be done in earth, as it is in heaven" (Matthew 6:10, KJV). He said that Christ's People had already become citizens of God's kingdom, yet God's kingdom can never come in its fullness here on earth: That will happen only in heaven.

Augustine entitled his new work *The City of God.* Few books have had a greater impact on human history. It explains how all events are moving toward an ending planned by Almighty God and how God is still in ultimate control of all earthly affairs.

Meanwhile things were worsening in Rome. The last reigning assistant emperor over the western half of the empire was removed from his throne in 476. A so-called imperial court moved to the nearby Italian town of Ravenna, but as a real power in world politics the old Roman Empire was finished. Nearly all of Europe, North Africa, and the Middle East were mired down in conflict and confusion. During those same dark years controversy and persecution also racked Asian centers of Christ's People in and around the Persian Empire.

Out of the wreckage of the old Roman Empire arose a new center of power: the bishops of Rome. All along these church leaders had claimed to be more important than the bishops leading

## The Wisdom of Augustine

One of Augustine's most famous books, *Confessions,* tells about his own struggles with sin. Some consider this to be the first autobiography.

The greatness of Augustine's thoughts can be seen from this striking fact: Since the Reformation five centuries ago, when Protestants broke away from the Roman Catholic Church, these groups have disagreed about many things; yet both look to Augustine's writings for some of their clearest understandings of Christianity.

A familiar thought of Augustine reads, "You have made us for yourself, O Lord, and our hearts are restless until they rest in you. You have put salt in our mouths that we may thirst for you."[1]

Augustine may have also been the first to voice this ancient prayer:

Eternal God, you are the light of minds
    that know you;
    you are the joy of hearts that
    love you;
    you are the strength of wills that
    serve you.

Grant us:
    so to know you that we may truly
    love you;
    so to love you that we may truly
    serve you;
    for in serving you is perfect freedom.[2]

Christian communities in other cities. These Roman bishops felt they were the spiritual heirs of the great apostles Peter and Paul. Now historical events were beginning to give them an even higher profile.

For many years Christ's People had been calling their bishops *papa* meaning *Father*. Gradually this title of love and respect settled in a special way on each bishop of Rome; in English the same word becomes *pope*.

One of the greatest of all the popes was Leo I (c.400–461). Twice he stood up to outside invaders to save his people and his city from utter disaster. In 452 Attila the Hun led his marauding horsemen from what is now Afghanistan and southern Russia into Italy. Some say the Huns, a fierce tribe, had already wiped out 200,000 of the world's 20 million Christians. Yet somehow Pope Leo persuaded Attila not to attack Rome.

Another threat arose only three years later—this time, not by land but by sea. The Vandals were a tribe originally from Scandinavia who had already caused great havoc in North Africa; now they sailed toward Italy. Pope Leo met the Vandal king at the gates of Rome and begged them to spare his city. For two weeks the Vandals treated Rome so roughly that they gave a new word to our language: vandalism. Yet they did not burn the city or massacre all its people. They took only a few hostages for ransom and plundered only a few of the many Roman churches. As a result the Romans felt that their good bishop had saved them once again.

Pope Leo I also showed his power and importance in quite a different way. In 451 Christians from many far-flung places were holding meetings near the capital city of Constantinople to settle a controversy about how Jesus the Christ could be both human and divine. Leo sent them a position paper, and his ideas had a great influence on the final outcome. (His position and two others are explained in the box on page 34.)

Another truly great Christian leader arose a century and a half after Leo I; he was Pope Gregory I (c.540–604). At the time of his election he was a middle-aged monk, and he did not really want to be pope— especially when an epidemic was raging through the city of Rome. Yet Gregory accepted the challenge and accomplished much; in only 14 years as the bishop of Rome he:

- Helped save the city from a hostile takeover.
- Promoted good church music (even today choirs sing "Gregorian chants").
- Reorganized the pastors and congregations in his area including their boundaries, finances, worship services, and calendar of holy days.
- Wrote Bible study guides, manuals on pastoral care, and biographies of great Christians that would be read for centuries.

- Sent out missionaries to Spain and England.

- Used his preaching and diplomatic skills in dealing with many problems.

Led by such great popes as Leo I and Gregory I, the Roman Catholic Church began to take on the shape it would retain for centuries to come. The word *catholic* means *universal* or *general;* these were Christians who lived in many different places, but all of them recognized the special leadership of the bishop of Rome.

Pastors among Roman Catholic believers more and more came to be called *priests.* Over time this term came to carry the idea of a go-between who could connect a person with God. Christians were beginning to lose the feeling that they themselves could go directly to God through Jesus the Christ—confessing their sins and asking for guidance, blessing, and protection.

Roman Catholics placed great importance on the things Christ had taught them to do, such as baptism and the Lord's Supper. Gradually these (and several other religious ceremonies) came to be known as *sacraments,* a word that originally meant a Roman soldier's loyalty oath. More and more these sacraments came to be seen as a means by which a person received God's grace through Jesus the Christ. Roman Catholics began to wonder: *If you have never been baptized, if you do not take part in the Lord's Supper, there is a big question as to whether you are really one of Christ's People.*

During those same centuries of historical development many people came to see the Roman Catholic Church as the only channel through which grace comes down from heaven. They thought: *If you are outside the true Church, then you are outside the grace of God.*

Such sweeping claims were easier to maintain when great Christians such as Leo I and Gregory I were leading the Roman Catholic Church. But not every pope could hope to be as noble or as talented. Leo III, the pope who crowned Charlemagne, was a weak leader who had been ambushed and beaten up by his enemies just the year before. The reason why Charlemagne had come to Rome in the first place was to put this poor Leo back in place as pope.

This brings up another new center of power that had arisen after the fall of the old Roman Empire: the new nation of the *Franks.* On that Christmas Day 800, Charlemagne knew that his Frankish forefathers had already been Christians for more than three centuries. Clovis (c.466–511), the founder of their nation, had followed the advice of his queen (see page 32) in leading his whole tribe to become Christ's People.

It is easy enough to trace the continuing influence of King Clovis across western Europe: Many French kings of later centuries used the

French form of his name, *Louis*. Many German kings after his time used the German form of his name, *Ludwig*.

Yet descendants of Clovis himself were very few by the time Charlemagne's grandfather, Charles Martel, became the king's general. In 732, near the Frankish city of Tours, General Charles Martel—*Charles the Hammer*—won a great battle against enemies of Christ's People. Therefore it is not too surprising that the great general's grandson eventually became the greatest King of the Franks.

# NO ROMAN EMPEROR IN CONSTANTINOPLE?

Roman emperors still reigned in Constantinople for a thousand years after no emperors were left in Rome. History proved that Emperor Constantine, a Christian, had made a wise choice in moving his imperial capital eastward. The eastern half of the old Roman Empire enjoyed many years of glory after the western half had all but disappeared. This eastern realm came to be known as the Byzantine Empire, after Byzantium, an older name for the city of Constantinople.

One of the greatest of all the emperors, east or west, was Justinian (483–565). A staunch Christian, he led his imperial scholars to make a thorough compilation of the many Roman laws; the *Code of Justinian* is still the basis of much civil law today. Emperor Justinian also rebuilt the Church of Holy Wisdom, which after having stood in Constantinople for two hundred years burned down early in his reign. This great church built by Justinian's architects is still standing after 15 centuries (although it subsequently was turned into a Muslim mosque and then into an historical museum).

At this point one might wonder: If there was still a Roman ruler in Constantinople at the time of Pope Leo III, why did he feel the need to crown Charlemagne as emperor in Rome? There is not one simple answer to this question.

Part of the reason was geography, part was politics, and part was religion. The farther away Christ's People got from Constantinople, the less attention they paid to the emperor ruling there. From time to time (as was the case in 800) the person reigning in Constantinople happened to be an empress not an emperor and that made some people respect the Byzantine Empire even less.

The eastern half of the old Roman Empire had not been able to protect the western half from being overrun by many different tribes. One of the most powerful of these people groups turned out to be the Franks. Clearly the ruler of the Franks had become more important even in Rome than the so-called Roman emperor or empress (more properly called the Byzantine emperor or empress) in faraway Constantinople.

There were also religious reasons why Pope Leo III as bishop of Rome distanced himself from the Empress Irene who was then reigning in Constantinople. Christian ways of worshiping continued developing differently in the two halves of the old Roman Empire. The eastern half had been torn apart by many arguments among the Christians. Sometimes the emperor or empress had followed "the right way" (according to the view from Rome), sometimes not. During the time when Charlemagne ruled the Franks, the whole Byzantine Empire had long been caught up in a fierce controversy as to whether or not pictures and statues of Jesus the Christ and his followers should be used in churches.

During the early centuries of Christ's People the bishop of Constantinople had been considered just as important as the bishop of Rome. But when Nestorius (c.381–c.451), a famous preacher and monk from Iraq, was appointed bishop of Constantinople, trouble broke out. It started in what seemed a very innocent way. In one of his Christmas sermons, Bishop Nestorius took note of how important Jesus' mother, the Virgin Mary, was becoming for some Christians. (Many new believers had formerly worshiped goddesses; maybe this had something to do with the special attention they were beginning to give to Mary.)

Here is what Bishop Nestorius actually said: "When I came here, I found a dispute among the members of the church, some of whom were calling the Blessed Virgin Mother of God, while others were calling her Mother of man. Gathering both parties together, I suggested that she should be called Mother of Christ, a term which represented both God and man, as it is used in the gospels."[4]

Unfortunately this honest attempt at peacemaking came to the attention of Cyril (died 444), bishop of Alexandria in Egypt, an irritable man already upset because he was not considered as important as the bishops of Rome or Constantinople. Quickly he seized the opportunity to criticize Bishop Nestorius: "If Mary was not the Mother of God," he thundered, "then this means that what she bore was not divine!"[5]

Misrepresenting the facts, paying huge bribes to imperial officials in order to get his own way, and calling meetings where decisions were made before his opponents had had time to arrive, this dishonest Egyptian bishop soon stirred up much religious controversy. After the troublemaker himself was dead the new bishop who succeeded him turned out to be even worse: He openly paraded through the streets of Alexandria with his mistress beside him.

Angry arguments about exactly how Jesus could be both human and divine spread outside the Byzantine Empire. In Asia this dispute split Christ's People into two warring camps. The fierceness of the conflict and the character of some Christian leaders of those days is revealed in the nicknames given by enemies to some of the bishops who opposed them: the Cat, the Mad Dog, the Wild Boar, the Leper.

For the majority of Christians an official decision was made at the Council of Chalcedon, a meeting held near Constantinople in 451. There were basically three different opinions on the subject of Christ's humanity and divinity, that of Pope Leo I (and others), that of Nestorius (with other Asians), and that of believers in Africa and Syria. A position paper sent by Pope Leo I of Rome had great influence on those attending. Most

| Pope Leo I (and others) | Nestorius (and other Asians) | Christians in Africa & Syria |
| --- | --- | --- |
| Jesus is fully human and fully divine, two natures in one person, "without confusion, without change, without division, without separation." Key Verse: "Christ … being in the form of God, … was made in the likeness of men … and became obedient unto death … every tongue should confess that Jesus Christ is Lord" (Philippians 2:5–8,11, KJV). | If Jesus is not truly human, then how can he be the savior of humankind? Christ the divine person and Christ the human person lived together in Jesus. The human Christ would be destroyed, while the divine Christ would live on. Key Verse: [Jesus said] "Destroy this temple, and in three days I will raise it up.… But he spake of the temple of his body" (John 2:19,21, KJV). | Jesus cannot possibly have two natures; his divine nature swallowed up his human nature "like a drop of wine in the sea." Key verse: "For it pleased the Father that in him [Jesus] should all fitness dwell" (Colossians 1:19, KJV).  |

of Christ's People agreed with Leo in holding to the views shown in the first column in the box on page 34. (In fact most Christians still hold to those same views today, whether they are Roman Catholics, Protestants, or Eastern Orthodox.) But most Christians in Egypt, Ethiopia, and Syria agreed with the views shown in the third column. And most Christians in Persia and elsewhere in Asia followed Nestorius's views shown in the middle column.

Bishop Nestorius never intended to start a new church or denomination among Christ's People; maybe nobody else did either. Yet that is what happened. Those who agreed with Nestorius have been nicknamed *Nestorians* ever since (although they do not like that name). Christ's People in Egypt came to be known as the *Coptic* Church, from an old-fashioned form of the word *Egyptic*. Many of Christ's People in Syria got the nickname *Jacobites* from the name of one of their early leaders (they do not like their nickname either).

## A Martyr in Arabia

In that part of the Middle East now known as Saudi Arabia, sometime in the early 500s an invading army stopped a man along the road. "Are you a Christian?" they demanded.

"Yes," he replied.

"Then hold up your right hand!" He did, and they lopped it off. "Are you still a Christian?"

"Yes," he said.

"Then hold up your other hand!" He did, and they cut it off, too. "Now are you still a Christian?" they jeered.

In a firm voice he cried, "Yes, in life and death I am a Christian!"

So they cut his feet off and left him there to die beside the road.[6]

This split among believers could hardly have come at a worse time. Besides all the troubles Christians were facing in the wreckage of the old Roman Empire, Christians in Asia had fallen onto hard times as well. Throughout those early centuries the words *Persia* and *persecution* often seemed to go together, especially when Persians were warring against so-called Christian enemies. Many of Christ's People in Asia became such brave martyrs or faithful witnesses that those killing them sometimes became believers too. Yet repeated bloodbaths sapped the strength of many Christian communities in Asia.

Now the rise of great controversy gave new reasons for conflict as Christian fought against Christian over how to describe Jesus the Christ. Christ's People began to use the ugly words *heresy* and *heretic*. Heresy originally meant *choice*. A heretic, therefore, is someone who chooses to believe differently from the majority of Christians. How sad when Christ's People begin to decide that there is no room for differences among them!

A present-day church historian has described the result of all the controversy in these striking words: "What should have been a spreading flame bearing light and warmth from the center to the ends of the earth turned instead into a wheel of fire spinning out of control and casting off blazing masses of incendiary counter-movements."[7]

## ANOTHER EVEN BIGGER SPLIT

As if things were not already bad enough, a bigger split soon divided Christ's People in Asia and Africa from those in Europe. The division started in Arabia but rapidly spread to other countries and other continents as well.

Today it is hard to imagine there were once three Christian kingdoms in Arabia. Nevertheless this was the case. Even if for political reasons an Arab king himself might not profess his faith as a Christian, his wife the queen was more than likely to be numbered among Christ's People.

Unfortunately these early Christians of Arabia made two great mistakes: They depended too much on military support from the great Christian kingdom of Ethiopia across the Red Sea in Africa. And they were too slow to translate the Bible into their own Arabic language.

Around 570 a "Christian" army attacked Arab tribes living in and near the desert town of Mecca. An old Bedouin sheikh led his forces to an unexpected victory over the invaders. That same year the old sheikh welcomed a new grandson named Muhammad.

Growing up as he did in Arabia during the late 500s, it is not surprising that Muhammad (570-632) had mixed feelings about Christ's People. Some things he liked about them; some he didn't. Since he and his fellow Arabs had no scriptures in their own language it was easy for strange ideas to creep in (such as the mistaken idea that Christians worshiped a Trinity composed of God the Father, Jesus the Son, and the Virgin Mary).

Besides that, the boy Muhammad must have heard many stories about how his own grandfather, an elderly sheikh, had once led desert warriors in fighting off a foreign army that tried to conquer Mecca. And who were those marauding foreigners? They called themselves Christians.

Like other Arabs before and after him, Muhammad had several wives. One of his favorite wives was a Coptic Christian named Mariya. She was the only wife who bore Muhammad a son that lived past infancy. If little Ibrahim had not died as a toddler, if he had grown up to become Muhammad's successor coached by a Christian mother, how different world history might have been.

Other history books describe in full detail how Muhammad came to feel he had been selected by God as a prophet and spiritual leader, how he urged his neighbors to throw away the many images they had been worshiping in Mecca and turn instead to the one Lord God, how he encouraged them to follow much that Jesus had taught by word and example. Yet Muhammad also spoke out sternly against believing that Jesus was the Son of God or the Savior of the world. Muhammad stressed his belief that God is One and that God has no son.

This new faith came to be known as Islam, a word that means both *peace* and *submission.* Its followers called themselves Muslims, those who claimed to submit to the one Lord God, Allah, and in submitting found peace.

When Muhammad died without direct heirs in 632 his family and followers had some squabbles. Yet they soon pulled together enough to start spreading their newfound faith. They used their military might to force almost all Arabs to become Muslims. Within the same calendar year, Arab horsemen defeated the armies of the two most powerful nations in their part of the world: the Persian Empire and the Byzantine Roman Empire.

Arabs were offered no other choice than to follow Islam. In contrast, non-Arabs were give a choice and often were treated kindly by the conquering Muslims who swarmed out of the desert. Sometimes non-Arabs even greeted Arab armies as liberators. The Persian Empire had from time to time fiercely persecuted Christians; now the power of the persecutor was finally broken. Even though the Byzantine Empire was officially Christian, those who lived inside its borders sometimes suffered because of heavy taxes. And if some of Christ's People were not "the right kind" of Christians, the Byzantine Empire might persecute them too.

Certain history books say that the invading Arab armies of the 600s and 700s gave people only two choices: "Islam or die!" The truth is more complicated because the Muslim approach was subtler than that. Most Christians in areas conquered by Muslims could still go on being Christians but they:

- Paid extra taxes.

- Could not serve in the military.

- Could not be witnesses in court trials.

- Sometimes could not build new churches.

- Sometimes had to wear special marks on their clothing.

- Could not criticize or oppose Muslims in any way.

- Could not try to get Muslims to follow Christ.

Actually some of Christ's People in Asia found they could get along quite well with their conquerors. Under Muslim rule Nestorian Christians almost had a monopoly on the medical profession. Fortunately Christian scholars had translated many ancient Greek writings into languages of Asia. They proceeded to teach the contents of these books to Muslim students. Later on it would be Muslim scholars who would reintroduce ancient Greek learning into western Europe.

Muslim military conquests were breathtaking in their speed. By the mid-600s these fierce horsemen from the desert had already conquered all of the Middle East, much of western Asia, and half of North Africa. By the early 700s they had stretched their boundaries all the way across North Africa and had even swung up into Europe. (An evidence of this conquest is the European use of Arabic names such as *Gibraltar.*) All of what is now Spain and Portugal fell to Arab armies. In 732 General Charles Martel, the grandfather of Charlemagne, led his Frankish troops to fight a horrendous battle which was the only thing that kept France from falling to the Muslims as well. (So both Charlemagne and Muhammad had grandfathers who fought off foreign enemies.)

The policies of Muslim governments took a little longer to grind down the Christian communities in their midst, but in the long run they were just as effective as the cavalry campaigns. Between 600 and 800, Christ's People lost about half of their major centers of population and power. Throughout the Middle East, all along the southern shores of the Mediterranean, and even in southwestern Europe only scattered pockets of Christian resistance still remained.

Thus the Muslims caused a deeper split among Christians than the followers of Christ had managed to cause among themselves with their hairsplitting discussions and mean-spirited disputes. That wide swath of Muslim conquest across the Middle East and the Mediterranean completely cut off Christ's People in Europe from those in Africa and Asia.

Even within Europe itself Muslim armies and navies often made it hard for Christians east and west to stay in contact. This made it even easier for differences to grow between Christ's People in the two halves of the old Roman Empire. In fact Muslim opposition to pictures and statues of God may have influenced the great controversy among Christians in the Byzantine Roman Empire as to whether or not such images should be used in worship.

## WHAT ABOUT THE GOOD NEWS?

All of this sounds pretty bad: Christians becoming Muslims, Christians fighting Muslims, Christians fighting other Christians, cities sacked and burned, kings and soldiers becoming Christians (or not) for political advantage, bishops paying bribes to get their own way, Christian leaders flaunting immoral lifestyles. Did anybody among Christ's People remember who Jesus the Christ really is, or what He did for them, or what He commissioned them to do?

Yes. That is the good news. Even during those tumultuous centuries, many Christian men and women were faithfully "holding forth the word of life" (Philippians 2:16, KJV).

For example there was a scholar named Jerome (c.345–420). He often got into arguments with his famous colleague Augustine, but he also used his great scholarship to a better end than arguing. Jerome moved to a retreat center in Bethlehem, the city where Jesus was born, to find the peace and quiet he needed to finish an important job. By that time Latin had replaced Greek as the language most widely used. Jerome prepared the best and most complete translation of the entire Bible to date. It was written in the common or *vulgar* language; the Vulgate, it was called, because common people could read it. (Jerome could hardly have guessed there would still be religious people using his translation 15 centuries later.)

In Armenia, that small Christian kingdom lying between the Black Sea and the Caspian, a man named Mesrob (354–439) went Jerome one better. First he had to invent an alphabet for the language of Armenia; only then could he work with other scholars to translate the New Testament into Armenian.

Throughout those troubled centuries, more and more of Christ's People took refuge in monasteries and convents. But even these retreat centers were not free of outside disturbance as one monk learned. Born in Damascus and named after one of Jesus' original disciples, Andrew of Crete (660–732) became a monk as a teenager. During a 23-year period in the 600s, his monastery near Jerusalem was raided three times by invading armies: first by the Persians, then by soldiers of the Byzantine Empire, and finally by Arabs.

While still a young man, Andrew became an important church official in Constantinople, the Byzantine capital. Then he was appointed bishop of Crete in the Mediterranean (which explains how he got the rest of his name). One of his duties was to organize the island's defenses against invasion by hostile armies.

Since Andrew of Crete knew so much conflict in his lifetime, it is no surprise that he thought of human life as a battle—not only against outward enemies but against inward foes as well. He expressed his beliefs in many hymns, one of which appears on page 40.

A brother and sister are another two good examples of faithful Christians during difficult times. Benedict and Scholastica were twins born in Italy near Rome. Scholastica founded a convent or spiritual retreat center for women. Her brother Benedict founded a monastery or spiritual retreat center for men. Benedict also compiled a list of rules for monks to follow—rules that kept the best of all that had developed out of the monastic movement while laying aside some of its extremes. Here are two examples of those rules:[9]

> Idleness is enemy of the soul. Therefore the brothers should have specified periods for manual labor as well as for prayerful reading.

> All guests . . . are to be welcomed as Christ, for he himself will say: 'I was a stranger and you welcomed me' [Matthew 25:35].

Benedict's rules became the basis for a large increase in the number, size, and strength of monasteries and convents. During dark and stormy years these Christian retreat centers stood as lighthouses of wisdom and mercy.

A great missionary monk named Abraham of Kaskar (c.491–586) regulated and improved the monastic movement in Asia much the same as Benedict did in Europe. A great Persian bishop named Mar Aba (died 552) reorganized and strengthened Christ's People in Asia similar to what Pope Gregory I did in Europe.

Some of the finest examples of Christian men and women during these times of tumult are the missionaries such as Patrick (c.389–461) for whom St. Patrick's Day is named. Born into a deacon's family in Roman Britain, Patrick was kidnapped as a youth and carried off to pagan

Ireland. While tending pigs there, he came to a personal relationship with the Lord Jesus Christ. Several years later he managed to escape. Yet after coming back home to Britain he could not forget Ireland, and eventually Christ called him back there as a missionary.

After Patrick and others led the way in influencing most of the Irish to become Christ's People, many Irish missionaries moved out to other places. Columba (c.521–597) set up a monastery and missionary training center on the windswept isle of Iona, just off the coast of Scotland. Columba's successors traveled out from Iona with the Good News to Scotland, England, France, Switzerland, and Italy.

Leaders of the Roman Catholic Church, such as Pope Gregory I, sent out other Christian missionaries. One of the greatest of these was Boniface (which means Doer of Good), an Englishman who contributed significantly in bringing Germany to Christ. Named Winfrith at birth (c.680-754), he and his sister Lioba (c.700–782) became missionaries to the continent of Europe in their middle years. One of the stories about Boniface recounts how he challenged the Norse god of war. Christian advance continued through the efforts of other Christians like this brother and sister until virtually every tribe in western Europe decided to become a part of Christ's People.

There was also good news from Africa: Nubia, an area including what is now southern Egypt and northern Sudan, became a strongly Christian kingdom during the 500s.

A little known and often forgotten fact: *Christ's People in Asia did as much or more than Christ's People in Europe to spread the Good News about Jesus the Christ.* This may be because those called Nestorians did

## Power Encounter Under an Oak Tree

Beginning in what are now Belgium and the Netherlands, Winfrith (or Boniface) had little success at first. Then he moved on to Germany, where many pagan tribes worshiped Thor, the Norse god of war. To challenge this god, Winfrith well publicized that he would chop down a holy oak tree that was dedicated to Thor.

As Winfrith began to chop down the sacred oak, German men and women held their breaths expecting him to be struck by a thunderbolt from heaven. But nothing happened except the old oak, rotten at the core, crashed down and broke into four pieces. Winfrith led the awestruck Germans in using the wood to build a chapel.

Winfrith sent for his sister Lioba who persuaded 11 English nuns and monks to join her in Germany. Lioba and the other nuns started schools and hospitals; Winfrith and the other monks preached the gospel while working as farmers.

Forty years later, Winfrith returned along with 50 other Christians to the hardhearted people in Belgium and the Netherlands. There was still little openness to the Good News and Winfrith and his colleagues were martyred for Christ.

much of the outreach and most other Christian groups have known little about them.

Chapter 2 tells of bold Christians who took the Good News to Iraq, Iran, Armenia, India, and perhaps as far as Afghanistan. By 547 there were already believers in Sri Lanka, an island nation off the southern tip of India. Asian Christians even dared to evangelize the fierce Iranian Huns, clan cousins of Attila's hordes that were devastating Europe.

A seminary and missionary training school at Nisibis was one of the greatest centers for Christian advance. Located near the banks of the Tigris in northern Iraq, it started out humbly in an old caravansary on the camel-train route. The students crowded three to a tiny room so they could learn how to better serve their Lord. After the campus was greatly expanded and improved, the number of students reached a thousand or more. Besides its main department of theology, the Nisibis seminary also featured a school of medicine, a clinic, and a working farm.

Three characteristics made this school special:

• Students were taught to dig into the Bible to learn what it actually says (rather than learning fanciful and figurative interpretations).

• Students were held to stiff standards or Christian morality.

• Many students were sent out as missionaries.

Even after changes in religion and politics caused the great Nisibis school to close, its spirit lived on through other schools and monasteries in Asia.

Perhaps the most amazing achievement of Asian Christians during those centuries of conflict was that by 635 they had established a beachhead in the world's largest city—Xian, capital of China! (The ancient imperial city of Xian has become newly famous in recent years as the place where archaeologists have discovered an underground cache of thousands of terra cotta warriors still faithfully guarding the tomb of their emperor.)

Christ's People from western Asia arrived in eastern Asia at an opportune time. Many scholars of Asian history consider the T'ang Dynasty to be The Golden Age of ancient China. The T'ang emperors, of mixed Chinese and Turkish descent, were new rulers open to new ideas. They welcomed Christianity as a friendly rival to Buddhism, Taoism, and Confucianism.

The leader of the first group of missionaries to arrive at Xian in 635 was a monk named Alopen. Later on Christ's People became so numerous and so important that there were even Christian generals in the Chinese army. One of these military leaders had a son, Ching-ching, whose Bible name was Adam. Ching-ching became a bishop and translated several parts of the Bible into Chinese. He also became such a famous scholar of languages and literature that Buddhists came from faraway places to learn from him. (There is even a slight possibility that through Ching-ching's influence a few Christian ideas may have filtered into later forms of Buddhism such as Zen and Nichiren.)

# NEW BEGINNINGS

Thus 12 centuries ago Christ's People had come through hard times with new hopes for the future; they felt new encouragement from new beginnings.

Besides the hope of successful Christian expansion into China, the Christians of Persia were also flourishing under Muslim rule. Timothy I, perhaps the greatest of all the Persian bishops, even dared to hold friendly debates with such great Muslim rulers as Caliph Mahdi and Harun al-Rashid, the famous caliph of *1001 Arabian Nights.*

Once Caliph Harun al-Rashid suddenly turned to Bishop Timothy (c.778–c.823) and asked him, "Tell me briefly which religion is the true one in God's eyes."

How could such a double-edged question be answered? To say "Islam" would be to deny the Christian faith. To say "Christianity" might mean imprisonment . . . or worse.

Bishop Timothy never blinked an eye. Without hesitation he replied: "That religion of which the rules and precepts correspond with the works of God."[10]

Wise Christians also served under the most powerful king in Europe 12 centuries ago: Charles the Great, or Charlemagne. From faraway York in the north of England, the King of the Franks summoned a learned man named Alcuin (c.735–804) to head his palace school and library. Alcuin also revised older translations of the Scriptures and wrote commentaries on the Bible.

Sometimes by force, sometimes by persuasion, Charlemagne brought many Europeans to profess faith in Christ. He made new laws to protect the poor and needy. He insisted that every monastery in his realm offer lessons in reading, writing, and mathematics as well as in music. He sent out royal representatives two by two to check on local officials and make sure that all was being done according to law and justice.

Charlemagne set a high standard for a Christian king. In him many Christians saw realized the ideals of that famous book by Augustine, *The City of God.* Certainly Pope Leo III (died 816) recognized Charlemagne's greatness: That was why he crowned the Frankish king and proclaimed a new beginning of what would later come to be known as the Holy Roman Empire.

Perhaps no other ruler has tried harder than Charlemagne did to use his great power for the good of Christ's People.

But . . . what would happen when Charlemagne was gone? Christians east and west had already learned to their sorrow that while imperial power could be used for their advantage it could also be used against them.

Outside Europe what would happen to Christ's People in Africa and Asia . . . mere Christian islands in a sea of Islam? Could they hold out against continuing Muslim pressure?

An even more worrisome thought: What would happen to that lonely Christian outpost in faraway China? Would it become firmly planted in Chinese soil?

Only the coming years would reveal the answers to these and other questions facing Christ's People of 12 centuries ago.

# KEY EVENTS

## 400 TO 500

In Bethlehem, Jerome completes the best Latin translation yet of the entire Bible.

Invading tribes sack Rome; North African Bishop Augustine writes *The City of God* and many other important books.

Mesrob and others put the Armenian language into writing and then translate the New Testament.

When Nestorius becomes bishop of Constantinople, he arouses controversy over Christian beliefs.

Patrick spreads the Good News in Ireland.

Bishops of Rome emerge as leaders of Christ's People; they begin to be called *papa* or Father (pope).

Attila the Hun and his army wipe out perhaps as many as 200,000 Christians; Pope Leo I saves Rome from attack.

Christ's People are once again fiercely persecuted in Persia.

The Council of Chalcedon defines how Jesus can be both divine and human; Christ's People in Asia and Africa disagree with this definition, resulting in major splits among believers; "Nestorian" Christians emerge.

There are now three Christian kingdoms in Arabia.

The western half of the old Roman Empire comes to an end.

A great seminary and missionary training center begins at Nisibis in Persia.

Queen Clotilde influences Clovis, King of the Franks, to become one of Christ's People.

## 500 TO 600

Christ's People have now translated the Scriptures into 13 different languages.

Irish monasteries become strong centers of learning, spirituality, cultural preservation, and missionary outreach.

Justinian, a great Byzantine (or Eastern Roman) emperor, compiles Roman laws and rebuilds the Church of Holy Wisdom in Constantinople.

Benedict, with the help of his sister Scholastica, brings renewal and reform to the monastic movement in Europe.

In Africa, Nubia becomes a strong Christian kingdom.

Mar Aba brings renewal and reform to "Nestorian" Christians in Asia; Abraham of Kaskar revives the monastic movement among them; Nestorians carry the Good News to many parts of Asia.

Christianity reaches Sri Lanka, the island nation to the south of India.

Columba begins an important missionary training center on the Scottish isle of Iona; Christ's People go out from there to the European continent.

Pope Gregory I sends out missionaries, improves church music, and brings renewal and reform among Roman Catholic Christians.

## 600 TO 700

In England, Queen Bertha influences King Ethelbert to listen to Christian missionaries.

In Arabia, Muhammad announces himself as God's messenger; he starts a new religion, Islam.

After the death of Muhammad, his Muslim followers quickly spread their religion into new areas.

Alopen and other "Nestorian" Christian missionaries begin their work in Xian, capital of the Chinese Empire (then the largest city in the world).

Within the same year, Muslims defeat armies of both the Persian and the Byzantine empires.

Muslim conquests drive a wedge between Christ's People in Europe and those in Africa and Asia; the number of Christ's People in Asia and Africa begins to fall because of Muslim pressures.

Nestorian Christian doctors, lawyers, teachers, merchants, bankers, and high government officials still have great influence under Muslim rulers in Asia.

Roman Catholic Christians and Eastern Orthodox Christians continue to steadily drift apart.

Muslims overpower all of the Middle East and North Africa and prepare to cross over at Gibraltar and attack Europe.

## 700 TO 800

Andrew of Crete defends his island against Muslim attack; he writes a hymn that describes the Christian life as a constant battle.

Winfrith (Boniface) and his sister Lioba become missionaries in Germany, Belgium, and the Netherlands; he dies a martyr.

In a great battle at Tours, the Frankish General Charles Martel halts the Muslim advance into Europe.

Christians in the Byzantine Roman Empire are bitterly divided on whether or not to use *icons* (images) in worship; eventually they decide that icons are valid as visual aids.

Ching-ching (Adam) translates parts of the Bible into Chinese and becomes a great scholar of languages and literature, influencing even Buddhist leaders.

Timothy I, perhaps the greatest of the Persian bishops, holds friendly debates about religion with Muslim caliphs.

Charlemagne, grandson of General Charles Martel, rules the Franks and most of western Europe.

Charlemagne asserts his power to help Christ's People; he forces many Europeans to become Christians (at least in name) and brings Alcuin from England to aid in a Christian revival of learning.

## Otto I
### Emperor of the Holy Roman Empire

# 4. A NEW MILLENNIUM
## (800-1000)

**M**any readers may remember the fears surrounding the change to a new millennium as the year 2000 drew near. There were predictions that every computer in the world would crash at the stroke of midnight on December 31, 1999. Followers of certain religious groups felt sure that the world would come to an end at the moment all four digits on the calendar flipped over simultaneously.

All of those mistaken ideas about Y2K were minor compared to the gathering fears as 1000 approached. Many Christians read the Bible with foreboding: "And when the thousand years are expired, Satan shall be loosed out of his prison, and shall go out to deceive the nations which are in the four quarters of the earth" (Revelation 20:7–8, KJV). They wondered: *What disasters might the powers of evil bring forth in the new millennium?*

Additionally, some Christians were fearful about facing not only the unleashing of Satan but also the end of the world. Imagine St. Peter's in Rome filled with trembling, weeping worshipers, as Pope Sylvester II led a midnight service on December 31, 999. Many of those present stretched full length on the polished marble floor, hardly daring to breathe, closing their eyes in expectation of a sudden blast from the Angel Gabriel's trumpet that would announce the dreaded Judgment Day.

In general, what was the situation for Christ's People as the first Christian millennium came to an end?

Here is a brief summary:

- Christ's People in eastern Asia virtually faded away to nothing.
- Christ's People continued to grow and spread all the way across the vast continent of Europe—northward into the Arctic Circle, eastward to the Ural Mountains that marked Europe's traditional border with Asia.

- Christ's People in the Middle East, western Asia, and southern Asia still held their own against tightening Muslim pressures.

# DISAPPOINTMENT AND DISAPPEARANCE

Since the late 400s, Christ's People had been traveling through some far-flung parts of the Chinese Empire. By 635 Christian missionaries had already reached Xian, the great imperial capital. Soon after that churches and monasteries dotted the Chinese landscape. How could it be that Christ's People in China then faded away to almost nothing during the two centuries between 800 and 1000?

While no one knows for sure, here are several possible explanations:

- The great T'ang Dynasty that had welcomed Christianity to China was no more. The Golden Age of ancient China ended with a long series of weak T'ang emperors. Then the Chinese Empire fell apart as rival warlords battled for power.

- Too many Nestorian Christian leaders were foreigners. Even Ching-ching (or Adam), the famous scholar (see page 42), was a descendent of a minority group on the fringes of the empire. Many other bishops and monks who served in China came from Iran, Iraq, or other parts of Asia—not from China itself.

- These foreign Christian leaders probably tended to use their own languages when preaching or teaching. Very few parts of the Bible were ever translated into Chinese.

- Monks may have been a mixed blessing in China. Unlike in Europe, where Christian monks were often the only literate people, the ancient Chinese were a highly educated people. Also many Chinese were Buddhist monks. Thus being a Christian monk in China gave no special advantage.

Whatever the reasons, when six Christian leaders from the Middle East were sent on a fact-finding mission in 980, they could locate only one Christian in all of China. Probably there were a few more, but the disappointing fact remains that within three centuries Christ's People had all but disappeared in the Far East.

# PERSISTENCE UNDER PRESSURE

We know very little about Christ's People in India ten centuries ago. From what happened later we know they were still there; we just do not have (or have not yet discovered) any records from that period in their history.

The same thing could be said concerning Christ's People in Africa. We know that most Christian communities in areas now called Libya, Tunisia, Algeria, and Morocco vanished under persistent Muslim pressure. In contrast we know that both Ethiopia and Nubia continued to be strongly Christian kingdoms, even though few details are known as to what was really happening there between 800 and 1000.

In some ways the situation for the ancient Coptic Church of Egypt a thousand years ago was much the same as it is today: holding out against strong Muslim pressure. Around 1000 a fanatical teenage ruler (al-Hakim, called "the Crazy Caliph" even by Muslims) burned crosses and either destroyed churches or ordered small mosques built on their flat roofs. Egyptian Christians were required to wear five-pound wooden crosses around their necks; many of them were forced to become Muslims.

Christ's People in Syria, Iraq, and Iran were a little better off than those in Egypt. As markers of their minority status in Muslim society they only had to wear yellow clothes and shirt patches, not heavy crosses. No new churches could be built; no Christian was allowed to appear in the marketplace on Friday, the Muslim day of worship; no Christian school-aged child was allowed to learn Arabic, the language of the Muslims' holy book. Sometimes government officials would launch a period of harsher persecution. But more often they just let Muslim mobs have their way—harassing Christians, razing Christian grave markers to the ground, and looting Christian churches and monasteries.

Throughout the centuries of Christ's People, it has often been said that religious persecution has a purifying effect. Sometimes that has happened, but it was not necessarily so with Christians in western Asia at the close of the first millennium. Instead there were sad signs of decay within. Monks were secretly taking wives, bishops were bribing caliphs in order to discredit other bishops, and one bishop even tried to steal a copy of the Four Gospels (perhaps because its golden cover was studded with jewels).[1]

Saddest of all, those usually called Nestorians seemed to have lost their enthusiasm for spreading the Good News. Would this loss of missionary momentum be permanent? Or would Asian Christians once again become bold witnesses for Christ?

Not everything was dark in western Asia as the first Christian millennium came to an end. At least Christ's People were still there. Many of them held important places in Asian society—doctors, lawyers, merchants, bankers, and even prime ministers under Muslim rulers. A few historical records seem to suggest that the total number of Christians in Iraq, Iran, Syria, and nearby areas might even have grown a bit during those hard centuries of Muslim pressure.

# GOOD NEWS IN EUROPE?

To find some really good news about Christ's People ten centuries ago, we need to turn again to the continent of Europe. More than at any previous time, at this point the future of Christians seemed to be closely linked with the future of the various European tribes and nations.

However at first glance the state of Christ's followers did not look very good. When Charlemagne, that noble Christian ruler, was crowned emperor by the pope in 800, many had hoped that he would make a new beginning, bringing untold benefits to Christ's People in Europe. In spite of his good start, less than 30 years after Charlemagne died his empire split up again into petty warring kingdoms.

Throughout this time, Muslims were still continuing their westward advance; in the year 902 they took control of Sicily. The largest city in Europe at the time was Cordova—perhaps the largest city in the world. This magnificent city was the capital of the Muslim caliphs who held all of Spain and Portugal in their grip. Cordova boasted magnificent palaces, a huge library, city parks, paved and well-lit streets, and good water and sewage systems.

The rest of the European continent was not so fortunate. It was between 800 and 1000 that the feudal system developed in Europe. Ordinary people became serfs, which was little better than being slaves. Serfs could not move from the land where they were born; they had to pay their landlord a portion of their crops. In turn each landlord had to pay his dues to a warlord who might be a king, a duke, or a count. When the warlord went into battle, all of his underlings had to help pay military expenses and also had to equip and lead their own serfs as soldiers.

To escape such bloody and uncertain times, many Europeans took refuge in monasteries and convents. But even these spiritual retreat centers had changed. In a way the monastic movement became a victim of its own success. When people chose to spend their remaining years as monks or nuns, they turned all their property over to the institutions where they would be living. When other Christians died, they left large gifts to monastic centers. Thus some monasteries became immensely rich; sometimes their leaders, called abbots, were so tempted by worldly wealth and power that they began to act about the same way as other landlords (or even warlords) of that era.

How about the head of all Roman Catholics, the bishop of Rome? Gone were the days of such great Christian leaders as Pope Leo I and Pope Gregory I. Now whichever Italian warlord happened to hold physical possession of the city of Rome could force his underlings to choose whomever he wanted to be the pope. So what if somebody else was already the pope. If a warlord had enough troops at his command, he could either kill the pope or run him out of town and then elect a new pope.

During the 800s one mentally unbalanced bishop of Rome had a former pope's body dug up, dressed in princely robes, set on a throne, and brought to trial as a criminal. Between 891 and 955 there were no less than 20 different popes. One rich Italian woman controlled the choice of popes for 60 years: She was the mother of one pope, the murderer of another, and the mistress of a third. When her grandson became pope in 955, he drank a toast to the devil!

As if having leaders no one could respect was not bad enough, Christ's People in Europe were facing an even bigger problem during those years: the Vikings. You perhaps have laughed over the comic strip "Hagar the Horrible." In reality these hardy seafarers from the Scandinavian countries of Sweden, Norway, and Denmark were nothing to laugh about. This is evidenced by what Alcuin, Charlemagne's librarian and school-master, wrote concerning one of the first Viking raids on a noted Christian center:

> Never before has such terror appeared as we have now suffered from a pagan race. Behold, the church . . . splattered with the blood of the priests of God, despoiled of all its ornaments, . . . given as a prey to pagan peoples![2]

Why did Vikings attack churches and monasteries? Because these Christian centers were rich, and the Vikings were poor.

Sometimes there were leaders among Christ's People who managed to fight off these fierce sea-wolves for awhile, such as England's famous King Alfred (849–c.901). (Alfred also translated parts of the Bible into the language of his people.) Eventually the Vikings ravaged the coasts of England, Scotland, Ireland, and almost all the countries on the mainland of Europe including southern European countries around the Mediterranean Sea. They also penetrated the areas now known as Russia, Ukraine, and Belarus—all the way southward to Constantinople, capital of the Byzantine Roman Empire.

Many of these bloodthirsty raiders remained in the new lands they had plundered. And many of them became curious as to why their own gods had previously left them poor, whereas the god of the Christians had let the Christians grow rich. They called this new God *Hvita Kristr* or the "White Christ," in contrast to their own gods who were red with the blood of their enemies.

As more Vikings settled in Europe, more heard the Good News—the message of salvation through Jesus the Christ. But it took awhile for the message of Jesus to spread among these fierce newcomers who now controlled or threatened many parts of Europe.

# CHRISTIANS WEST AND EAST

Before continuing the story of Christ's People in Europe, we need to take note of the fact that European Christians of that period were more and more breaking apart into two different groups. This divide has never been resolved.

History books often speak of this division as being between East and West. To be more exact, at its beginning the split was between Christians of both *western* and *southwestern* Europe on the one hand (Spain, Portugal, France, the British Isles, the Netherlands, Belgium, Germany, Switzerland, and Italy), and Christians of *southeastern* Europe on the other (Greece and nearby areas). Later this first group of Christ's People spread into *northern* and *central* Europe, while the second group spread into *eastern* Europe. The first group became known as the *Roman Catholic Church;* the second group became known as the *Eastern Orthodox Church.*

The main differences between these two groups are shown in the box below. Strangely enough, no one of these main differences actually started the controversy. Instead it was partly a power struggle and partly a disagreement over a single Latin word.

## Catholic or Orthodox—What's the Difference?

|  | Roman Catholic | Eastern Orthodox |
|---|---|---|
| **Name** | *Roman* refers to being led by the pope, the bishop of Rome. *Catholic* means universal or general. | *Eastern* refers to the eastern or Byzantine Roman Empire. *Orthodox* means glorifying God in the right way. |
| **Language** | Latin everywhere. | Mainly Greek, but other languages as well. |
| **Problem** | Humankind broke God's law by falling into sin. | Humankind broke God's image by falling into sin. |
| **Solution** | Christ came to earth and died on the cross to pay the penalty for our sin. | Christ came to earth to restore the image of God in humankind. |
| **Major emphasis** | The death of Christ. | The resurrection of Christ. |
| **Leaders** | Priests remain single. | Pastors married. |
| **Earthly rulers** | Less powerful than the bishop of Rome. | More powerful than any bishops. |

Some of Christ's People in southwestern Europe had become worried that the full divinity of Jesus was not being properly emphasized. To protect against this danger, they had started repeating as part of their creed: "The Holy Spirit comes to us from *both the Father and the Son.*" In Latin this change adds only one word, *filioque,* to the creed, yet that one word caused problems of great proportion.

Christians in southeastern Europe reacted angrily to the revised wording with cries like, "You're tampering with a creed half a millennium old, an ancient statement of beliefs that everybody agreed on!" or "What will you start trying to mess with next?"

In the mid-800s lack of unity reached the boiling point when two powerful bishops disagreed over which of them should hold the greater power. By appointment of the Byzantine emperor, a man named Photius (c.820–c.892) had just replaced Ignatius as bishop of Constantinople, the most important Christian leader in the empire. Meanwhile in Rome, Pope Nicholas I (c.825–867) insisted that he had the right to approve all bishops and that he recognized Ignatius as still being bishop of Constantinople.

The split between the two groups had been growing and widening for many years, but the very public ruckus between Bishop Photius and Pope Nicholas added to it. Through the next two centuries and beyond, Christians on both sides tried repeatedly to patch things up, but the gap continued to widen.

As a matter of fact, this major division continues even to our own day. We have already seen how doctrinal disagreements and Muslim conquests drove a wide wedge between Christ's People in Europe on the one hand and Christ's People in Asia and Africa on the other. Chapters 4 through 6 of this book will divide the history of the church in Europe as two separate stories: the Eastern Orthodox Church and the Roman Catholic Church. Beginning in chapter 7 we will add the stories of many different Protestant and evangelical Christians that emerged during and after the Reformation.

# GOOD NEWS IN THE EAST

For Eastern Orthodox Christians of ten centuries ago, the heart and center of the world was the great city of Constantinople. Even today, though it has been a Muslim city called Istanbul for 550 years, tourists come from around the world to see traces of Constantinople's Christian heritage.

One of these Christian landmarks is the Church of Holy Wisdom, first built by the Emperor Constantine and then rebuilt by the Emperor Justinian. Another famous site was outside Constantinople when it was first established but has long since been enclosed within the walls of the expanding city. This is the Church and Monastery of the Studium. Monks living there became known as *the Sleepless Ones*, because teams of them took turns singing God's praises or kneeling in prayer every hour of the day and night.

Monastic poets of the Studium wrote many great hymns and devotional classics of the Eastern Orthodox Church. One of the most famous monks was Simeon, later nicknamed Simeon the New Theologian (949–1022). Like Augustine before him, Simeon lived only for pleasure until he came into a personal relationship with Jesus the Christ. Even after becoming one of Christ's People in the late 900s, he often argued with other Christians; in fact, he left the Studium because of a quarrel.

Yet Simeon wrote magnificent poetic lines with a strangely modern sound, urging every Christian to experience a personal encounter with God. An example of one of Simeon's devotional classics is located in the adjacent box.

## A Devotional Classic from the Studium

I know that He who is far outside the
   whole creation

   takes me within Himself and
   hides me in His arms,

   and then I find myself outside the
   whole world.

I, a frail, small mortal in the world,

   behold the Creator of the world,
   all of Him, within myself;

   and I know that I shall not die, for
   I am within the Life,

I have the whole of Life springing up
   as a fountain within me.

He is in my heart, He is in heaven:

Both there and here He shows Himself
   to me with equal glory.[3]

           — *Simeon the New Theologian*

Many monks of the Studium suffered and even died as martyrs, mainly because of the long and bitter controversy about whether or not images should be used in worship. These images are often referred to as *icons*—a Greek word.

Those who supported the use of icons in worship finally won the long struggle. Their thoughts went something like this: *If we can't make pictures of Jesus, we tend to forget that the divine Son of God really did become a human being like us. Also, the earthly beauty of the icons turns our minds toward the heavenly beauty of God. They are visual aids to help us worship and learn.*

Within Eastern Orthodox churches anywhere in the world there are many pictures. Some show Jesus or his mother; some show other biblical characters; some show great Christians who lived after Bible times. The purpose of these icons is not to be worshiped as if they were idols. Rather as Eastern Orthodox Christians often say, "Icons are like windows through which we can see God."

Members of the Eastern Orthodox Church place great emphasis on glorifying God through worship, as reflected by the word *Orthodox*, meaning "glorifying God in the right way". Not only do a worshiper's eyes see the beauty of icons: The worshiper's ears also hear glorious unaccompanied singing. Even the worshiper's nose savors sweet incense and the smoke of many candles. All of the senses combine to create an atmosphere of awe and mystery. The magnificent pageantry of an Eastern Orthodox worship service definitely played a part in spreading the Good News about Jesus the Christ.

Among the first Orthodox Christians who went out as missionaries to central Europe were two brothers—Cyril (c.826–869) and Methodius (c.815–885), They grew up in an important family at Thessalonica in northern Greece. Land and sea travel brought many Slavic people from the north to that great Grecian seaport. While the two brothers were getting a good education, they also got acquainted with their Slavic neighbors.

When missionaries were needed to go northward, Cyril and Methodius seemed an obvious choice. Even before they left home, Cyril developed the first Slavic alphabet; this Cyrillic script is still being used today to write Russian and other languages.

After the two brothers reached what is now Slovakia, they told many Slavic people the Good News about Jesus the Christ. It seems likely that Cyril worked with others to translate the entire Bible into the local language. After Cyril died at the early age of 43, Methodius continued their work for many more years—without great success, but paving the way for others to follow. These brothers have since been given the honored nickname Apostles of the Slavs.

During their work among the Slavs, Cyril and Methodius ran into problems with Roman Catholic missionaries. One of the main points of disagreement was what language should be used in worship. Roman Catholics insisted that only the Latin language be used in worship services everywhere as a means of unifying worshipers. Eastern Orthodox missionaries saw an advantage to using whatever language was spoken by those who became a part of Christ's People.

When a king in Slovakia finally decided to follow the Roman Catholic way of worshiping, many Eastern Orthodox Christians took refuge in Bulgaria. Boris, king of the Bulgarians, was baptized as a member of the Eastern Orthodox faith in 864. A strong Slavic Christian movement developed in his kingdom and spread from there to Serbia and other parts of the Balkan Peninsula. These areas in southeastern Europe then became like a bridge extending northward from Constantinople—a bridge for an even greater geographical expansion of Eastern Orthodox Christians.

This expansion eventually included the royal family of the Russ (ancestors of the Russian people, as well as spiritual ancestors of the Russian Orthodox Church). The Russ were descended from Vikings who had come from the north. No one knows for sure how Princess Olga (died 969) first heard the Good News about Jesus the Christ. Before becoming a Christian she was known as a beautiful and capable woman—clever but cruel. After her husband, Prince Igor, had died she ruled the Russ in the name of her young son. It was then that she began thinking seriously about the Christian faith.

An ancient chronicle says that in the mid-900s Princess Olga traveled all the way to Constantinople and was baptized there by the Byzantine Emperor himself. After returning to her home capital city of Kiev, she tried with little success to influence her son to become a Christian.

Things were different with her grandson, Prince Vladimir (died 1015). During his reign over the Russ in the 980s, a delegation of Muslims came to visit him. They flattered Vladimir with comments like, "You are a wise and prudent prince. Yet you have no religion."

Prince Vladimir then began a serious consideration of the various religions being followed by nearby tribes and nations. He turned down the Muslims' offer when he heard they ate no pork and drank no wine. Roman Catholic missionaries encouraged frequent fasting; this had little appeal for a Russ with hearty appetites. When Jewish neighbors came calling, Prince Vladimir challenged them, in effect saying, "How can you hope to teach others, when your God has allowed you to be driven out of your own ancient homeland?"

The turning point came when Vladimir sent special ambassadors to Constantinople. They gave the following report of an Eastern Orthodox worship service held in the great Church of Holy Wisdom:

> We did not know whether we were in heaven or on earth.
> For on earth there is no splendor or beauty greater than
> this, and we are at a loss how to describe it. We only know
> that God dwells there among men. For we cannot forget that
> beauty.[4]

It was not long before Prince Vladimir was baptized as a Christian. More than that: He commanded all of the Russ to be baptized as well. One of the arguments that convinced him to lead all of the Russ to become Eastern Orthodox Christians ran something like this: "If the Greek faith were evil, it would not have been adopted by your grandmother Olga, who was wiser than all of us."

Can thousands of men and women be forced simultaneously to become Christ's People? Not really. Yet history reveals an interesting fact: Often when an entire tribe or nation at least goes through the motions of becoming Christian, this formal action gives the Good News a wider opportunity to work in individual hearts and minds. The coming centuries would show that the Russian people did indeed become some of the staunchest followers of Jesus the Christ.

# GOOD NEWS IN THE WEST

Roman Catholic Christians were strongest in western and southwestern Europe, yet they too carried the Good News toward the East. And as had been the case earlier in England and in France, women often led the way. Here is a general pattern of what would happen in each geographical area:

- The first Christian missionaries often died as martyrs. (The highest spot in Budapest today is Gellert Hill, named after a bishop who was caged inside a barrel studded with nails and then rolled downhill into the Danube.)

- A Christian queen or princess would influence a husband, son, or grandson.

- For a time the whole nation seemed to vacillate between following Christianity and turning away from it.

- A strong king and bishop would work together to finish the job, making the whole nation Christian . . . at least in name.

In what is now the Czech Republic, it was a king rather than a missionary who died as a Christian martyr. Young King Vaclav (c.905–929) was on his way to church when his own brother murdered him. (If you ever sang the familiar Christmas carol "Good King Wenceslas" you were singing about young King Vaclav.) But the anti-Christian reaction in Prague did not last long. Two of the murderer's own children turned against their father: The son eventually became king and built 20 churches, while the daughter married a Polish duke and encouraged him to lead Poland to Christ.

Hungary was a harder case. The Hungarians' ancestors were Magyars, a fierce Turkish-related tribe that swept into Europe from Mongolia. Otto I (912–973), a German king who reclaimed the title of Holy Roman Emperor, stopped the Magyar invasion in a bloody battle near Augsburg. The Magyars then settled in the heart of Europe. Once again, as with several other people groups in Europe, a woman led the way to Christ when a Christian princess from Poland married a Hungarian warlord. In the year 1000 their son Stephen I (968–1038) was crowned as the first Christian king of Hungary; the pope himself sent King Stephen a royal crown.

Further North the Vikings were slow at first to turn to *Hvita Kristr*, their name for Jesus the Christ. The story of Anskar (801–865), a missionary to the Vikings, reveals just how hard it was for these fierce raiders to become Christ's People.

Born in northern France, Anskar was sent to a French monastic school when he was only five years old. As he grew up, he became known as a pious but practical person: Fellow monks often noticed him knitting as he prayed.

When Anskar was still a young man, a civil war in Denmark forced a Danish prince into France. The king of France promised to help the prince take back his throne, but only on condition that he and all of his followers become Christians. The French king also wanted to send a missionary with these newly baptized Vikings. Anskar, ever practical, saw no problem in letting an invading army run interference for the Good News, so he was tapped for the job.

The great plan came to nothing; the exiled prince never set foot in Denmark again. But Anskar did. Three years later, when Swedish merchants invited him to visit their city, he set off at once. Even though North Sea pirates attacked the ship and took all he had, Anskar eagerly landed in Sweden and founded the first church in all of Scandinavia. Later he started two more churches in Denmark; yet none of these Christian beachheads actually amounted to much. Anskar earned his title of honor—The Apostle of the North—not so much for what he did, as for what he tried to do and inspired others to do when conditions became more favorable.

From childhood Anskar's greatest hope had been to die as a martyr. On his deathbed he felt he had failed his Lord. Then God sent him a vision, assuring him that he had indeed been "faithful unto death" (Revelation 2:10, KJV).

Even when Vikings came to Christ, many of them saw him only as a stronger warrior than their old gods, rather than as Prince of Peace and the Savior of the world. This perception was reflected in their art showing Jesus as a conquering king even when nailed to the cross.

Vikings who moved to other countries sometimes turned to Christ sooner than Vikings who stayed in their own Scandinavian homelands. Northern France became known as Normandy, because the North men settled there. Early settlers in Iceland held a great council in the year 1000 and decided—in a relatively peaceful manner—to become Christ's People. In those same years other Viking seafarers were moving on to Greenland and even to North America.

Generally speaking, the journey of the Vikings turning to Christ was a matter of fits and starts, of fire and sword:

- In the mid-900s a king of Denmark was baptized, but then he had to face a revolt among his own subjects.

- In the 990s a king of Sweden announced he was a Christian, but later turned back to his old religion.

- Another king united much of the coast of Norway under the banner of the Cross, but then died fighting pagan enemies in the year 1000.

As the first Christian millennium ended, much was still in doubt between *Hvita Kristr* and the blood-red gods of the Vikings.

In other parts of Europe there was still good news. Women such as Hrotsvit and men such as Theodulph of Orleans were using God-given talents to share the story of Jesus the Christ through drama and song.

The first dramas in church history—in fact, the first dramas of any kind written by anyone in Europe since the 300s—were the brainchild of a talented German nun. A brilliant woman named Hrotsvit (c.940–c.1002) lived in a convent at Gandersheim. *Hrotsvit* may have been only her pen name as it means "Strong Voice" in one of the old languages of Germany. Hrotsvit did all of her writing in Latin and also described herself in that language as "The Strong Voice of Gandersheim."

Hrotsvit was better educated than most women of her times. She studied many ancient works written both by Christians and by famous classical authors of Greece and Rome.

Besides dramas, Hrotsvit wrote long historical poems. Her subjects included Bible stories, heroes and heroines who died as Christian martyrs, and an account of the times in which she lived. One of her most famous dramas tells about the earliest Christian monks in Egypt and about a beautiful but immoral woman named Thais who became a believer. Hrotsvit died just after the turn of the first Christian millennium. More than eight centuries later, her story of *Thais* would be made into a famous French novel and then into an even more famous grand opera.

Theodulph of Orleans (c.760–821) was born in Spain and spent most of his life in France. Although he was a great Christian poet, pastor, bishop, and schoolmaster, none of this did him much good when he was accused of being on the wrong side in a power struggle.

While he was in prison, Theodulph wrote a great hymn describing that famous Sunday when Jesus rode in triumph into the city of Jerusalem. Theodulph showed his own humility by writing (in a stanza no one sings any more) that he and all of Christ's People should be like the little donkey Jesus rode that day, in humbly making themselves available for the Master's use.

According to a beautiful old legend, the king of France heard this hymn being sung on Palm Sunday. He asked who the writer of it was, and then released Theodulph from prison. A portion of this hymn is shown on page 60.

## A Hymn by Theodulph of Orleans

All glory, laud, and honor to You,
Redeemer, King,

to whom the lips of children made
sweet hosannas ring!

You are the King of Israel and David's
royal Son;

You come now in the Lord's name, the
King and blessed One!

The company of angels are praising
You on high,

as we on earth, and all things created,
make reply.

The people of the Hebrews with palms
before You went:

our praise and prayer and anthems
before You we present.

To You, before Your passion, they sang
their hymns of praise;

to You, now high exalted, our melody
we raise.

As You received their praises, accept
the praise we bring;

You take delight in all that's good,
O good and gracious King!

*-tr. John Mason Neale, 1854 (alt.)*[5]

A French duke deeded his favorite hunting ground at Cluny to a group of monks who founded a new monastery. They tried diligently to follow the rules set down by Benedict many centuries earlier. As the years passed, some of these monks moved out from Cluny to start many new-style monastic establishments. Until that time, Benedict's rules had mainly been followed by individual monks and individual monasteries; now for the first time this movement for renewal and reform applied the same rules to all of the new monasteries, thus tying them together into a close fellowship or *monastic order.*

As the millennium drew to a close there seemed to be renewed hope for the sadly abused position of the pope or bishop of Rome. There also seemed to be renewed hope for persons of ability to rise above the feudal system that held nearly all of European society in its grip ten centuries ago.

This chapter began with the story of a worship service at St. Peter's in Rome just as the year 1000 was about to begin. Pope Sylvester II who led that midnight worship service had once been known as Gerbert, the son of a French serf. As a monk, he had found many opportunities for learning and advancement. When he went to study in Spain, he discovered how much knowledge Muslim scholars could share with Christ's People of Europe. He brought this new knowledge back to northern France, where he became the head of a cathedral school.

When Gerbert was made the new pope, he followed a fairly new custom in choosing a new name for himself. Even the name he selected gave hints of future greatness: According to tradition, Pope Sylvester I had been the Christian bishop who had baptized the great Emperor Constantine. Under the wise leadership of Pope Sylvester II, Christ's People of Europe entered the second Christian millennium with renewed hope.

# KEY EVENTS

✌

## 800 TO 900

In Rome, Pope Leo III crowns Charlemagne as the new Roman emperor; many are hopeful of a new beginning for Christ's People.

Viking sea-raiders from Scandinavia begin attacking coastal areas of Europe.

Theodulph of Orleans writes the hymn "All Glory, Laud, and Honor."

Soon after Charlemagne's death, his empire splits up into warring kingdoms; the feudal system arises over most of Europe.

Christ's People in China and North Africa gradually fade away to almost nothing.

Anskar tries (with little success) to spread the Good News among the Vikings.

Pope Nicholas I in Rome and Bishop Photius in Constantinople argue, worsening the divide between Christ's People East and West.

Most "Nestorian" Christians in Asia lose their enthusiasm for spreading the Good News; yet they continue to hold their own against Muslim pressures.

Cyril and Methodius invent written Slavic languages, translate the Scriptures, and try (with little success) to spread the Good News in Slovakia.

Roman Catholic Christians suffer through a series of weak and wicked popes as their leaders.

King Alfred fights off Viking raiders in England and translates parts of the Bible into the language of his people.

## 900 TO 1000

Muslims continue to advance, gaining control of Sicily.

A new monastery at Cluny, France, becomes a model for renewal and reform in the monastic movement.

Simeon the New Theologian writes devotional classics at the Monastery of the Studium near Constantinople.

Vaclav (Wenceslas), youthful king of the Czechs, is murdered on his way to church.

Some of the Vikings begin to follow *Hvita Kristr,* "the White Christ"; others still follow their old gods and goddesses.

Hrotsvit, a nun in Germany, writes the first church dramas.

Princess Olga of the Russ travels to Constantinople and decides to become one of Christ's People.

Otto I, a German king, stops a Magyar invasion of Europe and reclaims the title of Holy Roman Emperor.

King Vaclav's nephew leads the Czechs to become Christ's People.

King Boris leads the Bulgarians to become Christ's People.

Prince Vladimir, grandson of Princess Olga, leads the Russ to become Christ's People.

Almost no Christians are now left in China.

"The Crazy Caliph" persecutes Christ's People in Egypt.

A Norwegian king uses great force to make his people become Christians.

Pope Sylvester II (Gerbert) gains new respect and arouses new hopes as the leader of Roman Catholic Christians.

## BORGUND STAVE CHURCH

Built in 1150 in Norway, this church was modeled
after a pagan temple and dedicated
to the Apostle Paul.

# 5. The Best and Worst of Times
## (1000–1200)

"**I**t was the best of times, it was the worst of times, it was the age of wisdom, it was the age of foolishness."

With these striking words Charles Dickens began his famous novel, *A Tale of Two Cities*. Dickens was writing about France and England of the 1700s. These contradictory statements could also be used as a fitting summary for the years between 1000 and 1200. Certainly Christ's People who were living eight centuries ago experienced both the best of times and the worst of times, both great wisdom and utter foolishness.

As we have explored the first 12 centuries of church history, we have seen a combination of lights and shadows, of good news and bad news. These vivid contrasts continued even more vividly during the next two centuries.

## THE BEST OF TIMES

### The Vikings

During this time Christ's People experienced amazing growth in the cold northern lands of the Vikings. For a time in the early 1000s a Viking king reigned over England, Denmark, and Norway; in all three of those countries he used his power to help spread the Good News about Jesus the Christ. His name was Canute.

Many schoolchildren have read about King Canute (c.995–1035). According to an ancient story he had his throne placed at the edge of the sea to show that even he could not control the tides (in spite of what his flattering courtiers said). If that strange event really happened it would have been in character, for Canute was brought up as one of Christ's People; he knew that supreme power on earth and in heaven rests only with God.

Vikings had settled in a part of France known as Normandy. So when William the Conqueror crossed the English Channel in 1066 and won the Battle of Hastings, it was Viking fighting against Viking, Christian against Christian. Under Norman kings of England, Christ's People continued to grow and spread in that island nation.

King Olaf of Norway tried to bring his people to Christ, but with limited success . . . until after he had died in 1030 fighting his enemies. Not long after that, Norwegian Christians began to honor him as a Christian martyr, calling him *Saint* Olaf. Like Christ himself, King Olaf's influence was stronger and wider after his death.

The people of Sweden were slower to accept Christianity than in other Viking countries. In the city of Uppsala stood a great temple, the center of pagan worship. A historian of the 1000s described the gruesome sacrifices offered there:

> Nine heads are offered from every living creature of the male sex. By the blood of these the gods are appeased. The bodies are hung up in a grove not far from the temple. Dogs and horses may be seen hanging close by human beings; a Christian told me that he had seen 72 bodies hanging together.[1]

King after king, bishop after bishop tried to move against the great pagan temple in Uppsala, but the stubborn Swedes resisted. Yet *Hvita Kristr* finally won the battle in the mid-1100s, . . . and from that time to now, this city has been the heart and center of Christ's People in Sweden.

It was also in the mid-1100s when King Erik IX of Sweden and an English bishop began working together to carry the Good News to Finland. As had happened so many times before, that first bishop died as a martyr. Yet Christianity continued to spread throughout northern Europe, although at first the change often came about only by force.

Christians of Europe kept on spreading eastward as well as northward. In Hungary after good King Stephen died in 1038, some of his people slid back into their old ways, but this revival of paganism did not last long. By the end of the 1100s the way of Christ had won the hearts and minds of most Hungarians.

## The Russ

At the beginning of the second Christian millennium, the Russ (ancestors of today's Russians) had been Christians (in name) for only about

12 years. After the entire nation of the Russ officially became "Christian" by command of their ruler Vladimir, there was much preaching and teaching that needed to be done. During the next two centuries pastors and monks faithfully spread the Good News about Jesus, so more and more of the Russ truly became Christ's People.

During the early 1000s a monk named Antony traveled to Greece so he could learn more about monastic life. Upon returning to his home country he began living in a cave on a hill overlooking the city of Kiev. Many other monks joined him there, until the Monastery of the Caves became the most famous Christian center in what is now Ukraine.

One of Antony's disciples was Theodosius, who lost his father when he was only 13. When the boy began to show Christian compassion by working in the fields alongside serfs and giving away his best clothing to the poor, his mother was horrified. Once he tried to join a group of pilgrims bound for Jerusalem and his mother had him pursued, punished, and dragged back home.

One day when his mother was away, Theodosius ran off to Kiev, where Antony took him in at the Monastery of the Caves. His mother sternly demanded that he return home. Young Theodosius replied, in effect: "If you ever hope to see me again, Mother, you'd better become a nun yourself!"[3] She did.

Eventually Theodosius became the leader, or abbot, of the famous Eastern Orthodox monastery that had been founded by Antony, his spiritual father. Abbot Theodosius was always noted for insisting on humility and poverty as illustrated in the above box.

After Vladimir, the ruler of the Russ who first chose the Eastern Orthodox Church over other ways of worshiping, changes were made. Christian princes of the Russ started many schools, so that their people could learn to read the Bible. They founded many institutions to help the sick, the poor, and the needy. They even ended the death penalty.

In the early 1100s one of Prince Vladimir's descendents ruled the Russ, Prince Vladimir Monomakh. He was a strong Christian layman who gave wise spiritual and practical counsel (see examples, page 66).

## Lessons from Abbot Theodosius

• Once when the monastery cook complained about running short of wood for the kitchen fire, Abbot Theodosius quietly took a hatchet and began chopping up logs. Although he was the abbot, he did not feel he was above doing menial tasks.

• If Abbot Theodosius found that a monk had stored away extra food or clothing, he threw it in the fire. Said he: "It is wrong for us, who are monks and have renounced the world, to collect property in our cells. How can a monk offer God a pure prayer if he has hidden possessions? Are you deaf to the words of our Lord, 'For where your treasure is, there will your heart be also'?"[2]

## The Europeans

Reform of the monastic movement had begun at Cluny in France during the 900s. This surge of renewal continued in the 1000s and 1100s. Christian monks cleared forests and drained swamps; they developed new breeds of cows and sheep; they cultivated types of grain that would grow well in various areas. All of this land-use technology they shared with the communities that grew up around each monastery.

Bernard of Clairvaux (1090–1153), a monastic leader who became one of the best-known Christians, was born into a noble French family. He grew up to be a young man noted for physical beauty, compelling personality, and eloquent speech. At the age of 22 he felt God calling him to become a monk. So great was his influence that a total of 30 men including his father, his brothers, and several of their friends became monks on the same day.

Three years later Bernard was sent out as an abbot with 24 others to start a new monastery. They selected a spot called the Valley of Wormwood, a place overrun with thick forests where robbers lurked. Bernard renamed this place *Clairvaux*, meaning "The Valley of Light." By the hard physical and spiritual labor of Bernard and his fellow monks the valley became a center of life and learning.

A new monastic order grew up all over western Europe under the influence of Bernard of Clairvaux. Before his death in 1153 there were no less than 162 other monasteries related to his; by 1200 there were some 500 of them. When Bernard preached, it is said that mothers hid their sons and wives hid their husbands, lest they be carried away by his eloquence and decide to become monks.

Bernard became a character of international importance. He advised kings and helped settle disputes between them. He influenced the selection of popes. Yet he himself remained a simple abbot devoted to the spiritual life. Some people call him "the father of Christian mysticism," because of his emphasis on a close inner relationship with God.

"The reason for our loving God," Bernard once said, "*is* God. Yet every soul that seeks God . . . has already been anticipated by Him. God sought you before you began to seek God."[5]

Monastic communities made contributions in other ways also. During the 1000s Eastern Orthodox Christians developed a system called "chanting by signs." Russian believers continued to use this way of writing down church music until the 1600s, when they began learning from other European Christians about a better method.

In its earliest form this better method was developed in the early 1000s by Guido d'Arezzo (c.990–1050), an Italian monk who wanted to help choirboys learn music without having to hear it first. He invented a way to write musical notes on four parallel lines with spaces showing where the notes came on the scale.

The pope heard about Guido's invention and asked to see it for himself. Guido described their meeting: "The pope was glad to see me. He leafed through my book and did not move until he had learned to sing a verse which he had not seen before."[6] With the addition of a fifth parallel line and other improvements, Guido d'Arezzo's system of writing music is still used today.

Another contributor to the arts was a multi-talented German abbess named Hildegard (1098–1179). She was the youngest of ten children in a noble Christian family. When she was only eight years old, her parents gave her as a tithe to God placing her in the care of a nun. In adulthood Hildegard and other nuns founded a convent at Bingen on the Rhine where she eventually became its head.

Starting at age 43, Hildegard produced an amazing array of writings and music: biographies of great Christians, books on Christian doctrine and Christian ethics, devotional classics, an encyclopedia of medicine and natural science, hundreds of letters to people from every level of society, the first known morality play, at least 70 songs, and even what is considered by some music scholars to be the first opera ever composed.

In addition, at the age of 60 Hildegard began making preaching

## From the Pen of Hildegard of Bingen

Fire of the Spirit, life of the lives of creatures,

spiral of sanctity, bond of all natures,

goal of charity, lights of clarity,

taste of sweetness to sinners, be with us and hear us.

Composer of all things, light of all the risen,

key of salvation, release from the dark prison,

hope of all unions, scope of chastities,

joy in the glory, strong honor, be with us and hear us.[7]

tours up and down the valley of the Rhine. Kings and popes affirmed her ministry, even when she challenged them toward reform. Other Christians, however, sometimes felt uncomfortable about having a woman in the pulpit. During all of this time Hildegard continued to serve faithfully as abbess, for a total of 43 years.

Hildegard was only one of several women who made outstanding contributions, both in the arts and in the monastic movement between 1000 and 1200. Queen Margaret of Scotland (1046–1093) founded many monasteries and led a strong church reform movement. Princess Anna Comnena (1083–1150), daughter of a Byzantine emperor, wrote the most complete history of her times. During the 1100s an Austrian nun known to us only as Frau Ava ("Mrs. Ava") composed a poetic version of the New Testament. And a saintly French abbess named Heloise (c.1100–c.1173), once the beloved of the controversial Professor Pierre Abelard, later wrote him many eloquent letters of support and wise counsel; she also established several new convents.

Not only did Christians of eight centuries ago experience renewal of the monastic movement: There were also strong movements to reform Christ's People as a whole.

One of the most unusual Christian leaders of that period in history was Pierre Valdes (or Peter Waldo), a wealthy French merchant who became a follower of Jesus the Christ in the 1170s. Like Zacchaeus in Bible times, Valdes gave his riches to the poor. He also had two priests translate parts of the New Testament into the local language, so he could teach the Scriptures to ordinary people.

As he gained followers, he sent them out two by two as Jesus did, preaching from village to town. Both women and men became preachers known as the *Waldenses* or *Waldensians*. These earnest Christians suffered much opposition and persecution; yet they have continued as a distinct group of Christ's People down to the present day. Some people have called this group *Protestants before the Protestant Reformation.*

During the two centuries between 1000 and 1200, the Good News about Jesus was spreading northward and eastward in Europe. Christ's People were making positive changes in human life and society. Many Christians—kings and monks, preachers and teachers, businessmen and missionaries—were setting outstanding examples for others to follow. Was this not the best of times?

# THE WORST OF TIMES

How sad that after the wise and respected Pope Sylvester II died in the year 1003, those who came after him again brought shame and disgrace to Christ's People whom they were supposed to be leading. It was just the same as before: Whoever held physical control of Rome could also control the choice of the next pope. One of the lowest points came when a 12-year-old boy became Pope Benedict IX in 1033. A few years later he decided he was tired of being the pope, so he sold the job to someone else for a thousand pounds of silver.

King Henry III of Germany (who also claimed the title of Holy Roman Emperor) stepped in to clean up the mess in Rome. But then this caused a new problem: Was it really any improvement if the next pope were selected on the basis of military might from Germany, rather than on the basis of military might in Italy?

A remarkable man named Hildebrand (1020–1085) had a lot to do with bringing strength and respectability back to the office of pope. Born into a poor Italian family, Hildebrand received a good education at a monastery in Rome where his uncle was the abbot. Later he traveled to Germany and served as secretary to a bishop there.

Back in Rome again, Hildebrand became the power behind the throne. Over a period of 24 years, under six different popes, he was the heart and brain of a movement for reform and renewal among Roman Catholics. During the 1050s he helped set up the process for selecting popes that has been generally followed ever since.

Certain important bishops were named as *cardinals;* the word originally meant "hinge" because the administration of church business hung on those leading bishops like a door on its hinges. Hildebrand persuaded the pope to start appointing cardinals from places other than just Rome, so that military power over the city would no longer automatically include power to choose the pope. For nine and a half centuries since then, all of the cardinals have gathered each time a new pope is chosen as the leader of Roman Catholics all over the world.

By 1073 Hildebrand himself became pope, with the name of Gregory VII. He kept on trying to improve the situation—this time, by freeing himself and other Christian leaders from too much German influence. One of the most famous scenes of church history took place at the Castle of Canossa in the winter of 1077. For three days Henry IV, the young king of Germany, stood in the snow begging the elderly Gregory VII to receive him and pardon him for challenging the pope's right to appoint bishops.

Hildebrand won that round but lost a later one when King Henry drove him out of Rome. The popes who followed Gregory VII continued the struggle against earthly rulers. No doubt they left their mark on church history; yet, is struggling for earthly power what a leader of Christ's People really should be doing?

Beyond the internal struggles and scandals involving various popes, the divide between Roman Catholics and Eastern Orthodox deepened. By

1054 the pope and the bishop of Constantinople were mutually saying to each other, in effect: "You have no place among Christ's People."

Even as reformers brought needed improvements among Christ's People, some of those same movements for change clearly got out of hand. Arnold of Brescia (c.1090–1155), an abbot in northern Italy, preached against earthly power for popes and bishops. When he was driven out of Italy, he studied for a while with Pierre Abelard, a controversial professor in France. Upon returning to Rome in 1144, Arnold led a revolt against the pope and set himself up as an earthly ruler. A German king helped the pope capture Arnold; he was burned to death, and his ashes were scattered over the waters of the Tiber.

Even more dangerous than Arnold of Brescia and his followers were the *Cathars.* The Greek word *cathar* means "pure"; from it have come such words as *catharsis.* This strange movement started in Greek- and Slavic-speaking areas of southeastern Europe but then spread with strength into Italy and France during the 1100s.

The Cathars were good men and women whose lives of purity and poverty showed up the wealth and easy living that had corrupted many of Christ's People. They claimed to be following the teachings of the New Testament, yet their beliefs were far from Christian. For them God was good and the world was bad; therefore God could not have been the Creator of the world. According to the Cathars, Jesus was an angel with a phantom body; therefore Jesus could not have died on the cross and risen again from death.

By 1200 they numbered tens of thousands in western Europe. So many of them lived around the city of Albi in southern France that they were given the nickname of *Albigenses.*

# AN AGE OF WISDOM

While some who called themselves Christians were straying into power struggles and peculiar systems of belief, other Christians were experiencing a revival of learning.

One of the forefathers of this enlightenment was Anselm (c.1033–1109). He was born in Italy but first became an important Christian leader in Normandy. After the Normans had conquered England, he was called at the age of 60 to cross the English Channel and become archbishop of Canterbury.

Anselm was a good man, a kind teacher who taught that although God cannot be fully understand, God does not contradict clear thinking. He prayed like this, "O God, I do not try to understand You so that I can believe in You. Instead, I believe in You so that I can understand You."[8]

There is a story that an abbot questioned him about what to do with boys in the monastery school who remained naughty even when whipped. Anselm questioned in return: "What if you planted a sapling in a narrow corner so that it was hemmed in on every side? What would be the result of that?"

The abbot shrugged and answered, "A useless, twisted tree."

"That's exactly what you're doing to those boys!" cried Anselm. "You've hemmed them in. Their minds are filled with twisted thoughts because they can see no Christian compassion in you."[9]

One of Anselm's most controversial students was Pierre Abelard (1079–1142). Later as a teacher Abelard challenged his students to think for themselves; one of his books had the interesting title, *Yes and No.* "The first key to wisdom is frequent questioning," said Abelard. "For by doubting we come to inquiry, and by inquiry we arrive at the truth."[10]

Such a free spirit was sure to end up on collision course with the powers that be. All of his life Abelard had to struggle against those who were not as broad-minded as he. One of his fiercest opponents was none other than the saintly Bernard of Clairvaux. In reference to Abelard, Bernard tartly remarked, "The faith of a righteous person does not dispute: it believes."[11]

Yet the revival of learning in Europe could not be bottled up. Several universities or institutions of higher learning began to spring up in Europe during the mid-1100s: at Bologna and Salerno in Italy, at Paris and Toulouse in France, at Oxford and Cambridge in England, at Salamanca in Spain. (Muslims had already founded Al-Azhar University in Cairo almost two centuries earlier.) A favorite university textbook of theology was *Sentences* written by Pierre Lombard (1100–1160), a student of Pierre Abelard.

These early universities were basically groups of teachers and students who banded together to create a little "universe" of their own. They did not meet behind ivy-covered walls on grassy campuses; at first classes were taught in open squares, rented rooms, drafty sheds, or dark halls borrowed from a church or monastery. Students sat on damp, straw-covered floors to hear their professors teach; then they went out to find room and board anywhere they could. With no library, no lab, no dorm, no stadium, it was easy enough to move a university if some of the rowdier students caused problems among the locals!

The education of the average Christian of eight centuries ago was much different. Most European men and women of that period could neither read nor write; how could they learn anything beyond plowing and planting, harvesting and threshing?

Educated Christians did not forget about ordinary men and women. They reasoned: *Even non-readers have ears; they can hear music being sung and played in praise of Almighty God.* By the 1100s many organs were adding their thunderous tones to Christian worship.

Non-readers also had eyes. During the 1100s Christ's People throughout western Europe began to erect great Gothic cathedrals as visual aids to help ordinary folks worship and learn. Builders discovered how to put roof supports on the outside, so that inside the building a worshiper's eyes could soar upward like a soul seeking God. Standing 45 stories high (only a little lower than the Washington Monument), Strasbourg Cathedral was the tallest structure in Europe until the Eiffel Tower was built in the late 1800s. Many other cathedrals also rose like huge fingers pointing toward heaven.

The great airy spaces inside a Gothic cathedral were not left empty. Countless pictures, statues, and stained-glass windows showed biblical characters and stories from the Scriptures. "Paintings are the Bible for ordinary worshipers," an Italian monk once said.[12] A French peasant of the same period confirmed his words when she confessed: "I am a poor old woman who knows nothing, who cannot read. But in the church I see Paradise painted, and Hell where the damned broil."[13]

Towering cathedrals were not the only kinds of worship centers being built in Europe eight centuries ago. Round, whitewashed church buildings with dunce-cap roofs were erected on the islands of Denmark. Tall wooden stave churches, modeled after older pagan temples, dotted the countryside in northern lands where the fierce Vikings had finally become Christ's People (see page 62).

Christians of this period also used church drama to tell the Good News. There were:

- Morality plays much like parables, acting out virtues such as temperance or truth and vices such as gluttony or greed.

- Mystery plays dramatizing familiar stories from the Old and New Testaments.

- Miracle plays retelling stories about past Christians who were considered to be saints (some from Bible times, but more from later centuries).

This interest in saintly Christians of the past took strange forms. Some people began praying to saints (instead of to God) or asking the saints to pray for them. Some people began to think they had discovered something that had once belonged to a saint, or even a part of a saint's body; these *relics*, as they were called, became almost like objects of worship.

This concern with the human and the physical in worship eventually changed the way people felt about their faith. More and more people began to believe that the crucified body of Christ was actually present in the broken bread and red wine used in the Lord's Supper. More and more they began to feel that since the Virgin Mary was Jesus' mother, surely she could exert some influence over her Son; therefore, more and more prayers began being addressed to Mary.

Many Christians felt they could lead holier lives if they could only make a pilgrimage to the Holy Land, the setting for the events described in the Bible, or to places where saintly Christians had once lived. Ivetta of Huy (1157–1228) was a teenage widow in Belgium who opened her home as a hostel to help Christian pilgrims along their way. Her family wanted her to get married again, but instead she left her children in the care of her father.

Because of a power struggle with the king of England, an archbishop named Thomas à Becket (1117–1170) was murdered in Canterbury Cathedral at the end of 1170. By 1173 Thomas was already considered a saint and streams of pilgrims were riding or trudging toward Canterbury.

Pilgrimages may have begun as a way to help people act out their faith and to learn by doing. Yet pilgrimages also had an important connection with the sad fact that many events in the first two centuries of the second millennium were not just an age of wisdom: They were also quite the opposite.

# AN AGE OF FOOLISHNESS

A major event of this period of history has intentionally not been mentioned until now: the Crusades. Much good from these centuries can be overlooked by letting the Crusades cast their shadow over the late 1000s and throughout the 1100s into the 1200s.

For many years nearly everything taught or written about the Crusades was favorable. More recently both lessons and books have turned strongly in the opposite direction: They have presented nearly everything about the Crusades in an unfavorable light.

The truth lies somewhere in between. Taking a broad view of human history, it must be admitted that the Crusades were acts of monumental foolishness and cruelty. They brought disaster and dishonor upon many of those claiming to be Christ's People and great harm to other religious groups. The shame and strained relations they caused still trouble Christians today.

Admittedly in the beginning there were indeed some good reasons why Christians of western Europe would travel to the Middle East and attack Muslims who were living there. While *Arab* Muslims controlled places such as Jerusalem, Bethlehem, and Nazareth, Christian pilgrims were welcome. Arab innkeepers and tour guides in The Holy Land were happy to accept money from Christian as well as from Muslims.

Things changed drastically when *Turkish* Muslims took over the Middle East. The beginning of change was as early as 1009, when "the Crazy Caliph" tore down an ancient church built on the traditional site of Jesus' crucifixion, burial, and resurrection. The church was later rebuilt, but then Seljuk Turks began ruling the Middle East. These fanatical Muslims began making it unsafe if not impossible for Christian pilgrims to worship at the holy sites.

So the Crusades, or "cross war" (two words in the Indonesian language translate the one word "Crusades") began as an effort to free the Holy Land from Muslim control. The Crusaders believed they were rescuing this geographic area where Jesus died on the cross, so they wore crosses on their clothing.

The actual story of the Crusades can be quickly told. Many history books divide it into the First Crusade, the Second Crusade, and so on, but in reality it was all one long running battle. Starting in 1096, hundreds of thousands of European warriors, priests, and ordinary people—including women and children—traveled southward through Europe and eastward across the Mediterranean Sea. They attacked their foes with good success at first, because the Muslims were militarily weak and divided among themselves. By 1099 the Crusaders had captured Jerusalem, where they slaughtered everybody they could find.

For nearly a century European warrior-kings and their followers held a narrow strip of territory along the eastern end of the Mediterranean. In the later 1100s a Kurdish general known as Saladin united the Muslims, proclaimed a *jihad* or holy war, and drove the Crusaders out of all their holdings except a few coastal cities. There the Crusaders hung on for another century; then even these were lost.

Nearly all of the Crusaders were Roman Catholics. To them any other kind of Christian was almost as far from the truth as were the Muslims themselves. Many innocent Christians were massacred along with their Muslim neighbors when Crusaders took over in the Middle East.

Taking a broad view of geography and military history, the Crusades were only a small portion of the long-lasting conflict between Christians and Muslims. After two centuries of warfare, everything was pretty much back to the way it was . . . but countless thousands of Christians and Muslims had died along the way.

This period can be summed up with one good thing that *actually* came out of the Crusades, two more good things that *could* have come out of them, and three bad things that *did* come out of them.

**The one good thing that *actually* came out of the Crusades:**

1. *The Crusaders brought much good knowledge back to Europe.*
   As the surviving Crusaders straggled back home, they brought
   many new products, processes, and ideas. They savored the
   tastes of sugar and coffee, apricots and ginger. They found out
   about algebra and almanacs, about zero and other numbers
   that could replace cumbersome Roman numerals. They saw
   distant lands only dreamed of before; they learned more about
   maps and ships and all the other things they needed in order
   to develop a broader outlook on the world.

**The two good things that *could* have come out of the Crusades:**

1. *The split between Roman Catholics and Eastern Orthodox might
   have been patched up.* In the early 1090s the Byzantine emperor
   in Constantinople asked the help of Christians from western
   Europe in winning back the Holy Land from the Turks.
   Unfortunately the partnership did not go well.

2. *There could have been an end to the infighting of so-called
   Christians in Europe.* One reason why Pope Urban II (c.1042–1099)
   proclaimed the First Crusade in 1095 was that he despaired of
   any other way of getting various religious groups to quit fighting
   among themselves. But the disagreements continued.

**The three bad things that really *did* come out of the Crusades:**

1. *The Crusades permanently wrecked any hopes of reunion between
   Roman Catholics and Eastern Orthodox.* When the Eastern
   Orthodox emperor in Constantinople asked for help from western
   Europe, he got more than he bargained for. He did not expect the
   Crusaders to demand that he replenish their supplies. Nor did he
   expect them to set up their own kingdoms in the Middle East.

   Communications broke down and relationships worsened. Then
   just after the year 1200, an incredibly bad event occurred:
   Crusaders stormed the great Christian city of Constantinople.
   For three days they raged through its streets. They stripped
   the Church of Holy Wisdom of its gold and jewels. They let a
   prostitute dance on its altar, singing bawdy tunes. They raped
   and killed Christians . . . all in the name of Christ.

   Not only did this shameful act permanently poison the atmosphere
   between these two groups: It also struck a mortal blow to the
   Byzantine Empire. Constantinople remained a Christian city for
   another 250 years, but it never quite recovered from being so
   grievously injured by those who should have been friends and
   brothers in Christ.

2. *The Crusades drew lines in blood between Christians and Muslims.* Americans and Europeans tend to think of the Crusades as long ago; the Crusaders have long slept beneath their monuments and grave markers in quiet churches and cathedrals of western Europe. Yet to Muslims it seems like yesterday. The negative image that the Crusaders gave to Christianity has never been erased from minds and memories all over the Muslim world.

Even today the word *crusade* has a strongly negative connotation to Muslims. They do not think of it as a noble endeavor or a campaign to accomplish something good in the face of difficulty or danger. Instead they remember the bloodshed and slaughter. Throughout the Muslim world Christians know not to use terms like *evangelistic crusade* because of the negative impression that this very word can give.

When European and American soldiers gathered at the Persian Gulf to rescue Kuwait from aggression in 1991, their Iraqi enemies tried to smear their reputation with other Muslims by calling them "the new Crusaders." This happened even though the foreign minister of Iraq at that very time was a Christian rather than a Muslim.

3. *The Crusades lowered the entire moral temperature of Christ's People.* No doubt there were sincere men and women who joined the Crusades because of worthy motives, but more people joined the Crusades for personal gain. Besides the hope of plunder along the way and newly conquered lands at journey's end, Crusaders were given strange promises by those who should have been their spiritual leaders. They were told things like, "Go fight for the holy cross and all your sins will be forgiven!" This meant that human beings were "offering bargains" for something which in reality can only be offered by Almighty God; such offers of special pardon came to be known as *indulgences.*

Little wonder that many Crusaders strayed off the noble path they had taken. Along the way many of them treated Jewish people so cruelly that Jews sometimes committed suicide when they saw Crusaders coming. Those who bore the sign of the cross ruthlessly pillaged many towns and villages along the their route. When Jerusalem was conquered in 1099, the Crusaders killed so many people that blood flowed in the streets up to their knees. Crusaders even sacked the great Christian city of Constantinople.

One of the strongest of all indicators as to how badly the Crusades corrupted the moral health of Christ's People was that many great and noble Christian leaders urged fellow believers to become Crusaders. Even the likes of saintly Bernard of Clairvaux persuaded some to join this foolish cause.

# BEYOND EUROPE

This chapter began with a list of opposites, which were then applied to the story of those who called themselves Christians in Europe eight centuries ago. All of those same contradictory statements could also be made in telling the story of Christ's People in Asia and Africa during the same years.

This was a period of great turmoil all over both continents. Old empires were breaking up; new ones were forming, only to be dissolved again and then to reappear in a different shape.

Here is a brief review of several groups of Christ's People in Africa and Asia during the years between 1000 and 1200:

## Africa

In the mountains of the Horn of Africa, Christ's People hewed 11 churches out of solid rock. Nine centuries later thousands of worshipers still come to those ancient churches for religious ceremonies.

Christ's People to the south of Egypt were doing well enough. So were the Coptic Christians of Egypt itself—once they got rid of "the Crazy Caliph" in the year 1021. (A small sect in the Middle East, the *Druze*, still expects this unbalanced ruler to return as the leader of all true Muslims.)

## Western and Southern Asia

There were three communities of Christ's People in Syria at this time: Eastern Orthodox Christians related to the Byzantine Empire, breakaway Eastern Orthodox Christians nicknamed Jacobites, and so-called Nestorian Christians. All three groups were at least holding their own against Muslim pressures.

In southern India Christ's People were regarded as a respected and prosperous community. Yet more and more they were becoming just another caste in a rigid society, cut off from any meaningful opportunity to share their faith with others. These believers were the spiritual descendants of the Apostle Thomas, one of Christ's original 12 disciples, and so they came to be known as Thomas Christians.

## Central Asia

Some of the greatest battles were being fought in Central Asia during those turbulent centuries. Various ethnic groups and ways of worshiping struggled to get the upper hand. For instance one major Central Asian tribe, the Uighurs, changed from following Christianity mixed with two non-Christian religions, to following Christianity mixed with Buddhism; still later, almost all of them became Muslims!

Islam was the greatest rival to Christianity in this region. It spread eastward along the Great Silk Road toward China and southward as conquering armies began to invade India. Christian missionaries were also following those same old routes. Those known as Nestorians had recovered much of their former enthusiasm for spreading the Good News about Jesus. Most of these Nestorian missionaries were no longer monks but rather merchants.

The Keraits were a powerful Turkish-Mongolian tribe that roamed the river valleys near Lake Baikal, in what is now southern Russia and northern Mongolia. In the year 1009 their prince and 200,000 of his followers were all baptized as Nestorians. In later years of exploring church history, more will be heard about Nestorian Christians among the Keraits.

Of all the tribes during those centuries in Central Asia, the fiercest and most famous were the Seljuk Turks. They, too, may have been Nestorian Christians at first. Their earliest known leader was Seljuk, the man who gave his name to the tribe. By ancient tradition Seljuk had sons named Mika'il and Musa (Michael and Moses), and a grandson named Dawud (David). Bible names such as these were often used by Christ's People in Central Asia.

Eventually the Seljuk Turks became Muslims. They aggressively swept out of their ancient homelands and conquered much of the areas now known as western China, northern India, Pakistan, Afghanistan, Iran, Iraq, and Armenia. In 1071 the Seljuk Turks even captured the Byzantine emperor, routed his army, and seized vast amounts of his territory. This conquest is how the huge peninsula jutting out from Asia toward Europe got its present-day name: Turkey, land of the Turks. The once-proud Byzantine Empire shrunk to a small area surrounding its capital Constantinople.

As already mentioned, these conquests were one of the major triggers of the Crusades. When Christians tried to make their pilgrimages to the Holy Land, the Turks did not welcome them as the Arabs had. The Crusades were a severe form of retaliation.

The Christians of Asia were generally more advanced in medicine, science, art, and literature than those who had just arrived from Europe. Because the Roman Catholic Crusaders did not regard the Asian Christians as true believers, they were often as harsh in their treatment of these believers as they were of Muslims. Asian Christians did not feel any great improvement in their situation when they had to change Muslim masters for European masters.

In spite of everything, a significant portion of Christ's People in Asia still held on eight centuries ago. John Mason Neale, a famous church historian, remarked that around the year 1200, the great and powerful Pope Innocent III in Rome probably did not command the allegiance of many more Christians than did the chief bishop of the Nestorian Christians in Asia.[14] Census numbers are not available but according to highly educated guesses of church history scholars, by 1200 Christ's People had grown to more than 18 percent of the world's population, or 50 million out of a total of 270 million. Almost a fourth (12 million) of those calling themselves Christians were known as Nestorians.[15]

A Christian believer at this time may well have wondered:

• What will the coming centuries bring to Christ's People—in Asia, in Africa, in Europe?

• Will the next age be the best of times or the worst of times for Christians?

• Will the coming centuries be marked by wisdom or by foolishness?

# KEY EVENTS

## 1000 TO 1100

Stephen becomes the first Christian king of Hungary.

Icelandic Vikings peacefully become Christians; the Viking King Canute tries to help Christ's People in England, Denmark, and Norway.

In Central Asia, some 200,000 Keraits become Christ's People.

Even after dying in battle, the Viking King Olaf still influences many Norwegians to become Christ's People.

Christians among the Russ and in Italy develop separate methods for writing down church music.

The pope in Rome and the main bishop in Constantinople mutually excommunicate each other.

Christian rulers positively impact Russ society; Antony and Theodosius lead the Eastern Orthodox monastic movement.

Norman French Vikings replace other Vikings as rulers of England.

Seljuk Turks (whose founder seems to have been a Nestorian Christian) bring a harsher form of Islam to the Middle East.

Hildebrand brings new strength and respect to the office of pope; later he becomes Pope Gregory VII.

Queen Margaret founds new monasteries and leads church reform in Scotland.

Anselm, a great teacher in France, becomes archbishop of Canterbury in England.

Pope Urban II proclaims the First Crusade; Crusaders capture Jerusalem and large areas of the Middle East.

## 1100 TO 1200

Vladimir Monomakh, Christian Prince of the Russ, writes good advice for his sons.

Bernard of Clairvaux becomes an outstanding leader of the monastic movement in Europe.

Pierre Abelard becomes a noted but controversial Christian teacher.

Arnold of Brescia leads a revolt against Roman Catholic rulers.

Pierre Lombard, a pupil of Abelard, writes a theology textbook used in new European universities.

Hildegard of Bingen preaches and writes on many subjects, including music and plays to help ordinary people understand Christian teachings.

The pagan temple at Uppsala, Sweden is torn down; the Good News also begins to spread in Finland.

Anna Comnena, daughter of a Byzantine emperor, writes the history of her times.

European Christians build Gothic cathedrals with statues, paintings, and stained-glass windows to teach the Bible to illiterates.

Archbishop Thomas à Becket is murdered; many Christians begin pilgrimages to Canterbury and other places.

Pierre Valdes gives away his wealth and starts the Waldenses.

In Belgium, Ivetta of Huy helps pilgrims and lepers; in Germany, "Frau Ava" writes a poetic version of the New Testament.

Saladin drives Crusaders out of most of the Middle East.

The Cathars, a Christian look-alike movement, become especially strong in France.

## Francis of Assisi (1181–1226)

Perhaps more than anyone else, he tried to live a simple life
in imitation of Jesus the Christ.

# 6. What Might Have Been
## (1200-1400)

"**O**f all sad words of tongue or pen,
The saddest are these: 'It might have been.'"

The American poet John Greenleaf Whittier (a devout Christian, by the way) wrote those familiar lines from "Maud Miller" in 1854.

Whittier's haunting words seem to reverberate as we continue to explore church history in the 1200s and 1300s. Not that those two centuries were a sad time—rather, much that even now brings joy and hope to Christ's People had its beginnings during that period. Yet it was also a time of lost opportunities. Again and again we find ourselves facing such questions as: "What if . . .? What might have been?"

Perhaps the most momentous of all those "might-have-beens" among Christ's People six centuries ago was acted out on the stage of history in the vast continent of Asia.

## MONGOLS—FRIENDS OR FOES?

The very word *Mongol* sends a shiver down the spine of anyone who knows much about the history of Christianity. Knights in armor from so-called "Christian" countries were no match for fast-moving Mongol horsemen. Most church history books speak of the invasion of "the Mongol Horde" or "the Golden Horde" as being a terrible disaster for Christ's People.

In many ways this was true as the Mongols did indeed sweep out of Central Asia bringing death and destruction to many Christians on the continent of Europe, especially eastern Europe. Yet this rise of the

Mongols also brought unprecedented opportunities for Christ's People on the much larger continent of Asia. How did this come about?

Chapter 5 told about the Keraits, a Central Asian tribe who became Christ's People in the early 1000s. They were among many Asians whose way of worshiping has been nicknamed Nestorian. During the late 1100s, the Nestorian chief of the Keraits befriended a young Mongol prince who had to take over for his father at the early age of 13. That teenage warrior grew up to be Genghis Khan (c.1167–1227), fearsome leader of the Mongol Horde. Genghis himself was no Christian, either in word or in deed; yet he never got completely away from Christian influences.

Genghis took Christian wives for himself and his sons. The most notable of these was Princess Sorhatani (died 1252), niece of the Kerait chief who had taken the young Mongol under his wing. Sorhatani, a sincere and strong-minded believer, became the wife of Tolui, fourth son of Genghis Khan. In due time she also became the devoutly Christian mother of three mighty kings: a Great Khan of the Mongols, a lesser Khan of the Persians, and greatest of all the world-renowned Kublai Khan (c.1215–1294), emperor of China.

Another sign of Christian influence on the Mongols was evidenced in Genghis Khan's written law that includes this important sentence: "All people are to believe in one God, Creator of heaven and earth."[1] This sounds like an echo of the Ten Commandments or perhaps the Apostles' Creed. The Mongol "constitution" then goes on to forbid adultery and to free all priests—Christian, Buddhist, whoever—from taxation.

During the 1200s and 1300s most of the Mongol rulers were remarkably tolerant toward those who followed various ways of worshiping. Yes, the Mongols were fierce and cruel; yes, they slaughtered many of their enemies; yet they hardly ever tried to force anyone to practice (or stop practicing) a certain religion.

After sweeping conquests, various members of the Mongol royal family became the rulers of nearly all Asia, with each of them owing supreme allegiance to the Great Khan as their overlord. This meant that for about 150 years there was a measure of peace and stability all over Asia. Travel across Asia was easier than it had been for many years; the Great Silk Road and other land routes were generally open and protected from harm. Thus the situation throughout the world's largest continent during the 1200s and 1300s was similar to when Rome had ruled around the Mediterranean Sea, a situation that had greatly helped the early spread of Christianity.

Besides these two *positive* ways the Mongol conquest helped Christ's People, there was also a *negative* way it benefited them: During the mid-1200s, the Mongols came close to wiping out the power of Muslim rulers throughout Asia. Under the leadership of the three sons of Princess Sorhatani, for a brief time it seemed possible that most of Asia might decisively turn toward Christianity, as most of Europe had done back in the times of the Emperor Constantine nine centuries before.

Once more, as six centuries earlier, Nestorians were quick to take advantage of this unprecedented opportunity. Christian churches and monasteries arose in China. Actually all across Asia, from Constantinople to Beijing, Christian presence and influence reached what was perhaps its greatest height as shown in the map on page 86. History tells us of Asian Christian generals, princes, and prime ministers. It also gives us tantalizing hints that there might even have been Nestorians in faraway Korea, Myanmar, and Indonesia.

Roman Catholics in Europe also heard about the new opportunity offered by the Mongol conquest of Asia. Between the 1240s and the 1340s they periodically sent out small parties of missionaries. Some of these stopped in Azerbaijan, Georgia, Armenia, or India; others traveled onward all the way to the Far East. Sad to say, the two varieties of Christ's People in China often fussed and fought with each other. Yet both groups grew and prospered under Mongol rule.

The greatest among these early European missionaries was John of Monte Corvino (died 1328). According to Dr. Kenneth Scott Latourette, a noted church historian, this missionary:

> . . . almost single-handedly established the Roman Catholic faith in the capital of the mightiest empire of his time and to do so had journeyed farther from his home than ever any missionary of any religion is known to have done before him. . . . For single-hearted devotion and quiet persistence he deserves to be ranked with the foremost pioneers of all faiths and times.[2]

In the 1260s Kublai Khan, Mongol emperor of China, sent a message to the pope in Rome, asking for one hundred missionary teachers. He said:

> If they can come and show us clearly by reason that the Christian faith is better and truer than all the other religions, then I and all of my powerful leaders will become men of the Church.[3]

The pope, busy with other matters, sent only two missionaries— not a hundred. Even those two got discouraged and stopped along the way (or so Marco Polo reported when he finally arrived in Beijing ten years later). The story of Christ's People in Asia during the 1200s and 1300s is a story of countless such lost opportunities. Yet there continued to be flickers of hope; for instance consider the intertwining accounts of three outstanding Asian Christians.

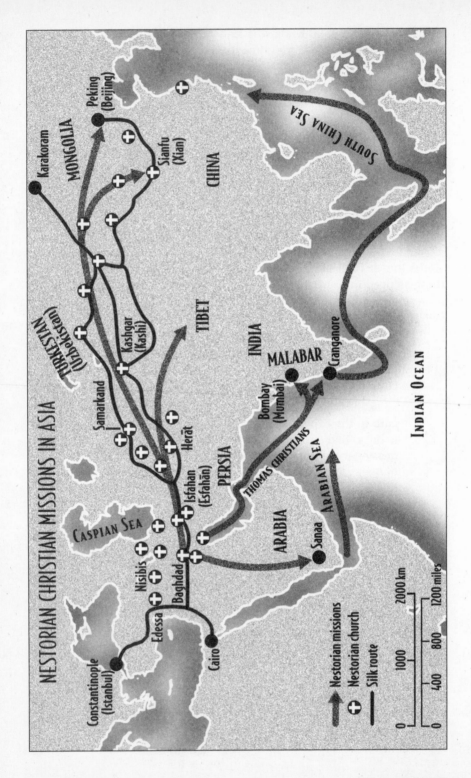

NESTORIAN CHRISTIAN MISSIONS IN ASIA

Karakoram
MONGOLIA
Peking (Beijing)
Sianfu (Xian)
CHINA
TURKESTAN (Uzbekistan)
Kashgar (Kashi)
TIBET
Samarkand
Herāt
Isfahan (Esfahān)
PERSIA
INDIA
MALABAR
Cranganore
Bombay (Mumbai)
THOMAS CHRISTIANS
Caspian Sea
Nisibis
Baghdad
ARABIA
Sanaa
ARABIAN SEA
Arabian Sea
Edessa
Cairo
Constantinople (Istanbul)
SOUTH (CHINA SEA)
INDIAN OCEAN

Nestorian missions
Nestorian church
Silk route

2000 km
1200 miles
1000
800
400
0

Born in eastern Turkey, Bar Hebraeus (1226–1286) was the son of a Christian doctor of Jewish descent. His mother may have been Arabian, for he also had an Arabic name. As a child he moved with his family to Antioch, that great Syrian city from which the Apostle Paul had once been sent out as a missionary. The boy studied under teachers from two main divisions among Christ's People in Asia during those times: the ones nicknamed Nestorians and the ones nicknamed Jacobites.

Bar Hebraeus himself was barely out of his teens when he became a Jacobite bishop; yet he always tried to stay on friendly terms with all believers. Throughout his life he served in many ways as a peacemaker among Christians in conflict. He also wrote an important book of church history without which we would know much less than we do about Christianity in Asia.[4] For instance, Bar Hebraeus was the first to record any information about two other outstanding Asian Christians—Mark and Sauma.

Around 1250, a son was born into a devout Mongol Christian family near Beijing. They gave their boy the New Testament name of Mark. In the capital city of the great Chinese Empire Mark met a Mongol companion named Sauma. Both of these youthful Christians gave away everything they owned and became Nestorian monks. In the late 1270s they set out on a pilgrimage to Jerusalem, meeting various delays along the way.

While they were enjoying the friendship of fellow believers in what is now Iraq, the leader of the Nestorian Christians died and Mark was unexpectedly chosen as his successor. The young Chinese Mongol was shocked: "I can't even speak the holy Syriac language used in your worship services," he protested.[5] Yet time proved that his fellow Christians had made a wise choice. Through many years of difficulty and persecution Mark the Mongol shepherded Christ's People scattered across Asia.

By 1287 Mark's friend Sauma was also a Nestorian bishop. When the Mongol ruler of Persia hoped to join Christians of Europe in an alliance against Muslim foes, he sent Bishop Sauma as an ambassador to visit the pope, the king of France, and the king of England. He was warmly received, but the plans for a great East-West alliance came to nothing. (Just four years later, the last Crusader holdout in Asia fell to Muslim soldiers.)

Like so many others, this flicker of hope never quite burst into flame. The great Mongol Empire broke up into warring factions. Many of the Mongols themselves turned to Islam instead of Christianity.

In the late 1300s, in what is now Uzbekistan, a general called Tamerlane (c.1336–1405) arose who was no kin to the former ruling family. By lying and killing he built an Asian empire nearly as widespread as that of Genghis Khan two centuries earlier. But Tamerlane showed none of the tolerance of those earlier Mongols. Instead, he ranks with Hitler and Stalin as one of the most monstrous mass murderers of human history. He wiped out Muslims who dared to oppose him, but he seemed to take special delight in killing Christians. By 1400 the number of Christ's People in Asia had once again been reduced to what it had been centuries before: only a few scattered pockets of believers, mostly in the Middle East and in India.

# LOSSES SOUTH AND EAST

It was not only in Central Asia and East Asia that Christ's People of this time suffered disastrous losses. This period in church history was also one of discouragement and defeat both in Africa to the South and in Russia and Ukraine to the East.

The Nubians, those hardy black-skinned people who live to the south of Egypt, had built their own strong kingdom by the century of the 200s. Then in the 500s Nubia became a Christian nation. After holding out against Islamic pressure for many years, Nubia finally fell to the Muslims in 1366. Nubian Muslims of today, living near the famous High Dam at Aswan and in other parts of modern Egypt, know little about their ancient Christian heritage.

Destruction in Russia and Ukraine came not from Muslims but from Mongols. One group of them known as The Golden Horde invaded eastern Europe. By December of 1240 they had captured and sacked Kiev, the center of Eastern Orthodox Christianity. Onward they stormed—into Poland, Germany, Hungary, Austria, and the Balkan Peninsula as far as the Adriatic Sea. Only the death of the Great Khan in faraway Central Asia caused them to pull back and regroup.

For 200 years Russians and Ukrainians lived under Mongol masters. Gradually the center of Eastern Orthodox Christianity shifted from Kiev in Ukraine to Moscow in Russia.

One of the greatest Russian Christians was Sergius of Radonezh (c.1314–1392). Born to a noble family, young Sergius (or Sergei) left home and entered a dense forest to live as a Christian hermit. At first he was completely alone in his woodland hut; later he tamed a bear as the companion of his solitude.

Other devout Christians gathered around Sergius and almost forced him to set up the Monastery of the Trinity. This monastery became not only a spiritual retreat center but also a positive force in Russian society. The great Russian icon painter Andrei Rublev was inspired by Sergius to create matchless masterpieces of Christian art. The prince of Moscow was inspired by Sergius to start a long fight against foreign Mongol overlords that eventually drove them out of Russia.

Through it all Sergius himself remained a deeply spiritual Christian. When administration of his monastery or other worldly concerns became too much for him, he would retreat in silence once again to his humble hut in the forest. Even as abbot, he dressed in rags. By the time of his death in 1392, Sergius had led an entire nation toward a closer relationship with Jesus the Christ.

Throughout the 70-year existence of the Soviet Union during the 1900s, millions of Russians traveled to Red Square in Moscow so they could view the tomb of Lenin. Yet even when Communism was at its height, many more millions of Russians traveled to *Sergeyev Posad,* about 25 miles north of Moscow, so they could view the tomb of Sergius.

Many devout and notable Russian believers lived under Mongol domination. Yet this period of Asian influence cut Russia off from many new currents of thought and action that were stirring in the rest of Europe. There was never any renaissance of art and learning in Russia; neither was there ever any Protestant Reformation.

# THE MOST POWERFUL POPE

For Roman Catholics in western Europe, the 1200s began on a high note. Pope Innocent III (c.1161–1216) was one of the most capable and learned men ever to become the bishop of Rome. Educated at the new universities in Paris and Bologna, he was a gifted musician, able lawyer, and eloquent speaker in several languages.

Innocent was only 37 years old when he was elected pope. During the early 1200s he reached a pinnacle of power. If a king disagreed with him, he would *excommunicate* the king. This meant the king was considered "out of communication" with Christ's People until he made things right: He could not attend church or partake of the Lord's Supper. Furthermore, Pope Innocent would sometimes place an entire country under *interdict* because of disagreements with that country's ruler. When an interdict was in effect, no worship services, Christian weddings, nor Christian funerals could be held; for many Roman Catholics, this seemed like a living death, with the fires of hell sure to follow.

Pope Innocent summoned a professor from a medical school in France to build a model hospital in Rome. He often pointed it out to visitors. Other state-of-the-art hospitals were built on the same plan in France, Germany, and England.

In 1215 Pope Innocent assembled 400 bishops and 800 abbots, plus many other priests, secretaries, and experts—the largest council of Christian leaders up to that time. The pope's stated purpose was to reform the Roman Catholic Church. Many wise decisions came out of this great Fourth Lateran Council:

- Every bishop was to provide good preachers for all the churches in his area, so all of Christ's People could hear the Word of God.

- In order to provide good preachers, every cathedral school was to employ competent teachers.

- Every form of moneymaking based on spiritual matters was forbidden: no charge to view the relics of Christians long dead, no payment for indulgences or special offers of forgiveness.

- Every Roman Catholic was to confess his or her sins to a priest at least annually.

Other decisions made at Rome in 1215 were not as positive. Jewish people were ordered to wear special marks on their clothing and to live only in special areas. This anti-Semitic prejudice was a bitter fruit of the Crusades: Fighting in the Holy Land had caused many Crusaders to remember that most Jews had rejected Jesus, who came to earth both as Jewish Messiah (or Christ) and as Savior of the world.

During the 1200s and 1300s, several countries of western Europe took further steps of discrimination against Jews—sometimes driving them out altogether. As a result the coming years saw a steady migration of millions of Jewish people toward central and eastern Europe, North Africa, and the Middle East.

Another result of Pope Innocent's council in 1215 was a formal statement of the doctrine of *transubstantiation*. To those who hold this doctrine the word means that the bread and wine used in the Lord's Supper actually become the broken body and spilled blood of Jesus— even though it still looks and feels and smells and tastes like bread and wine. This teaching was intended to give new significance to Christ's solemn words, "This is my body which is given for you: this do in remembrance of me" (Luke 22:19, KJV). Yet for many ordinary people, the Lord's Supper had become a sort of sacred magic trick. They began to call it the *mass*, from *Missa est* or "Go forth," the final words spoken by the priest. They also took the Latin words *Hoc est corpus Meum* meaning "This is my body" and turned them into . . . "Hocus-pocus."

One of the many "might-have-beens" in relation to Christ's People of six centuries ago is this: What if the good decisions made by Pope Innocent III and his great council had made a wider impact than the not-so-good steps that they took? All of church history in later centuries might have been quite different.

Even though Pope Innocent exercised his mighty power over kings, German emperors often opposed him. To counterbalance German influence, Innocent and his successors tried to build up other rulers, especially the king of France. This tactic brought unexpected consequences a century later: In the early 1300s French troops invaded Italy, kidnapped an elderly pope, and mistreated him. When a Frenchman was elected as the new pope a year later, he decided for his own safety to stay close to home.

For 70 years all of the popes were French, and all of them lived at Avignon in southern France. An abortive attempt to move the pope back to Rome ended in failure. Then some Roman cardinals decided to elect their own pope, thus bringing about an even worse result: For the next 40 years, from 1378 to 1417, there were two popes, one in Avignon and one in Rome, each excommunicating the other. In a situation like that, is it any wonder that many people forgot the moves toward reform and other good results of the great council assembled by Pope Innocent III?

# A BITTER AFTERMATH

In addition to discrimination against Jews, another negative side effect of the Crusades was the tendency to adopt a Crusader mentality toward anything or anybody you might happen to disagree with. This attitude was reflected in many ways:

- When Spanish and Portuguese armies began driving Muslims back southward toward Africa, they did so in the spirit of a Crusade; they believed they were Christ's soldiers, fighting for the true religion.

- When Prussians, Lithuanians, and other tribes living near the Baltic Sea resisted the majority of Europeans in becoming Christ's People, German knights mounted a Crusade, forcing them to become Christians (at least in name) or to be sold as slaves. (Once again women led the way in erasing the last non-Christian holdout in Europe: In 1386 the king of Lithuania agreed to become a Christian so he could marry a Christian princess who was heir to the throne of Poland.)

- Russians living near the Baltic Sea claimed to be Christ's People, but to Roman Catholics they were not "the right kind." Therefore Crusaders took advantage of turmoil caused by the Mongol invasion and attacked them too. Only a heroic defense led by Alexander Nevsky kept Russia from being divided into two warring camps of so-called Christians. (The widest street in present-day St. Petersburg is called *Nevsky Prospekt*, in honor of this long-ago national hero.)

- There were also the Waldenses (or Waldensians) and Albigenses (or Cathars) who claimed to be Christians. Roman Catholics disagreed and said they were following some type of heresy or beliefs that were different from those of the majority. At first the Christian majority used only teaching and persuasion against these groups. When this failed, they used harassment and imprisonment and then a Crusade against the area around Albi in southern France. The Albigenses were virtually wiped out; the Waldenses took refuge in the high mountains of Switzerland and northern Italy.

- The *Inquisition* was another evidence of the Crusader mentality. During the 1200s this new system of religious courts of justice was set up to be directly accountable to the pope. The inquisitor was prosecuting attorney, judge, and jury all in one. He was not required to tell the accused person who made the accusation. In some cases he could even use torture to force a confession. If the heresy was great enough, he could turn the guilty over to civil authorities to impose the death penalty.

# WAR AND PLAGUE

One of the reasons Christian leaders encouraged Europeans to go on Crusades was to unite them against a common foe so they would stop fighting each other. It did not work out that way. For instance, in 1337 France and England started what came to be known as the Hundred Years' War. (Actually this on-again-off-again conflict lasted a little longer than a century.)

In October 1347 the European continent was struck by something far worse than war. A ship docked in Sicily with most of its crew dead, dying, or suffering from headaches and chills, high fevers and heavy coughs, and black swellings that oozed blood and pus. No one knew what caused the Black Death, as people began to call it. They had no idea that fleas on shipboard rats brought the germs of the bubonic plague to Europe.

The Black Death spread rapidly all over Europe. Doctors caught it from their patients and died alongside them. A person might be healthy at bedtime and dead before morning. Bodies piled up in the streets because too few people were left to bury them or because everyone was too afraid to touch the foul corpses.

The death toll surpassed anything before or since in human history. The plague would rage through an area and die down except in densely populated cities. It might lie dormant during the winter only to break out again the next spring.

"A third of the world died," so wrote a contemporary observer. "And no bells tolled, and nobody wept, no matter what his loss, because almost everyone expected death."[6] Modern studies have confirmed that some 20 to 40 million people, including one out of every three Europeans, died between 1347 and 1351. In Constantinople the death rate was 88 percent; in Paris 800 people died each day.

Some of the ways people tried to ward off the plague were almost as ugly as the plague itself. So-called Christians turned against their Jewish neighbors, claiming that Jews had brought on the Black Death. In one town several hundred Jews were locked up in a wooden house and the house was set on fire. In another city 2,000 Jews were marched out to the cemetery and offered a stark choice: Become a Christian or be burned to death!

Many of Christ's People felt that God had sent the plague as a punishment for their wickedness, much like the Flood in Old Testament days. Priests organized great prayer-walks, begging for God's mercy . . . and without realizing it, giving the germs more opportunities to spread among crowds of worshipers. Sometimes prayers with words did not seem to be enough: People stripped to the waist and beat themselves with iron-spiked whips, letting their blood flow as a sacrifice for sin.

Eventually the Black Death diminished (although it had a tendency to reappear in certain areas every ten years or so). It left many scars. One of the greatest "might-have-beens" is this: What might those many millions of Europeans have accomplished if they could have reached a normal span of life? Would they have brought greater good among Christ's People? Or greater evil?

Generally speaking, Christian leaders were not regarded positively during the plague years. Many priests were accused of being too frightened to minister to the sick, hear confessions from the dying, or give decent burials. There were exceptions: Nuns at a city hospital faithfully cared for victims of the plague. As these gentle nurses caught the horrible disease and died, other nuns bravely took their places.

Because so many had died, many material goods were left unclaimed and people fought over them. Along with greed, there was a renewed fear of God and a heightened awareness of God's commands. Many couples that had been living together hastily got married. Gamblers turned their dice into prayer beads.

This overwhelming invasion of death into daily life caused a change in the whole outlook of Christ's People in Europe. Wealthy Europeans set up private chapels where they paid a priest to repeat prayers all day long for the soul of a dead loved one. Art and literature took on a darker tone, frequently showing a preoccupation with death or dying.

# LIGHTS IN THE DARKNESS

Even during these two centuries of death and darkness, many true Christian men and women were shining "as lights in the world" (Philippians 2:15, KJV), pointing the way toward God and heaven. Several examples are showcased in the box below.

Two of the brightest among these light-bearers in Europe were a Spaniard named Dominic (c.1170–1221) and an Italian named Francis of Assisi (c.1181–1226). The lifetimes of these two men ran parallel: Both were born to wealthy families in the later 1100s, both were not understood by their parents, both died (too young) in the 1220s, and both founded new monastic orders of *friars*, meaning "brothers."

Unlike monks who mainly stayed in monasteries, friars went out among the common people, teaching and preaching the Good News about Jesus the Christ. Monks sometimes grew rich because of gifts made to monasteries; friars wore simple robes and often went barefoot, staying alive by begging for food. Many friars bravely took to the road as Christian missionaries, winning new converts in Ukraine, in Central Asia, even in faraway China.

## Men and Women with Influence

**Elizabeth of Hungary** (1207-1231) was a king's daughter who was married at 14 and widowed at 20. She ministered to the poor and sick, using her wealth to establish a hospital.

**Dante Alighieri** (1265-1321) wrote one of literature's masterpieces, *The Divine Comedy.* This long dramatic poem gives a vision of the world to come, but its stated purpose is to help Christ's People know better how to live their lives in this present world.

**Meister Eckhart** (1260-1327) and his pupil **Johann Tauler** (1300-1361) were Dominican friars whose teaching and preaching in Germany helped prepare the way for the Protestant Reformation two centuries later.

**Bridget** (Birgit or Birgitta) of Sweden (1303-1373) and her husband of 30 years experienced a new personal relationship with Jesus the Christ. Her husband became a monk; Bridget founded a new monastic order for women. She spoke out for religious renewal and reform and became one of the greatest Scandinavian writers of her time.

**Catherine of Siena** (1347-1380) had a passion for bringing the lost to Christ. She ministered to prisoners, lepers, and victims of the plague. She urged renewal and reform; she even dared to advise popes. When criticized, Catherine said that God had affirmed her work with these words: "Does it not depend on My will where I shall pour out My grace? With Me there is no longer male or female, lower and upper classes, but all are equal in My sight."[7]

Dominic's new monastic order, the *Dominicans*, became especially known as the preaching friars. They emphasized getting a good education so they could give strong reasons for following the true faith. As Roman Catholic Christians began to take a harder line toward heretics, unfortunately an earnest Dominican preacher sometimes found himself becoming an agent of the dreaded Inquisition.

The *Franciscan* friars placed more emphasis on a deeper spiritual life than on higher education. Yet they too taught the common people. One of the most beloved traditions among Christ's People worldwide was started by Francis himself as a way to teach through a vivid visual presentation: On Christmas Eve of 1223, near the little Italian town of Greccio, Francis arranged for a living nativity scene.

Francis also cared about those who did not know that the Christ had been born in Bethlehem as the Savior of the world. He sent several Franciscan friars on a mission trip to Morocco, where they all died as martyrs. More than once Francis tried to sail to Muslim lands. In 1219 he actually succeeded in getting an audience with the sultan of Egypt. This Muslim ruler did not become a Christian, but he was impressed with Francis' bravery and sincerity, refusing demands from his advisers that Francis should be executed. Instead he sent Francis back home with a present of a carved ivory horn that is on display even today in Assisi.

Giovanni Fidanza, later known as Bonaventure (1217–1274), became a Franciscan friar at the age of 17. He was the new order's greatest promoter and theological teacher, a peacemaker in troubled times, and the official biographer of Francis of Assisi. He described his spiritual leader:

> In beautiful things Francis saw Beauty itself, and through Beauty's traces imprinted on creation he followed his Beloved everywhere, making everything a ladder by which he could climb up and embrace the One who is utterly desirable.[8]

Clare of Assisi (1194–1253) was Francis's female counterpart, a beautiful teenage girl who dedicated her life to Christ and started a Franciscan monastic order for women, the *Poor Clares*. Her father had died as a Crusader; her mother had made a pilgrimage to the Holy Land. Clare influenced many other wealthy Italian women and girls to join her in giving all their riches to the poor. When Clare became a nun, Francis himself cut off her long golden hair. (Visitors to Assisi can still view Clare's tresses today.) The two of them were close friends in Christ, yet they always kept the strictest vows of total sexual abstinence.

Perhaps not as well known as Francis, but a greater missionary was Ramon Lull (c.1235–1315). Born to a wealthy family on the Spanish island of Majorca, the young Ramon lived only for pleasure. One day in his 30s while writing a sexy song, he saw a vision of Jesus on the cross. This started a process that changed his entire life.

Unlike Francis of Assisi, Ramon became a great scholar and author, writing an astounding total of 321 books, most of them having something to do with winning Muslims to Christ. "Fighting them as Crusaders is not the way," Ramon counseled; "instead, we must win them with love and prayers, tears and blood."[9]

Ramon realized how ignorant most European Christians were about the Muslim world. He spent years studying the Arabic language and urging others to do the same. He also encouraged Christ's People to learn all they could about the geography and culture of countries where Muslims lived.

But studying and teaching about missions was not enough. Time and again Ramon Lull put his theory into practice by traveling to North Africa and sharing the Good News there. A few people listened and became believers; others chased him away under threat of death. Sometimes he could minister only in hiding; other times he stood up in the marketplace and boldly challenged Muslim beliefs. Still putting his life on the line at the age of 80, he was stoned to death in 1315 by a Muslim mob in what is now Algeria. (It is interesting to note that during the 1990s a strong Christian movement arose among some of the native Berber peoples of Algeria near the very place where Ramon Lull died a martyr.)

Friars and missionaries were not the only ones bringing light in the darkness six centuries ago. Some scholars say that the great theologian Thomas Aquinas (1225–1274) did more than anyone of his time to save Christianity from ruin. Putting his towering intellect to work for God, Thomas Aquinas showed his fellow believers how they could reconcile Christian faith with modern learning. "We look at everything from the standpoint of God," he wrote. "When we study theology, we are in part studying God Himself and in part studying other beings insofar as they are a part of God's plan."[10]

Born into an aristocratic family in the southern Italian town of Aquino, Thomas was named for one of the twelve apostles. When he announced his intentions to enter the monastic life, his family affirmed his decision at first. Then they were shocked to find out he planned to join the strange new order of Dominican friars. So they locked him up and tried to make him change his mind, even tempting him with prostitutes. Thomas finally escaped and made his way to Paris where he enrolled in the university.

As a student he was overweight, solemn, and quiet; fellow collegians teased him by calling him "The Dumb Ox." A professor silenced them all by saying that one day "The Dumb Ox" would bellow so loudly that he would shake the whole world!

The professor was right. During the 1200s Christ's People in Europe had become reacquainted with ancient learning from the Greeks and Romans and were struggling to fit Christian teaching with Aristotle's teaching. Thomas Aquinas worked to reconcile the two. Today Christians of every kind are still studying his great book on Christian doctrine entitled *Summa Theologica*.

The list of outstanding Christians of this period would not be complete without the man who has been called "The Morning Star of the Protestant Reformation," John Wyclif (c.1328–1384). In the 1370s Wyclif (or Wycliffe) was one of the leading professors at Oxford University, then as now one of the world's great centers of higher learning. He spoke out against ways he felt his fellow Roman Catholic Christians were going astray, such as:

- Making the Lord's Supper into something magical.
- Paying a priest to pronounce forgiveness of sins.
- Recognizing anyone other than Jesus the Christ as Head of the Church.
- Hoping to be made right with God in any other way than through faith in Christ.

It is understandable why many religious leaders including bishops, abbots, archbishops, and popes fiercely attacked Wyclif. Fortunately for him, he lived in times when priestly power was not too popular in England and therefore he had powerful defenders in high places (such as John of Gaunt, Duke of Lancaster, who was the son, uncle, and father of kings). Even so he lost his honored position as an Oxford professor and thereafter lived quietly as a village priest.

Yet John Wyclif did not remain silent. During the last years of his life he worked with others to prepare the first complete translation of the Bible into the English language. He trained preachers and teachers—some of them clergymen, some of them laymen—to go out and share the Word of God with the common people. Their enemies mocked them calling them Lollards, meaning "mumblers". When John Wyclif died on New Year's Eve in 1384, no one had any idea how widely his radical ideas would spread.

For a time Wyclif had served the same noble employer (Duke John) as Geoffrey Chaucer (1340–1400), honored by later generations as one of England's greatest poets. Both Wyclif and Chaucer used the Midland dialect of English, thus helping it to become the most widely accepted form of the language. And in Chaucer's renowned *Canterbury Tales* the description of a faithful country parson has been seen by many as a disguised tribute to the Lollards—perhaps even a veiled word-picture of John Wyclif himself.

During Wyclif's last years, a teenage princess came from what is now the Czech Republic to marry the teenage king of England. Young Queen Anne (1366–1394) encouraged many of her fellow Czechs to study at English universities. Both she and her countrymen were much taken with the revolutionary ideas of John Wyclif. After both the old professor and the young queen had died, some of these same students carried those radical thoughts back home to Prague as seeds of the Protestant Reformation.

Six centuries ago most of England and most of Europe were not ready for the teachings of John Wyclif. Forty years after Wyclif died, his body was dug up, he was condemned as a heretic, his bones were burned, and his ashes were scattered into a nearby river. That river flowed into a larger river and that larger river flowed into the sea. Some Christians have seen these facts of geography as a parable of how the influence of the bold "Morning Star of the Protestant Reformation" was destined eventually to spread throughout the world . . . but not during his own times.

What if . . .? What might have been?

# KEY EVENTS

## 1200 TO 1300

Crusaders sack Constantinople, capital of the Byzantine Empire.

Pope Innocent III calls the Fourth Lateran Council to reform the Roman Catholic Church.

Dominic and Francis of Assisi start new monastic orders of friars, or wandering monks.

The Inquisition, a system of religious courts of justice, begins rooting out heretics.

Mongols, a tribe influenced by Christ's People, bring stability to Asia, making travel easier; they also sweep across eastern Europe and rule Russia for two centuries.

Sorhatani, a Christian princess, becomes the mother of three mighty Mongol rulers, including Kublai Khan.

Missionaries, both Nestorian and Roman Catholic, travel to many parts of Asia.

Bar Hebraeus writes church history and promotes peace among Asian Christians.

Thomas Aquinas writes *Summa Theologica*, one of the greatest books of theology.

Kublai Khan asks the pope to send 100 missionaries to China; the pope sends only two.

Bonaventure, an outstanding Franciscan, writes the official biography of Francis of Assisi.

Sergius of Radonezh leads Russian Christians to new heights in religious art, spirituality, and national unity.

Mark and Sauma, Mongols from Beijing, become outstanding leaders among Asian Christians.

Ramon Lull urges and exemplifies loving outreach toward Muslims.

## 1300 TO 1400

John of Monte Corvino becomes an outstanding Roman Catholic missionary to China.

Roman Catholic popes begin to live at Avignon in France.

Many western Europeans discriminate against Jews; many Jews migrate to central and eastern Europe, North Africa, and the Middle East.

Dante Alighieri writes a long dramatic poem about this world and the world to come.

By their preaching and teaching in Germany, the Dominican friars Meister Eckhard and Johann Tauler help prepare the way for the Protestant Reformation.

England and France begin the Hundred Years' War.

Bridget of Sweden founds a new monastic order for women and becomes one of the greatest Scandinavian writers of her time.

The Black Death (bubonic plague) wipes out a third of the population of Europe; survivors take a darker outlook toward life.

Catherine of Siena urges reform, advises popes, and ministers to prisoners, lepers, and victims of the plague.

An abortive attempt to move the pope back to Rome results in two popes who excommunicate each other; the pope returned to Avignon, but cardinals in Rome elected a new pope.

Professor John Wyclif challenges several Roman Catholic teachings; with friends he translates the entire Bible into English and sends out preachers to explain the Scriptures to ordinary people.

Queen Anne of England encourages her fellow Czechs to study Wyclif's teachings and take them back home to central Europe.

The Mongol ruler Tamerlane almost wipes out Christ's People in Asia.

## THOMAS À KEMPIS (c.1380–1471)

He wrote *The Imitation of Christ*, one of the
all-time favorite devotional classics.

# 7. On the Brink of New Worlds
## (1400-1500)

Five centuries ago Christ's People in Europe seemed to be teetering on the brink of something strange and new and full of wonder.

By the year 1500 the world as we know it was already beginning to take shape. All over Europe people were reading printed books, the same as we do today. The Italians were beginning to use forks along with knives and spoons. The English were beginning to write with black-lead pencils. Many people in Europe now realized that somewhere out there to the West and South lay other great continental shapes, and some were even beginning to refer to these shadowy unexplored regions as "America."

Much that was new had already come into their experience during the century of the 1400s: new ideas, new lifestyles, new discoveries. Yet in a way everything seemed to be on hold, in breathless anticipation of something newer still. All the new arts and sciences being cultivated by the original "Renaissance men" (and Renaissance women as well), all the new landfalls being made by bold seafaring explorers—all of this seemed to be pointing the way toward something still beyond the horizon in the unknown future.

But . . . what was that something?

## EUROPEAN RENAISSANCE: GOOD OR BAD?

Church history is different from general history, as Christ's People must look at historical events from a special perspective. Regarding the Renaissance, most regular history books include high praise for this notable period. The conventional wisdom is that the Renaissance brought western Europe out of the backward and bleak Dark Ages.

Likewise Christ's People can find much to appreciate in the revival of art and learning that began in Italy during the 1400s. Without the Renaissance:

- No scholarly study of ancient languages and manuscripts would have laid the foundation for all Bible translations of the past 500 years.

- No mass-produced books, magazines, or newspapers would be available to us. The secret of printing with movable type had been hidden somewhere in China for centuries until a German named Johann Gutenberg (c.1397–1468) rediscovered it in the mid-1400s. The first book he printed was the familiar *Gutenberg Bible* of 1456; about one-fourth of the original 200 copies are still in existence today.

- No *Last Supper* by Leonardo da Vinci, no *Praying Hands* by Albrecht Dürer, no *Sistine Madonna* by Raphael, no *Pietà* by Michelangelo (along with countless other masterpieces of religious art) would exist to bless us with their beauty.

Yes, in some ways Christians can be thankful for the Renaissance. Yet in other ways the Renaissance was a disaster for Christ's People.

When scholars rediscovered the learning of ancient Greece and Rome, they also rediscovered the joys of paganism. Feeling that the Ten Commandments and the Apostles' Creed no longer concerned them, many "enlightened" men and women fell into grossly immoral lifestyles. Even leaders among Christ's People did not escape the moral drift of the 1400s.

To give them credit, many Roman Catholics realized that changes needed to be made. In 1414 they assembled the largest council of Christian leaders yet: Thirty thousand people thronged into the small Swiss city of Constance and some 5,000 attended the council sessions.

This important conference straightened out the tangled situation of having two rival popes at the same time. An earlier council had worsened things, so that for a few years there were three "Roman" popes living in three different cities! Finally the Council of Constance succeeded in reducing the number once again to only one pope enthroned in Rome.

It is questionable how much good this did. In the following years the popes of the Renaissance were some of the worst ones. Of course many of them were learned men who encouraged art and learning; the world-famous Sistine Chapel, for instance, is named after Pope Sixtus IV (1414–1484), who had it built. Yet Sixtus is also the pope who arranged political assassinations and appointed six of his own young nephews as cardinals.

Even worse was the Spanish-born Rodrigo Borgia (1431–1503), who became Pope Alexander VI: He bribed cardinals to win his election as pope in 1492. He also openly paraded his many mistresses and children (including the infamous Lucrezia Borgia and her warlike brother Cesare Borgia). Borgia's successor rejected the custom of renaming himself after a Christian saint; instead, he took the name of a pagan Caesar and became Pope Julius II (1443–1513).

With such negative examples, it followed that many bishops and priests of the 1400s cared more about hunting, gambling, moneymaking, and skirt-chasing, than about their spiritual responsibilities as shepherds of Christ's People.

In spite of this, there were still many ordinary Christians who sincerely followed their Lord:

- Lady Julian of Norwich (1343–c.1423) recovered from a near-fatal illness to write a devotional classic—*Revelations of Divine Love*—the first known book in the English language penned by a woman. Lady Julian lived alone as a hermit in a room attached to a church where she devoted her entire life to prayer and meditation. One of her prayers is in the adjacent box.

> ### A Prayer of Lady Julian
>
> "God, of Your goodness, give me Yourself; for You are sufficient for me.... If I were to ask less, I should always be in want. In You alone do I have all."[1]

- Margery Kempe (c.1373–c.1439) was an English merchant's daughter who never learned to read or write. After a near-death experience (like Lady Julian), she spent the rest of her life urging others—sometimes with shrieks and cries—to enter into a closer relationship with God like hers. Although she had a husband and 14 children, she made long religious pilgrimages to half a dozen different countries and worshiped in Rome, Assisi, and even Jerusalem. Late in life she dictated her colorful autobiography, the earliest known English book of this type.

- Joan of Arc (1412–1431) was born to a French farm family during the Hundred Years' War. Starting in her early teens, Joan heard mystical voices that she interpreted as coming from saints and angels. At age 16 she followed what she believed to be God's will and offered herself as commander of the French army against the hated English invaders. At first she was amazingly successful, but then she fell on harder times. Betrayed into the hands of the English, Joan was condemned as a heretic; she died by fire while shouting "Jesus!" A quarter century after her death Joan's guilty verdict was reversed. By 1920 the Roman Catholic Church had even named Joan of Arc a saint.

It was during the times of these corrupt Renaissance popes that a new system of religious courts of justice began to function in Spain, the infamous Spanish Inquisition. Through the years many Spanish Muslims and Jews had professed faith in Christ; now Spanish friars began following up on popular suspicion that some converts were Christians in name only. There was also an ulterior motive: a plan to drive Jewish people from Spain entirely, while making them leave all their wealth behind. Secret trials, paid informers, hellish tortures, and bribed witnesses were used in an effort to root out so-called heretics. Fires with human fuel lit up the plazas of cities and towns all across Spain.

## COULD ANY REFORMER SUCCEED?

In western Europe the 1400s began and ended with two would-be reformers among Christ's People, both of whom showed remarkable courage. They both enjoyed great initial success and strong support from high officials. Then the tide turned against them and they were burned alive as heretics like charred bookends at the beginning and end of the century.

The first martyr bore a name that sounded funny to those who understood his native language: Jan Hus (c. 1369–1415). In Czech his name meant "John Goose" and Hus often made a play on words with that name. The saying "Your goose is cooked" was first used in connection with this brave Czech Christian's death by fire.

Born to a poor family in what is now the southern part of the Czech Republic, Jan Hus earned two academic degrees and became rector of Charles University in Prague. In 1402 he was appointed to preach at Bethlehem Chapel near the university. Although called a chapel this historic building is big and barn-like, so Hus could preach to packed crowds of 3,000 or more.

He preached about some of the same things that had been bothering John Wyclif in the late 1300s; Czech students at Oxford had brought Professor Wyclif's revolutionary ideas back home to Prague. Hus preached that Christ is the only Head of the Church, and that all Christian teachings must agree with the Bible. Yet he did not so much attack the *beliefs* of his fellow Roman Catholics as he did their *lifestyles*.

To make sure everybody got the point, Jan Hus hung vivid posters on the inside walls of Bethlehem Chapel, contrasting Jesus the Christ with bishops and cardinals and popes of his own time. Christ carries his cross; the pope rides a fine horse. Christ washes his disciples' feet; the pope demands that worshipers kiss his feet.

Ordinary men and women of Prague loved it. And Hus in turn loved them, caring for them as a true pastor should. At first the Czech king, egged on by good Queen Žofie (c.1378–1428), supported Hus in his bold preaching. Then power politics became involved in the situation and the pope in Rome threatened to put the whole city of Prague under the dreaded interdict. Pastor Jan Hus could not bear to see his beloved flock deprived of any opportunity to worship together or to partake of the Lord's Supper, so he voluntarily left Prague and settled in a small village. From there he wrote pastoral letters filled with encouragement and advice.

When a great council assembled in 1414 on the shores of Lake Constance, the Holy Roman Emperor gave Hus a promise of safe conduct if he would come and present his views. Hus came to Constance . . . and was promptly thrown into a dark prison cell right next to the sewage system. See the adjacent box for a few quotations from Jan Hus while in that foul prison—letters and statements that sound like echoes of the Apostle Paul awaiting execution in Rome. Hus never had a chance; his opponents shouted him down when he tried to protest that he had never taught the strange ideas of which they accused him. Finally on a summer's day in the year 1415, he was burned to death, boldly singing a prayer to Jesus the Son of God.

As both John Wyclif and Jan Hus (and others as well) have been credited with saying, "Truth is mighty and will prevail." Ideas of renewal and reform did not die with Jan Hus. His Czech followers took up arms rather than be forced back to their old ways of worshiping. One of their generals was nearly blind; he even used his visual impairment to good advantage in planning a surprise night

### Echoes from Prison

Compare these written and spoken words from Jan Hus with Paul's second letter to Timothy in the New Testament:

"Dearest brother! Be diligent in preaching the gospel and do the work of a zealous evangelist. . . . Labor as a good soldier of Christ. First of all, live a devout and holy life, and then teach faithfully and truly. . . . Do not refuse such help as you can render to others."[2]

"O most holy Christ, draw me, weak as I am, after Yourself, for if You do not draw us we cannot follow You. Strengthen my spirit, that it may be willing. If my body grows weak, let Your grace go before me, . . . for without You I cannot go for Your sake to a cruel death. Give me a fearless heart, a right faith, a firm hope, a perfect love, that for Your sake I may lay down my life with patience and joy. Amen."[3]

attack. Again and again Roman Catholic Christians mounted military crusades against Hussite Christians; the stubborn Hussites struck back, turning their farm carts into war-wagons like forerunners of today's armored tanks.

Finally in the 1430s the two sides reached a compromise of sorts. Remnants of the battered Hussites got together with remnants of the 250-year-old Waldensian movement (see the adjacent box). The Waldenses began to realize that they had much in common with these persecuted Czech Christians. The two groups never quite merged, but a special relationship developed between them. Both movements helped prepare the way for the Protestant Reformation of the 1500s. Some of these persecuted believers would later re-emerge in church history as the Moravians.

The second would-be reformer, at the other end of the 1400s, was a slightly built Dominican friar with penetrating eyes and a huge hooked nose; his name Girolamo Savonarola (1452–1498). In Florence, the cultural capital of Renaissance Italy, Savonarola preached to such overflow crowds that he had to move from his own church into the downtown cathedral.

Even more so than Jan Hus, Savonarola spoke out against wrong lifestyles rather than wrong beliefs. He scolded the rich for oppressing the poor; he attacked pornography, prostitution, and many other social evils.

In 1494 the king of France invaded Italy. Sent as a civic ambassador, Savonarola succeeded in persuading the king not to attack Florence. After that the little friar's reputation grew dramatically. He influenced local lawmakers to reduce taxes, set up low-cost loans for the needy, and start closing down gambling halls.

The spring carnival time was traditionally an excuse for wild partying. At carnival time 1496, Savonarola organized thousands of boys into teams to walk through the city, singing hymns and gathering offerings for the poor.

Then Savonarola's successes started going to his head. He turned his youthful "bands of hope" into vice squads, spying on immoral people. During the carnival season of 1497 he sent out both boys and girls to gather anything that could be considered "sinful vanities": fancy costumes, wigs and cosmetics, books and manuscripts, paintings and musical instruments. Piling their collection into a pyramid 60 feet tall, the white-robed children then set everything afire.

Reaction against such a cultural revolution was swift. As with Jan Hus nearly a century earlier, power politics came into play. By May of 1498 Savonarola was being burned at the stake in the great piazza of Florence.

The story of Christ's People in western Europe during the 1400s seems rather depressing. Every movement toward renewal and reform was corrupted by worldliness and power politics and the final answer always seemed to be a martyr's death by fire.

# WERE THINGS ANY BETTER ELSEWHERE?

Outside of western Europe things were only marginally better.

A fierce new breed of Muslims had arisen in the Middle East, the Ottoman Turks. During a time of civil war, a misguided Byzantine emperor had first invited them into southeastern Europe. By the early 1400s Ottoman Turks were conquering the areas now known as Bulgaria, Serbia, Albania, and Hungary. Soon they were raiding the coasts of Italy, carrying off young girls for the sultan's harem.

Then in May 1453, Ottoman Turks captured the great Christian city of Constantinople. They killed the last Byzantine emperor; they made a virtual prisoner of the head of the Eastern Orthodox Church; they turned the Emperor Justinian's historic Church of Holy Wisdom into a mosque.

As disastrous as this was, some good came out of it. Christian scholars fled from Constantinople ahead of the advancing Turks. They took with them priceless ancient manuscripts. Some of them took refuge in western Europe, where they added new momentum to the ongoing Renaissance of art and learning. Others went the opposite direction and took refuge in Russia.

At that time Ivan III, also known as Ivan the Great (1440–1505), was ruling in Moscow. He was married to the niece of the last Byzantine emperor. Finally he succeeded in driving the last of the Mongols out of Russian territory. Gradually each Prince of Moscow began using the royal title *Tsar*, a Russian form of the old Roman name *Caesar.*

An Eastern Orthodox monk once wrote to the son of Tsar Ivan III:

> The church of Moscow, the new "third Rome," shines
> throughout the entire world more brightly than the sun. . . .
> Two Romes have fallen, but the third stands and a fourth
> can never be.[4]

Did Moscow really offer much hope for Christ's People as a new
holy city, replacing ancient Rome and medieval Constantinople? To a
certain extent, yes. Structures such as St. Basil's Cathedral in Moscow,
with its characteristic onion domes, began to arise as impressive
landmarks. Russian Orthodox worship services featured lengthy Bible
readings in the language of the people. Russian monasteries, even more
so than those in western Europe, became centers of art and cultural
preservation, as well as centers of caring for men and women in need.
Schools, hospitals, old folks' homes, and hostels for travelers were
among the ministries carried on by Russian Orthodox monks. As
Russian settlers moved eastward and northward toward Siberia, the
monastic movement encouraged colonization. A new village grew up
around each monastery.

Although Moscow seemed far away from England, France, and
Spain, this "third Rome" was actually within the continent of Europe.
What about Christ's People who lived outside the European continent?
Did the 1400s bring anything better for them?

# THE VOYAGE OF COLUMBUS: GOOD OR BAD?

Some readers will remember a time when schoolchildren celebrated
Columbus Day—a time when everyone was taught to think of those
early voyages of exploration as a glorious first chapter in the magnificent
story of America. On the other hand, many readers will recall a heated
controversy that flared up in 1992 over the five hundredth anniversary
of the first voyage of Christopher Columbus (c.1451–1506). Some people
still thought of it as a day to be celebrated, an event to be remembered
with profound gratitude. Others angrily insisted that the voyage of
Columbus marked nothing but the beginning of five centuries of invasion,
disease, exploitation, racism, and genocide.

The right perspective probably lies somewhere between the two
extremes. Here are a few thoughts and questions that might encourage
a more balanced view:

- Should the peoples of the Americas have been left to their own
  cultures and religions? This is a purely hypothetical question, for
  if Columbus and other European explorers had not found them,
  someone else undoubtedly would have.

- The reason King Ferdinand and Queen Isabella could afford to underwrite the expenses of Columbus' first voyage was that in early 1492 they had finally succeeded in driving the Muslims out of Spain. What if this centuries-long war had gone the other way? Would the Americas have been better off if they had been discovered and colonized by Muslim seafarers?

- Rather than becoming Christians (or Muslims), would the peoples of the Americas really have been better off if they had been left to follow their own religions . . . even though some of those religions called for a throbbing heart to be cut from the chest cavity of a still-living human victim?

- While many Europeans who came to the Americas were greedy and cruel, other Europeans came to the Americas out of a sincere desire to share the Good News about Jesus. Between 1493 and 1820 the Spanish government financed some 15,585 Roman Catholic missionaries to the American continents. Facts such as these must be balanced against the undeniable horrors of racism and slavery, treachery and plunder, infectious diseases and genocide.

- Christopher Columbus did not fit the stereotype of a sea captain with an eye for nothing but gold, glory, and girls. He never cursed or swore and he also went far beyond the customs of his time in conducting praise and prayer services aboard his ships. Some of his own thoughts are presented in the box above.

## A Christian Sea Captain

Christopher Columbus was a deeply religious man. Here, in his own words, is his Christian testimony: "I am only a most unworthy sinner, but ever since I have cried out for grace and mercy from the Lord, they have covered me completely. I have found the most delightful comfort in making it my whole aim in life to enjoy His marvelous presence."[5]

He explained his persistence in sailing West to reach the East: "Our Lord opened to my understanding (I could sense His hand upon me), so that it became clear to me that it was feasible to navigate from here to the Indies, and He gave me the will to execute the idea.... The Lord purposed that there should be something miraculous in this matter of the voyage to the Indies."[6]

Once he had met his first "Indians" (as he mistakenly persisted in calling them), Columbus reported: "I recognized that they were people who would be better ... converted to our Holy Faith by love than by force.... I see that they say very quickly everything that is said to them; and I believe they would become Christians very easily."[7]

# WERE THERE CHRISTIANS ELSEWHERE?

One outcome of the daring voyage of Christopher Columbus in 1492 was that long-separated people groups were being brought into closer contact with one another.

Columbus and other mariners in the service of Spain were not the only bold seafarers of those days: In 1493 the pope tried to avoid armed rivalry by drawing imaginary lines on the globe, dividing the New World between Spain and Portugal. (That is why Brazilians speak Portuguese while most other South Americans speak Spanish.) Columbus thought he had found "Indians" in the Caribbean, but Portuguese explorers of the 1400s voyaged all the way around Africa and discovered a new sea-route to the real India.

Christ's People followed close behind: They dared martyrdom in sharing the Good News with natives of the Canary Islands. Two years before Columbus sailed, Roman Catholic missionaries had already arrived at the mouth of the Congo in Africa. They also landed in Brazil precisely at the turn of the new century.

One of the most interesting of these meetings between long-separated peoples also came in 1500. When Portuguese explorers landed in southern India, they found around 100,000 Christians there. When they returned to Portugal, they took with them a man named Joseph as a fraternal representative of the age-old Thomas Christians (those who learned of Jesus the Christ through the Apostle Thomas). Joseph was living proof that Christ's People did indeed live in other places besides the continent of Europe.

Ten years earlier another interesting meeting between peoples had already taken place. In 1490 a delegation of three Thomas Christians had traveled overland from India to the Middle East. There they had made contact with those known as Nestorians and had discovered that their two groups had much in common even though they had been widely separated for centuries.

By 1500 Nestorians and other historic groups of Asian Christians such as the so-called Jacobites had reached their peak. The Nestorians have survived to the present era as a separate denomination of Christians, with perhaps a few hundred thousand believers in their Middle Eastern area of origin and about as many more scattered in other lands. Still rejecting their old nickname, they prefer to be called *The Ancient Church of the East.*

No one knows for sure why these groups never quite succeeded in taking their continent for Christ, as Christ's People in Europe had done. Some church historians have either dismissed the Nestorians as being unworthy of serious study because they were considered "heretics" or else have concluded that their failures grew out of faulty theology. Yet a careful reading of original sources shows that Nestorian beliefs were in fact closer to those of other Christians than most people have assumed.[8]

At one time they may have claimed as many as 6 percent of all Asians as their church members; why, then, did the Nestorian Christians never experience ultimate success? Perhaps it was because:

- Asia is so vast and Christ's People were often so isolated from one another.

- Persecution was fiercer and longer-lasting than anything European Christians ever had to face.

- Internal divisions among Christ's People (in Asia and elsewhere) weakened them.

- No Asian counterpart to Constantine or Charlemagne ever rose to sweep Christians into the seats of power.

Whatever the reason for the final decline, Christ's People should never forget their Nestorian sisters and brothers. For fully a millennium they kept the flame of missionary outreach burning across half of the face of the earth. Yet by five centuries ago the time had come for other groups of Christians to take up the task of bold expansion.

# GOOD EFFECTS OF THE RENAISSANCE

This chapter began with an explanation as to why the Renaissance was a mixed blessing for Christians. Fortunately the worldliness and secular humanism that flourished along with the revival in art and learning was not equally strong everywhere. The bad effects were most felt in Italy; as the Renaissance moved outward to the North and the West, more of its good effects began to show up among Christ's People.

## France and Spain

Professor Jacques Lefèvre d'Étaples (1450–1536) taught at the University of Paris about the beginnings of the Bible and Christianity. He urged a return to the way things had been centuries before; he encouraged his students to follow the Scriptures rather than manmade teachings.

Cardinal Jiménez (1436–1517), a Franciscan friar, tried to reform the Roman Catholic Church in his region and worked with other scholars to produce a multi-language edition of the Bible.

## England and Germany

Professor John Colet (1467–1519) delivered a series of groundbreaking Oxford lectures on the New Testament letters of the Apostle Paul.

Johann Reuchlin (1455–1522) published a state-of-the-art guide to reading and understanding the Old Testament in its original Hebrew tongue.

## Netherlands

*The Brethren of the Common Life* were a group of Christ's People (including women at first but later limited to men) who lived in communes or co-op dorms—much like monks, but without making a lifelong commitment. Also like monks, they devoted their lives to spiritual disciplines.

A strong emphasis on education made these Dutch Christians different from others in the monastic movement. Many of them became schoolteachers; sometimes they started their own schools. They supported themselves by almost anything having to do with books: writing, copying, binding, marketing, and after Gutenberg's great invention, printing them.

Many of the Brethren of the Common Life made their mark in the 1400s. One of them taught a German lad named Martin Luther (see chapter 8). Some of them became renowned as Christian scholars, Christian philosophers, Christian mystics. Three pupils of this unusual semi-monastic order deserve special mention:

- John of Wesel (c.1400–1489) was such an outstanding scholar and thinker that many contemporaries called him "the light of the world." He emphasized the authority of the Bible and taught that sinful men and women are justified by faith. "He who thinks to be justified by his own works does not know what it is to be saved," said Wesel.[9] He also rejected the granting of indulgences and the doctrine of transubstantiation. Like many who wanted reform, John of Wesel ended his long life in prison.

- Thomas à Kempis (c.1380–1471) wrote *The Imitation of Christ*, one of the most popular devotional books of all time (see the box below).

### Thomas à Kempis Writes About Jesus

Jesus has many who love his kingdom in heaven, but few who bear his cross.

He has many who desire comfort, but few who desire suffering.

He finds many to share his feast, but few his fasting.

All desire to rejoice with him, but few are willing to suffer for his sake.

Many follow Jesus to the breaking of bread, but few to the drinking of the cup of his passion.

Many admire his miracles, but few follow him to the humiliation of his cross.

Many love Jesus as long as no hardship touches them....

They who love Jesus for his own sake, and not for the sake of comfort for themselves, bless him in every trial and anguish of heart, no less than in the greatest joy.

And were he never willing to bestow comfort on them, they would still always praise him and give him thanks.[10]

It was first circulated in hand-written form soon after he wrote it in 1418. Since its first printing in 1471, this devotional classic has appeared in more than 3,000 editions.

• Desiderius Erasmus (1467–1536) was the son of a priest and an unwed teenager. Although a poor boy, he received a good education—first from the Brethren of the Common Life and then at the University of Paris. He used his sharp wit and sharper pen to show how far Christians of his time had strayed away from the teachings and example of their Lord. Seeing Pope Julius II ride into town at the head of an army, the young Erasmus muttered, "Whose successor is this? Jesus Christ's or Julius Caesar's?"[11] One of his many famous books is *In Praise of Folly*. No intellectual lightweight, Erasmus also published the first scholarly edition of the New Testament in its original Greek language. One of his famous quotations may be read in the box above.

> ## Erasmus's Hope for Christ's People
>
> I wish that:
> the Scriptures might be translated into all languages, so that not only the Scots and the Irish but also the Turk and the Saracen might read them and understand them.
>
> I long that:
> the farm-laborer might sing them as he follows his plow, the weaver hum them to the tune of his shuttle, the traveler beguile the weariness of his journey with their stories.[12]

# WHAT WOULD COME OF ALL OF THIS?

So much new learning! So many new ideas, new discoveries, new initiatives among Christ's People!

In 1493 the *Nuremberg Chronicle* was published; it was intended as a complete history from the beginning to the end of time. Those who compiled this remarkable book felt that nearly everything that could possibly be imagined had already happened. Yet there were still nagging doubts in their minds, so they left six blank pages at the back of the book on which to record all future events.

Though their outlook was rather limited, those diligent historians were at least looking toward the future. At the same time Christ's People were looking ahead. So much that had happened during the 1400s seemed somehow incomplete, still awaiting further developments.

What would the next century bring? Far more than they dreamed!

# KEY EVENTS

## 1400 TO 1500

Jan Hus urges reform among Christ's People in Prague; he is well received, then silenced.

The Council of Constance ends the conflict of multiple popes; it also condemns Jan Hus to be burned alive as a heretic.

Thomas à Kempis, a Dutch Christian, writes *The Imitation of Christ*, a favorite devotional classic.

Christian mystic Lady Julian of Norwich dies; she was known as the first English female author.

Joan of Arc, a teenage peasant girl, follows what she believes to be God's will in leading the French army to victory over English invaders; then she is betrayed, captured, and burned alive as a heretic.

Jan Hus's Czech followers are called Hussites; they fight against Roman Catholics and build a new relationship with the Waldenses.

Margery Kempe, a devout Christian, dictates the first known autobiography in the English language.

The Renaissance, a revival of art and learning, spreads from Italy to other parts of Europe with both positive and negative effects for Christ's people.

Ottoman Turks capture the great holy city of Constantinople, turning it into an Islamic center; Christian scholars escape to western Europe and Russia, taking along priceless ancient manuscripts.

Johann Gutenberg rediscovers the secret of using movable type; the first book he prints is the Bible.

Roman Catholic missionaries enter the Canary Islands, parts of Africa, and parts of South America.

Moscow claims to be "the third Rome" as a new center for Christ's People; Russian Orthodox churches and monasteries spread the Good News.

Renaissance artists produce great religious masterpieces such as Leonardi da Vinci's *Last Supper,* Albrecht Dürer's *Praying Hands,* Raphael's *Sistine Madonna,* and Michelangelo's *Pietà.*

Renaissance popes encourage art and learning, but also become some of the most immoral of all Christian leaders.

Scholars among Christ's People in England, France, Spain, the Netherlands, and Germany, bring about many positive results of the Renaissance.

The Spanish Inquisition begins to persecute Jews, Muslims, and so-called heretics.

The Thomas Christians of India make contact with the Nestorians in the Middle East and Roman Catholics in Europe.

Muslims are driven out of Spain; the end of this long war frees up money to support voyages of discovery.

Christopher Columbus sails to America, with the hope of leading other peoples to become Christians.

Savonarola preaches reform among Christ's People in Florence; he receives strong support at first, but then faces opposition and is burned alive as a heretic.

## LUTHER'S 95 THESES ON THE CHURCH DOOR

Dr. Martin Luther (1483-1546) posted an offer to debate questions
about basic Christian beliefs and practices.

# 8. REFORMATION AND EXPANSION: PROTESTANTS AND OTHERS
## (1500-1600)

Take a fresh look at a familiar word: *reformation*. What does it mean to *reform* something?

Today the usual meaning is to make a change for the better—such as an improvement in the morality of a political administration, the ethical standards of an institution, or one's own personal character and conduct.

Take a closer look at a familiar word. In its original sense, to *reform* something meant to form it again, to reshape it, to give it a new and different form. In this older meaning, the verb *reform* is somewhat similar to the present-day word *regroup*.

As we continue exploring church history and plunge into that crucial period known as the Reformation, we would do well to keep in mind the original meaning of reform. Many of Christ's People living four centuries ago must indeed have felt as if nearly everything was being dissolved or broken into pieces, only to be rearranged in startlingly new and different ways.

Did Protestants reform the Roman Catholic Church? No, Roman Catholics themselves did that. In many history books the Catholic response to the Protestant Reformation is called the Counter-Reformation; in other books (including this one) it is called the Catholic Reformation.

In some ways this movement toward renewal among Roman Catholics brought about great improvement; in other ways it only hardened the stance of Catholic Christians in opposition to Protestant Christians. Overall, the Catholic Reformation produced as dramatic and far-reaching a change among Christ's People as did the Protestant Reformation.

# WHAT WAS THE REFORMATION REALLY ALL ABOUT?

Because Christ's People are sinful men and women, every age brings the need for reformation. Earlier chapters in this book have described repeated cycles of renewal and reform among Christians during the first 15 centuries after Christ. Yet in spite of everything Christ's People in Europe kept slipping back into darkness and decay. Church leaders kept allowing worldly concerns to crowd out spiritual ministries. Beliefs and practices of Christians kept edging farther and farther away from the teachings and example of Jesus the Christ.

The continent of Europe in the 1500s was quite different than it was in earlier centuries. Bold astronomers such as Nicholas Copernicus (1473–1543) were changing the way men and women viewed the universe. New centers of wealth and commerce were growing in the cities. Royal rulers were chafing against demands made by the pope in Rome. Nation-states in the modern sense were slowly emerging.

Printing with movable type during the 1500s was as revolutionary as the introduction of the Internet during the 1980s and 1990s. In both cases it was impossible to stop the spread of new ideas. Books may have been expensive, but leaflets and broadsheets were not. People all over Europe were enjoying their newly acquired access to more information.

In such a rapidly changing environment, how long could traditional Christianity hold out? Many of its leaders were morally corrupt; many of its ideas seemed dated. To make things worse, the Ottoman Turks kept on advancing until they held all of the Middle East, much of southeastern Europe, and all of northern Africa; the Mediterranean had become a Muslim lake. By 1529 the Turks were even knocking on the gates of Vienna.

In the midst of this new age of new challenges, Christian leaders seemed content with the status quo. Pope Julius II (1443–1513), the same pope who was mocked by the young scholar Erasmus as being the successor of Caesar rather than Christ, continued with business as usual by commissioning Michelangelo to paint magnificent frescoes of the Creation and the Last Judgment inside the Sistine Chapel. A speaker at a council of Catholic leaders held in Rome during the early 1500s remarked, "Now nobody contradicts us, no one opposes us."[1] Indulgences were being offered at bargain prices to Christ's People everywhere to help pay for a new St. Peter's in Rome.

It is hard to imagine what might have become of Christ's People at this time if God had not done something truly amazing. Between 1500 and 1600, God's hand moved in human history to bring about more drastic changes than Christ's People had ever experienced. As a result, the 1500s:

- Saw Christ's People make a radical turn *back to the Bible* and to the original Christian faith.

- Marked the beginning of *several new groups* of Christians now known all over the world—Lutherans, Presbyterians, Episcopalians, and spiritual heirs of the Anabaptist movement (later known as Mennonites, Amish, and others).

- Saw the Roman Catholic Church undergo *dramatic change* and take on a new shape that would basically continue with little alteration for the next 400 years.

- Saw *Christians spreading* to many parts of the known world (after 95 percent of Christ's People had been concentrated in Europe).

Why did Christ's People have to split into so many different denominations? Why were the leaders of the Protestant Reformation unable to do what Wyclif, Hus, Erasmus, and other earlier reformers had done—stay Catholics while trying to work on improvements from the inside?

According to Bruce H. Shelley, one of today's leading church historians, the great divide between Protestants and Catholics can be summed up by how each group answers four big questions. Here are Dr. Shelley's questions, restated and reordered:[2]

**Where** do Christ's People find their source of authority? (In other words, where do they go for answers to important questions?)

**"What** must I do to be saved?" *(Acts 16:30, emphasis added).*

**Who** are truly Christ's People?

**How** should Christ's People live in this world?

The responses given by Catholics and Protestants are listed (in an extremely oversimplified form) in the box on page 120. Notice that the Catholic answer for questions 1 and 2 *repeats* the Protestant answer and *adds* to it. On the other hand, notice that for questions 3 and 4, the Catholic answer seems to be *narrower* than the Protestant answer.

This period of reform will be covered in two chapters: Chapter 8 tells about the Protestant Reformation country by country across the European continent (in a much abbreviated form); chapter 9 covers the Catholic Reformation, as it spread from Europe to other continents.

# THE PROTESTANT REFORMATION

Each year many churches celebrate the last Sunday in October as Reformation Day. In doing so they recall the last day of October 1517 when a Roman Catholic monk in Germany tacked a sheet of paper to a church door (the community bulletin board of those days).

## Four Major Differences: Protestant and Catholic

| | The Protestant Answer | The Catholic Answer |
|---|---|---|
| 1. *Where* do Christ's People find their source of authority? | In the Word of God, which is found in the Bible. | In the Bible *and* in the official teachings and traditions of the Roman Catholic Church. |
| 2. *"What* do I have to do to be saved?"* (Acts 16:30, emphasis added). | "Believe on the Lord Jesus Christ" (Acts 16:31, KJV). | "Believe on the Lord Jesus Christ" *and* behave in ways that are proper for a Roman Catholic. |
| 3. *Who* are truly Christ's People? | All those who truly believe on the Lord Jesus Christ. | Roman Catholics, in a fuller sense than other Christians. |
| 4. *How* should Christ's People live in this world? | By serving God in any useful calling, whether as an ordained minister or as a layperson. | The highest form of Christian living is to become a priest, monk, nun, or teaching sister. |

Who was that monk? The monk's name was Dr. Martin Luther (1483–1546); he was a learned professor at the local university.

What was printed on that sheet of paper? The notice he posted was an offer to debate a long list of questions about beliefs and practices of Christians; it is usually referred to as the *95 Theses.*

Why is this seemingly unimportant event still being remembered five centuries later as the beginning of the Protestant Reformation? Some of the questions Professor Luther brought up for debate had been brought up before, yet never with quite the same impact. You might even say that echoes of Luther's hammer blows tacking that notice to the church door are still being heard around the world today.

## PROTESTANTS IN GERMANY

In a book like this it is hard to do justice to Martin Luther, who has had more books written about him than any other person in church history except Jesus. Born to a German peasant family in the late 1400s, Martin Luther got a good education—first with the goal of becoming a lawyer, then as a Roman Catholic monk. Obsessed by the idea of God as a righteous judge, he desperately tried to find peace with God. Eventually he became a university professor of Bible and theology while also serving as local parish priest.

In his studies of the Scriptures, Dr. Luther became convinced that righteousness is not something we can achieve by our own efforts; instead, by faith we must receive righteousness as a gift from God. Along with this realization the young professor experienced a profound personal assurance of God's grace and mercy. "The noblest of all good works is to believe in Christ," Luther taught. "Good works do not make a person good, but a good person does good works."[3]

With his newfound understanding of biblical truth, Luther became especially upset with those who were selling indulgences. He had already been preaching and teaching against this practice for some time before he posted his notice, inviting debate on the issue.

The Protestant Reformation might never have happened without Johann Gutenberg's rediscovery of printing with movable type. Many of Luther's ideas were not new; he gave much credit to Jan Hus and John of Wesel. Yet those earlier would-be reformers did not have the help of printing.

In Luther's case, within two weeks his *95 Theses* had spread all over Germany; within a month his words had been translated and published in many other languages. All over Europe people were talking about the brash young professor who dared to question a system supported by long tradition. Many of those same people liked what they heard, for they were tired of being manipulated by greedy church officials.

Catholic leaders made several efforts to silence Luther, but their tactics had just the opposite effect. As opposition mounted, more and more people came to hear and approve Luther's revolutionary ideas. As he kept studying the Bible, Luther found more and more ways Christ's People had wandered far from Jesus' teachings and example. Luther reasoned that it was not true to say that all Christians must submit to the pope because Eastern Orthodox Christians had long been recognized as Christ's People, yet they had never submitted to the Roman pope.

For such teachings Luther was called to stand before Charles V (1500–1558), the Holy Roman Emperor, plus a whole roomful of religious and secular leaders. Pointing toward a table where Luther's books and pamphlets were piled high, the prosecutor demanded that he take back what he had written. Luther defended himself by asking that his writings be proved wrong by the Scriptures rather than by the word of a pope or a council. In a climactic court session, he cried out: "My conscience is captive to the Word of God. I will not take back anything, for to go against conscience is neither right nor safe. Here I stand! I cannot do otherwise. God help me! Amen."[4]

Across the centuries it is hard for us to realize how startling those words were when first spoken in 1521. The emperor's secretary retorted,

"If it were granted that whoever contradicts the councils and the common understanding of the church must be overcome by Scripture passages, we will have nothing in Christianity that is certain or decided."[5] He was right: One unintended byproduct of the Protestant Reformation was a period marked by much uncertainty and indecision.

By taking such a bold stance, Martin Luther brought himself into grave danger of dying by fire like earlier martyrs. Fortunately one of his princely followers spirited him away to safety in the remote Wartburg Castle, where he let his beard grow as a disguise. He was not idle while in hiding: During just 11 weeks of furious activity, he made a rough draft of the entire New Testament translated into everyday German.

Even five centuries later, his version of the New Testament is still readable. In later years he worked with other scholars to translate the entire Old Testament, also using the language of ordinary people. "I make Moses so German that no one would suspect he was a Jew," Luther boasted.[6]

For the rest of his life Luther was technically an outlaw—excommunicated from the church and liable to be imprisoned or executed by secular authorities. So many Germans supported him, from princes in their castles to farmers in their fields, that he was relatively free to teach, preach, and publish. He kept up a furious barrage of writing, turning out an average of one published work every three weeks. His media campaign marked the first full-scale use of the printing press being organized to mold public opinion.

Even Martin Luther's admirers will admit that he made many mistakes. He held too much to his Catholic background, when other Protestant Reformers were willing to give up tradition for the sake of biblical truth. He depended too much on earthly rulers for protection, even encouraging the slaughter of 100,000 rebellious German peasants. When he heard false rumors that Christians were being persuaded to follow the Jewish faith, he produced harshly anti-Semitic writings that have haunted Germans ever since.

Luther never intended to start a new Christian denomination. Even when he and his followers were compiling their statement of faith, they began by reaffirming the Apostles' Creed, the Nicene Creed, and other traditional documents from the history of the church.

For several years Luther hoped he could remain a Roman Catholic while reforming the church from the inside. This proved to be impossible; the Emperor Charles V so fiercely opposed Protestantism that he took up arms against it. Yet only a few years after Luther's death in 1546, even the great emperor himself was forced to make a concession: He agreed that each local ruler could decide whether people in that area would be Catholics or Lutherans.

Luther's lasting legacy does not consist only of a worldwide Christian denomination (which includes millions of Batak believers in Indonesia who do not use the name Lutheran but embrace Lutheran doctrine). He also blazed a path back to the Bible and to early Christianity as demonstrated by one of his followers who, when accused of teaching new doctrines, replied, "Oh no, they are 1,522 years old!"[7]

Martin Luther set new standards for Christ's people in many aspects of life: in Christian worship, in Christian family life (see the adjacent box), and in the firm conviction that *every true believer is a priest* before God. He even planted the seeds for a united German nation, by standing up against outside powers and by giving Germans a common language as they read the Bible in words they could all understand.

## PROTESTANTS IN SWITZERLAND

While nearly everybody knows something about Martin Luther, hardly anybody knows anything about Ulrich Zwingli (1484–1531). Zwingli was another great Christian leader whose influence on the Protestant Reformation might have been as great as Luther's if events had not combined to divide his followers and cut short his life.

In many ways Zwingli and Luther were alike. Each of them:

- Was born in the late 1400s (only seven weeks apart) to German-speaking peasant parents.
- Received a good university education, with Zwingli being more influenced than Luther by great Renaissance scholars such as Desiderius Erasmus (1467–1536).
- Devoted his life to Christian ministry, intending to be a faithful Catholic.

### My Lord Katie

As a Roman Catholic monk Martin Luther pledged himself to sexual abstinence. Yet the New Testament convinced him that such a lifestyle was not necessary for all full-time Christian workers, men or women.

With the help of friends, Luther found good husbands for several former nuns. Only one was left: Katherine von Bora, a redhead approaching her late 20s. She and Luther did not fall in love; rather, they grew to love each other deeply during two decades of marriage. The Luthers had six children, besides caring for several orphans.

Luther had great respect for his wife and jokingly referred to her as *My Lord Katie.* Another time he declared, "I would not give my Katie for France and Venice together."

He confessed, "In domestic affairs I defer to Katie. Otherwise, I am led by the Holy Ghost." According to Luther, they sometimes disagreed: "It is impossible to keep peace between man and woman in family life if they do not condone and overlook each other's faults, ... for who does not at times offend?"[8]

- Became convinced (each without much influence from the other) that Christ's People had strayed a long way from Bible truth.

- Began a gradual process of change in the areas of worship, daily living, and the ideal of a Christian family (Zwingli married a wealthy widow with three children).

- Was willing to call on earthly powers for protection against their enemies.

There were also differences between them. For example, Luther started his reform movement as a university professor in Germany; Zwingli started his as a city pastor in Switzerland. More so than Luther, Zwingli stressed changes in personal behavior and society, as well as changes in Christian beliefs and practices. Zwingli never forgot his peasant roots; he was a staunch Swiss patriot, even translating Psalm 23:2 "He makes me lie down in beautiful Alpine pastures."

*A question worth considering:* What might have happened to the budding reform movement if Luther and his friends had gotten together with Zwingli and his followers? It certainly was not for lack of trying: Once the two great Protestant leaders met and agreed on 14 out of 15 points of a joint statement. Strange to say, the one thing that separated them was the one thing around which all of Christ's People are supposed to meet together: the communion table.

Here is a summary of the two men's arguments about the Lord's Supper:

> Luther: Christ said, "This is my body." That means the bread and the wine really are Christ's body, . . . even though of course they do not change as Catholics say they do in the doctrine of transubstantiation.

> Zwingli: What Christ really meant was, "This signifies my body," or "This symbolizes my body." Of course Christ is present in the Lord's Supper . . . but so is he present everywhere that Christ's People gather.

Luther kept Catholic traditions unless *forbidden* by the Bible; Zwingli dropped Catholic traditions unless *taught* by the Bible. These different approaches sometimes led the two great Reformers in two different directions; see for instance the box on page 125.

Some parts of Switzerland responded favorably to Zwingli's teachings; some did not. Unfortunately a civil war broke out, with Swiss fighting against Swiss. Pastor Zwingli took up his sword to defend what he believed and died in battle at the age of 47.

The reform movement spearheaded by Zwingli continued, in Switzerland and elsewhere; there were further developments under different leadership. Some of Zwingli's spiritual heirs use the word *Reformed* as the name of their group of believers. More of them instead use the term *Presbyterian*, taken from a New Testament word meaning a church elder or leader.

A Christian reform movement quite different from Zwingli's also arose in Switzerland—during Zwingli's lifetime and under his influence. Some of Ulrich Zwingli's most trusted followers began to feel that he was still retaining too much from the past.

The slow pace of reform in Switzerland caused these dissidents to became impatient. They were especially concerned about the tradition of baptizing every baby born into a Christian family. They wondered: *Doesn't the New Testament teach that baptism is intended for a person who repents from sin and confesses faith in Christ?*

Feeling that their own infant baptism meant nothing, these earnest believers began baptizing one another a second time. They also expressed grave doubts about letting earthly governments decide which religion everyone must follow. Instead, they stressed that becoming one of Christ's People meant radical discipleship—an individual decision to give up everything and follow Christ. In addition, many of them believed that the New Testament forbade all use of force, even when facing their armed enemies.

Neither Zwingli nor Luther liked this new development . . . a fact that becomes plain from the nicknames flung at its followers, both in Switzerland and in Germany: "Revolutionaries!" "Rabble-Rousers!" "Dark-Corner-Preachers!" "Fanatics-That-Swarm-Like-Bees!" One nickname stuck: "Again-Baptizers," or "Anabaptists."

## Reformation on Wings of Song

Church music played a major role in the Reformation period. Martin Luther felt that offering praise to God had wrongly become the monopoly of a trained minority. So he wrote hymns in German, had weekly rehearsals for the entire congregation to learn four-part harmony, and included hymns and the use of musical instruments such as organs in worship services.

His early hymns put the Ten Commandments and the Apostles' Creed into German verse. His most famous hymn, "A Mighty Fortress Is Our God," was written during severe opposition, a raging epidemic, and his own poor health. Christians all over the world have been singing this so-called Battle Hymn of the Reformation for the past five centuries.

Other Protestant Reformation leaders held other opinions about music:

• Ulrich Zwingli and his followers smashed organs or had them carted out of churches.

• John Calvin preferred singing only the Psalms in unison. One of his followers developed the familiar tune beginning with the words, "Praise God, from Whom All Blessings Flow."

In spite of all the ridicule, Anabaptists found ready recruits—especially among the lower classes after Luther encouraged German princes to massacre rebellious peasants. Anabaptists sent out missionaries to many parts of Europe, urging people to become daring disciples.

No one great leader emerges in the early history of Anabaptists like Luther at the beginning of the Lutherans or Zwingli (and later, Calvin) at the beginning of the Presbyterian and Reformed churches. Why? Because most of the Anabaptist leaders were killed within only a few years' time. (See the box below.)

Christ's People four centuries ago had no concept of "live and let live." They were unable to see how there could be more than one right way to follow Christ—their way was that one right way. Such a rigid view paved the way to martyrdom. Catholics persecuted Protestants; Protestants persecuted Catholics; everybody persecuted Anabaptists.

With their brightest and best already dead, some of the early Anabaptists were easily led astray by extremists. One group eerily foreshadowed the Branch Davidian massacre at Waco, Texas in 1993: They announced that their German city was the New Jerusalem. Mustering an army, they crowned a new King David, complete with multiple wives as in Old Testament times. This bizarre incident brought shame to all Anabaptists, even after the fanatics themselves were wiped out by military force.

The Anabaptist movement might have mired down in extremism or faded away in disgrace if not for Menno Simons. A Dutch Catholic

## Anabaptist Martyrs

Newly-married Margaretha Sattler saw her beloved husband burned to death while pointing toward heaven as a sign of where his hopes lay. He was charged with the fact that both he and Margaretha had previously been members of religious orders, dedicated to lifelong sexual abstinence. Margaretha's turn came eight days later. Like many other Anabaptists, she was drowned in a river—a cruelty joke growing out of this group's insistence on baptism for believing adults.

A pregnant Anabaptist woman witnessed her husband's execution; she was spared only long enough for the birth of their daughter. From a jail in Antwerp, Belgium, the young mother wrote:

My dearest child, the true love of God strengthen you in virtue, you who are yet so young, and whom I must leave in this wicked, evil, perverse world. Oh that it had pleased the Lord that I might have brought you up!... Be not ashamed of us; it is the way the prophets and the apostles went. Your dear father demonstrated with his blood that it is the genuine faith, and I also hope to attest the same with my blood.... We shall meet hereafter.[9]

priest, Simons slowly accepted the ideas of the Protestant Reformers. Under his wise and cautious leadership, Anabaptists gathered new strength. No wonder the best-known name among Christian heirs of the Anabaptist tradition is *Mennonite.*

# PROTESTANTS IN FRANCE, THE NETHERLANDS, AND SCOTLAND

Chapter 7 of this book tells about Jacques Lefèvre d'Étaples (1450–1536), a famous professor at the University of Paris who helped prepare the way for the Protestant Reformation (see page 111). Among the many university students he influenced was a young man named John Calvin (1509–1564). Well trained in law and literature, Calvin was also influenced by his cousin, who had been influenced by the persecuted Waldenses.

Calvin was part of the second generation of Protestant Reformers; he was only eight years old when Martin Luther displayed his *95 Theses.* At an undated time Calvin (like Luther) had a deeply personal religious experience and became an earnest Bible student. Although Luther wrote a lot, he never compiled a complete and balanced statement of his beliefs. When Catholic pressure forced Calvin out of France, he took refuge in Switzerland and wrote the first edition of the most important book from Reformation times. Its title is usually translated *Institutes of the Christian Religion;* a better wording might be *Principles of the Christian Faith,* or *Instruction in the Christian Faith.*

At the age of only 27, Calvin produced this clear and systematic Protestant theology based on statements from the Apostles' Creed. He wrote in classical Latin and then translated his writing into clear, elegant French. Throughout his life Calvin continued to rewrite his book until its original 6 chapters had expanded to 79.

The very name *Calvin* sounds harsh to many Christians today because of a doctrinal system known as *Calvinism.* As usually understood, this refers especially to *predestination:* the belief that God has planned from the beginning of time who is *destined* to be saved and who is *destined* to be eternally lost.

Actually predestination was not unique to Calvin; many great Christians from Augustine to Martin Luther embraced it. Yet Calvin stated this doctrine more clearly than anyone else, so it is forever linked with his name.

Calvin did not stress predestination. Rather, his starting-point was the almighty power of God. He taught in effect, "If any of us are saved, it is because God does it, not we ourselves. The Bible says that all of us are lost in sin, so it is only by God's mercy that any of us are saved."[10]

Inclined toward the quiet life of a scholar, he never planned to become a prominent leader in human affairs. Other people almost forced him to "get into the game," as Calvin himself expressed it.[11] For many years he virtually ruled the Swiss city of Geneva, being strongly influenced by Augustine's famous *The City of God*. Before he came, Geneva had been known for its drinking, gambling, and other vices. Calvin reformed not only the faith but also the conduct of Genevans, so that John Knox, a famous Scottish Protestant, would later describe Geneva, as "the most perfect school of Christ . . . since the days of the apostles."[12]

John Calvin never held any title beyond that of local pastor. He did not force others to follow his beliefs; instead, he tried to persuade them—through his words and the passage of laws for the common good. He preached almost daily. He set up the first Protestant academy and became one of its teachers. He continued to write sermons, commentaries on nearly every book of the Bible, and thousands of letters. (Calvin had a gift for writing polite but forceful letters to kings and others in the seats of power.) All of this work continued through years of poor health, including migraine headaches.

Martin Luther and John Calvin never met, but they had a mutual respect for each other. Each of them appreciated what the other had written even though not fully agreeing with it.

Because Switzerland offered a measure of religious liberty, Protestant exiles from many countries flocked to Geneva. In this way Calvin had a far-reaching influence; he has been called the only international Protestant Reformer. He sent out many missionaries, concealing their names for security reasons as some mission agencies do today. These bold evangelists traveled on back-country roads and hid in attics while beginning underground congregations. Calvin even tried to reach beyond Europe: He sent two missionaries with a group of Protestants who were sailing for Brazil. Unfortunately this venture came to nothing because of the treachery of one of its leaders.

Since Geneva lies in the French-speaking part of Switzerland, it isn't surprising that Calvin and his followers had a great influence in France. At one time between 10 percent and 15 percent of all French people were Protestants, and most of these followed the Reformed faith. French Protestants were called *Huguenots*, a name of uncertain origin. Bitter struggles between Protestants and Catholics occurred in France during the later 1500s.

Calvin's type of Protestantism also had a strong effect in the Netherlands, where the Brethren of the Common Life had already prepared the way for renewal and reform. During this time Holland was under the rule of Catholic Spain. When a new king used the dreaded Spanish Inquisition to kill thousands of Protestants, the Dutch rebelled and eventually won their freedom.

Another country strongly influenced by John Calvin was Scotland. John Knox (c.1505–1572), the Scottish leader already quoted, came to Geneva as an exile. After listening and learning there, he traveled back home and virtually kindled a religious revolution. Scotland became one of the most staunchly Presbyterian nations in the world.

# PROTESTANTS IN ENGLAND

The story of the Protestant Reformation in England is quite different from the story of the Protestant Reformation on the European mainland. It originated not at a church or a university but in a king's palace. At first it mainly affected church government, not the actual beliefs and practices of Christians.

Henry VIII (1491–1547), king of England, was no Protestant. In fact, early in his long reign he produced a pamphlet (probably ghost-written by someone else) strongly opposing the teachings of Martin Luther. In return, a grateful pope named him "Defender of the Faith", a title used by English rulers ever since.

By the 1530s, the Defender of the Faith was losing his patience with the pope. For political reasons he had married his older brother's Spanish widow. Only one young daughter still lived from their marriage, and the queen was now getting into her 40s. Fearing trouble in the future, King Henry wanted a new wife who would give him a male heir to the throne.

Ordinarily the pope would have granted the king a divorce or an annulment as a courtesy. However, Henry's Spanish queen was also the aunt of Emperor Charles V, whom the pope did not dare to offend.

Finally King Henry took matters into his own hands. He realized that many English people were noticing how rich English churches and monasteries had become. He also realized that they resented having to send offerings to the pope in Rome. Making the most of this anti-foreign feeling, the king got laws passed naming himself and not the pope as head of the Church of England. The new laws made Thomas Cranmer (1489–1556), archbishop of Canterbury, the highest church official in the country. With Cranmer's help King Henry quickly got his first marriage dissolved and his second marriage legalized.

At first it seemed that little had really changed. The Latin language was still used in worship; the church was still governed by bishops. (This explains its other name, Episcopal, from *episkopos*, the New Testament word for a manager or overseer.) Christ's People in England were still Catholics, but English Catholics or Anglo-Catholics (or Anglicans) rather than Roman Catholics. However, several historical forces were working toward further change:

- William Tyndale (1494–1536) died a martyr's death for daring to produce a New Testament in everyday English. Yet only a few years after Tyndale's death, a large pulpit Bible was placed in every church in England. As more and more English began to read God's Word in their own language, they saw the need for change.

- Partly as a grab for power and money, King Henry did away with monasteries all over England. Many Catholics either left their faith or their country; some of them died as martyrs.

- As the English traveled to and from the European mainland, the teachings of Luther, Calvin, and other Reformers continued to spread.

- Henry VIII finally had a son, a sickly boy who succeeded him as King Edward VI. Those who ruled in the young king's name leaned toward the Protestant side, so the pace of Reformation increased in England. Archbishop Cranmer produced an Anglican confession of faith and new guide to worship, *The Book of Common Prayer*. For examples of prayers in this famous book, see the box on page 131.

After the boy king died at age 16, his older half-sister came to the throne. A genuinely devout Roman Catholic, Queen Mary I (1516–1558) believed it was her duty to persecute Protestants; among those burned at the stake during those troubled times was Archbishop Cranmer. Yet what Queen Mary actually accomplished during her brief reign was to cause many more English people to start hating Catholics. Ever since, she has been stuck with the nickname Bloody Mary.

The next ruler was Queen Elizabeth I (1533–1603), the only surviving child of King Henry VIII. Elizabeth felt no strong urge to support either side in a war of religion. Instead, she sought a "middle way." Anglicanism truly became a Protestant denomination, but one that still seemed closer to Roman Catholicism than did Lutheranism or Presbyterianism.

The English Reformation, for all of its strange beginnings, is important in church history far beyond the Church of England and far beyond the shores of England itself for two main reasons:[13]

1. The Anglicans opened the door for other kinds of Christians to emerge such as the Puritans whose spiritual heirs are the Congregationalists today. In coming centuries other important groups of Christ's People would arise in England: during the 1600s, the Baptists and the Friends or Quakers; during the 1700s, the Methodists; during the 1800s, the Salvation Army and various Holiness groups.

2. English-speaking people colonized and conquered many other countries or areas, bringing their ways of worshiping with them. One striking result of this historical movement is that more Anglicans or Episcopalians worshiped last Sunday in Africa than in the United States, Canada, and Australia combined!

## A Prayer Book for All Seasons

Perhaps the greatest achievement of the Protestant Reformation in England was *The Book of Common Prayer*, written and compiled by Archbishop Thomas Cranmer. Though worded in English of the 1540s, it still speaks to human hearts today.

Here are two samples from this incomparable prayer book:[14]

Blessed Lord, who hast caused all Holy Scriptures to be written for our learning, grant that we may in such wise hear them, read, mark, learn, and inwardly digest them, that by patience and comfort of Thy Holy Word we may embrace and ever hold fast the blessed hope of everlasting life, which Thou hast given us in our Savior Jesus Christ. Amen.

Almighty and most merciful Father, we have erred and strayed from Thy ways like lost sheep. We have followed too much the devices and desires of our own hearts. We have offended against Thy holy laws. We have left undone those things which we ought to have done, and we have done those things which we ought not to have done, and there is no health in us.

But Thou, O Lord, have mercy upon us miserable offenders. Spare Thou them, O God, which confess their faults. Restore Thou them that be penitent, according to Thy promises declared unto mankind in Christ Jesus our Lord. And grant, O most merciful Father, for His sake, that we may hereafter live a godly, religious, and sober life, to the glory of Thy holy name. Amen.

# PROTESTANTS ELSEWHERE IN EUROPE

This book can give only the briefest survey of the Protestant Reformation. Besides all of the important leaders already mentioned, each of the great Reformers also had a special colleague who succeeded him and continued his work. Luther had Philip Melanchthon (1497–1560); Zwingli had Heinrich Bullinger (1504–1575); Calvin had Theodore Beza (1519–1605).

Many leaders in other lands also deserve mention:

- The Calvinist John à Lasco led in the Reformation that seemed for a time to be sweeping across his native Poland; later he became a university professor in England.

- The Lutheran brothers Olav and Lars Petri led all of Sweden into the Protestant camp; others later followed their example in Denmark, Norway, Iceland, Finland, Estonia, Latvia, and Lithuania.

- Even in Italy, the geographical heart of Roman Catholicism, there were bold Reformers such as Peter Martyr Vermigli (1500–1562), who later became a university Bible professor in England and in Switzerland.

- Persecuted pre-Reformation groups—such as the Hussites in what is now the Czech Republic and the Waldenses in the high mountains of Italy, France, and Switzerland—came out of hiding and found that they had much in common with Reformation Christians.

- Many Hungarian students of both Luther and Calvin so influenced their native land that Hungary at one time had a strong Protestant majority.

Some of these gains of Protestantism, though, were only temporary; chapter 9 explains why.

# KEY EVENTS

## 1500 TO 1600

*The events listed here are covered in chapters 8 and 9; the number following each event indicates the relevant chapter.*

In Rome, Michelangelo paints the Sistine Chapel; foundations are laid for a new St. Peter's; several Catholic leaders urge reform. (9)

Antonio de Montesinos protests mistreatment of Native Americans by settlers in the Caribbean. (9)

Martin Luther launches the Protestant Reformation in Germany; his *95 Theses* captivates Europe. (8)

In Switzerland, Ulrich Zwingli begins church reform. (8)

Luther refuses to recant before Emperor Charles V and others; he later translates the New Testament into everyday German. (8)

Pope Adrian VI tries but fails to reform the Roman Catholic Church from the inside. (9)

Anabaptists spread in Switzerland and Germany, in spite of persecution by Catholics and Protestants. (8)

William Tyndale translates and publishes the New Testament in everyday English; he dies a martyr. (8)

Luther and Zwingli meet but cannot fully agree on their beliefs. (8)

King Henry VIII becomes head of the Church of England; a Bible is placed in every English church. (8)

Catholics carry the Good News to many parts of the Americas; Bartolomé de Las Casas defends Native American rights. (9)

John Calvin publishes the most complete Protestant theology: *Institutes of the Christian Religion.* (8)

Pope Paul III approves Ignatius of Loyola's new Jesuit order; Francis Xavier and other missionaries go to many parts of the world. (9)

Some Anabaptists fall into extremism, recover under Menno Simons' wise leadership, and become known as Mennonites. (8)

The Council of Trent begins to correct abuses among Roman Catholic Christians and strengthens their opposition to Protestantism. (9)

In England, Archbishop Thomas Cranmer publishes *The Book of Common Prayer.* (8)

Queen Mary I tries to make England Catholic again; many Protestants take refuge with John Calvin in Geneva, Switzerland. (8)

John Knox leads the Reformation in Scotland. (8)

In Spain, Teresa of Avila and John of the Cross work to improve spiritual life among nuns and monks. (9)

In England, Queen Elizabeth I tries to find a "middle way" between Catholics and Protestants. (8)

In France, Catholics and Protestants fight wars. (8 & 9)

Navies from European Catholic countries combine to defeat a Muslim fleet in the Mediterranean. (9)

In Japan, Catholic missionaries have great success; in the Philippines, they stop the spread of Islam. (9)

Dutch Protestants successfully rebel against their Spanish Catholic rulers. (8)

In France, the king finally ends the fighting between Catholics and Protestants. (9)

Catholic missionaries experience success in Africa, the Americas, and many parts of Asia, but new Japanese rulers begin to oppose Christianity. (9)

Many Orthodox Christians in eastern Europe recognize the pope, without becoming Catholics. (9)

The Thomas Christians of India come into a close relationship with Roman Catholics. (9)

**MARTIN LUTHER**

Luther translated the Scriptures into common German.

# 9. Reformation and Expansion: Catholics and Others
## (1500–1600)

**W**ell before the date usually given for the start of the Protestant
Reformation (October 31, 1517), concerned Roman Catholics were
making strong efforts toward renewal and reform. Chapter 7 mentions
how Cardinal Jiménez cleaned up much of the corruption among
Catholics in Spain. Even in Rome, small groups of Christian leaders
met to pray and plan for improvements. They spoke out against
unworthy and ignorant priests; they encouraged Bible reading and
church music; they tried to settle community disputes; they cared
for the sick and the needy.

For a time it seemed as if a thorough internal reform might even
bring protesting Christians back into the Catholic fold. In 1521 a
Dutch priest who had tutored the young Emperor Charles V was
elected as pope. Taking the name Adrian VI, the new pope tried to
stop the sale of indulgences as well as other unworthy practices. Yet
he could make little headway against other Catholic leaders in Rome
who were unwilling to give up their wealth and privileges. After less
than two years of frustration, Pope Adrian died in 1523. (Incidentally,
he was the last non-Italian pope until the Polish bishop Karol Wojtyla
became Pope John Paul II in 1978.)

In the 1530s Pope Paul III (1468–1549) appointed a study
commission whose report may have brought more aid and comfort
to Protestants than to Catholics, since it indicated that the Roman
pope and those surrounding him were the main source of the problem.
Pope Paul tried to act on some of the recommendations in the report,
but as before, political considerations got in the way of spiritual
concerns. In the 1540s Pope Paul made a last-ditch attempt to
bring Catholics and Protestants back together; it failed just as

earlier efforts had. Finally this reform-minded pope made two important decisions. He:

- Called for a new general council representing all Roman Catholics.

- Approved several new orders of full-time religious workers— especially The Society of Jesus, or the *Jesuits.*

# THE COUNCIL OF TRENT

There were political reasons for choosing the small town of Trent as the location for the general council called by Pope Paul III. The Holy Roman Emperor wanted the council to meet near areas in Germany that were under his control; the pope wanted it to meet near Rome. They compromised on Trent, in the mountains of northern Italy.

The Council of Trent met in three sessions, widely separated in time, between 1545 and 1563. The final session was delayed for several years by an elderly pope who insisted that he could do all the reforming himself, while retaining full power. More Italians attended the council than representatives from other countries; few Catholics came from northern and western Europe. Protestants were invited to one session, but soon left when their concerns were kept off the agenda by the majority.

What kinds of decisions were made by the Council of Trent?

Many of them were *positive:* There was to be no more selling of indulgences. Bishops could no longer get by with worldly lifestyles; instead, they were to regularly visit, instruct, and minister to those under their care. More seminaries were to be started for the training of devout Catholic priests. More missionaries were to be sent to share the Good News about Jesus all over the world.

Yet in many ways the Council of Trent hardened the stance of Catholics in opposition to Protestants. For centuries there had been a measure of freedom in the way Catholic teachings could be interpreted; after Trent, there was less room to wiggle. All of the doctrines opposed by the Reformers were reaffirmed (see the box on page 120 in chapter 8) and church members were taught:

- Men and women are not saved by faith alone; they must work with God to insure salvation.

- The bread and wine used in the Lord's Supper do become the body and blood of Christ.

- The Virgin Mary and all the other saints are still to be honored and mentioned in prayer.

- All Christian ministers must remain unmarried.

The Council of Trent set up several safeguards to make sure that no one would stray from the right path. They enlarged the role of the Inquisition in rooting out so-called heretics. They issued a list of books that faithful Catholics must not read (including three-fourths of all books printed up to that time).

Also on the forbidden list was any translation of the Scriptures into a local language. The only official Bible was to be the Latin Vulgate, and even that should not be made available freely to everyone. Of course worship services everywhere were to be conducted only in Latin.

At first it seemed the Council of Trent might weaken the power of the pope, but in the end its effect was just the opposite: The pope was the one assigned to see that the decisions of the council were carried out. After Trent, the center of the Catholic Church was more firmly fixed in Rome than ever before.

The Council came close to banning all music by living composers; many of the conferees insisted that only the ancient Gregorian chants should be used in worship. The music of a devout Italian choirmaster caused them to change their minds and approve "contemporary Christian music" of four centuries ago. That Italian was Giovanni Pierluigi da Palestrina (1525–1594), whose compositions are still being sung today. The adjacent box shows a part of the dedication Palestrina wrote for one of his many books of choir music.

All in all, the Council of Trent set the pattern for Roman Catholics all over the world—a pattern that would continue with little meaningful change until the 1960s, when another pope would call another general council.

## The Purpose of Church Music

"The function of music in the church is the seasoning of devotion by the added delight of sweetness of song and variety of harmony. The sharper blame do those deserve who misemploy so great and splendid a gift of God in light and unworthy things."[1]

# JESUITS AND OTHERS

During the 1500s many Roman Catholics showed a spirit of devotion that could be an example to any Christian of any age. They also set up new religious orders of two types:

- Some of them tried to encourage a stronger devotion to Christ among traditional monks and nuns.
- Others more nearly resembled the friars of earlier years; they sent out men and women to serve in Jesus' name.

A good example of the first type is the lifework of Teresa of Avila (1515–1582) and her younger associate John of the Cross (1542–1591). Both of them came from the city of Avila in central Spain and were Christian mystics, stressing an intimate personal relationship with Christ. Yet both of them also took practical steps to improve monastic orders—Teresa mainly working with nuns, of course, and John mainly working with monks.

A good example of the second type mentioned on page 37 is Angela Merici (1474–1540), a devout Italian woman who enlisted several friends to help her teach poor girls. Later this group developed into the Ursulines, the oldest and largest order of teaching sisters among Roman Catholics.

The most famous and most representative example of the second type of religious order is Ignatius Loyola (1491–1556), founder of the Jesuits. A worldly-minded Spanish soldier, Ignatius was recovering from a serious wound when he had a deep spiritual experience. After that he spent many years in preparation for ministry, humbly sitting in university classes with students half his age. Then he and a few close friends pledged to become Christian soldiers, going anywhere and facing any danger for the sake of Christ.

Roman Catholic leaders including the reform-minded Pope Paul III were a little suspicious at first: Were Loyola and his friends trying too hard to prove their courage and devotion? Finally the pope decided to approve The Society of Jesus. In doing so he commissioned the largest and most effective band of Christian missionaries the world had ever seen.

The Jesuits played a large part in winning back much of Europe to the Catholic way of worshiping. In doing so they earned a nickname: "the pope's shock troops." By the end of the 1500s, many formerly Protestant areas were back inside the fold.

The Jesuits—along with older religious orders such as the Dominicans and the Franciscans—played an even larger role in carrying the message of the cross to every known continent.

---

## Catholic Faith, Christian Devotion

**Teresa of Avila:** Let everyone understand that real love of God does not consist in tear-shedding, nor in that sweetness and tenderness for which we usually long (just because they console us), but in serving God in justice, fortitude of soul, and humility.[2]

**John of the Cross:** If we are guided by divine Scripture, we shall not be able to err, for He who speaks in it is the Holy Spirit.[3]

**Ignatius of Loyola:** Teach us, good Lord, to serve Thee as Thou deservest: to give and not to count the cost; to fight and not to heed the wounds; to toil and not to ask for rest; to labor and not to ask for any reward save knowing that we do Thy will. Through Jesus Christ our Lord.[4]

# CATHOLIC OUTREACH WORLDWIDE

Some Christians say that Francis Xavier (1506–1552) is the second greatest missionary (after the Apostle Paul) in all of church history. A Basque from Spain, Francis was among that small group of companions who joined Ignatius of Loyola in founding the Jesuits.

Xavier first served in Goa, a Portuguese seaport colony in India. Then he moved down the coast to work with people in the low-caste fishing community who had turned to Christ. Next he traveled to what are now parts of Malaysia and Indonesia. His most effective work was done during the 27 months he spent in Japan. When he died after only ten years of missionary service in Asia, he was trying hard to get into China.

Any time a missionary covers that much territory in that short a time, the question must be asked: Did he really lead those thousands of men and women to become Christ's People?

Yes and no. Xavier's standard operating procedure was to find a local translator (often a very poor one, as it turned out) and start teaching the Ten Commandments, the Lord's Prayer, the Apostles' Creed, and a few other simple prayers and statements of faith. No doubt many of his "converts" understood next to nothing about Christianity. Yet it was a beginning. At least they knew a little about Jesus the Christ. They could pray to the living God in their own language. And in Francis Xavier himself they had seen a living example of how a Christian ought to act.

As in Europe centuries earlier, when many people turned to Christ all at once, this set up a spiritual climate in which individual decisions could follow. Certainly Christians of other types have no room to criticize such eager Catholics as Francis Xavier and his missionary colleagues: It would be another 200 years before Protestant Christians would send out any significant number of missionaries at all.

Other Catholic missionaries followed up Xavier's spiritual beachhead in Japan. In 1579 they started a new settlement for Christians; it has since grown to be the great city of Nagasaki. Many Japanese people were quite open to the Good News about Jesus the Christ. Even some of their rulers were sympathetic, giving protection to new believers. By four centuries ago there were already tens of thousands of Christians in Japan—some historians say hundreds of thousands, even half a million.

China proved to be a tougher mission field. Portuguese seafarers set up Macao on an island off the coast of China, much like their colony of Goa on the coast of India. One missionary, looking longingly toward the mainland, cried out, "O Rock, Rock, when will you open?"[5]

The first Jesuit with any degree of success in China was an Italian named Matteo Ricci (1552–1610), who had earlier been a seminary professor in Goa. At first Ricci was only allowed to live and minister out in the provinces. Unlike Xavier and many other early Catholic missionaries, he settled down and learned the local culture and language.

At the turn of the century in 1600, Matteo Ricci got his long-hoped-for permission to enter the imperial capital. Very cleverly he made the Chinese emperor a gift of two clocks . . . without any instructions as to how to keep them running. The emperor was fascinated; he kept Ricci in his royal court as clock winder and mapmaker.

Jesuits and others served as missionaries in the Philippines. They found even greater response there than in Japan. Everywhere they went they set up new villages of Christian converts. Muslims had been spreading rapidly across the islands from the South to the North, but these early Catholics managed to contain them in a relatively small area. Even today, a majority of Filipinos claim to be Christ's People of one sort or another, while only a small minority follow the way of Islam.

Missionaries followed the fleets of Portuguese colonizers to what is now Indonesia. Unfortunately they did relatively little to reach out to the local people. *A question worth considering:* What if the Portuguese had been as eager in sending missionaries to Indonesia as the Spanish were in sending missionaries to the Philippines? Would Indonesia be the most populous Muslim country in the world today?

European Catholics also tried to spread the Good News in other parts of Asia including Korea and several areas of Southeast Asia.

In India during the 1500s there occurred another of those tantalizing "might-have-beens" of Asian church history. Strong Muslim rulers invaded from Afghanistan in the North, bringing together almost all of India under their rule. The most important of these Mogul emperors was Akbar the Great, who reigned from 1556 till 1605. Akbar was remarkably open-minded and rather dissatisfied with Islam. Several times he received Jesuit missionaries in his court for long discussions about matters of religion. Yet he never turned toward Christ, nor did any significant number of his people.

Missionaries had more success in western Africa, where the Portuguese had already been spreading the Good News in the Congo since the late 1400s. One African crown prince was sent to Portugal to learn how to become a Catholic priest; when he returned to the Congo, he was made the first bishop of his capital city. In the 1520s a priest moved from the Congo to Angola and started working there. Much as in Europe many centuries before, a king or a queen would become a believer and lead thousands to do the same, but then other kings and queens would oppose or even persecute Christians.

The first missionaries to Mozambique in eastern Africa were sent not from Europe but from Goa on the coast of India. A king and 400 of his people were baptized. Unfortunately this mission effort soon bogged down because of military struggles between Muslims and Portuguese.

The most spectacular spread of Christianity during the 1500s, of course, occurred in the Americas. By early in that century, Spanish and Portuguese conquerors had already overrun all of the Caribbean, the coasts of South and Central America, the southern borders of North America, and many inland areas of both continents.

Other history books tell of the killing and looting, the exploitation of land and people, the epidemics and genocides, and the racism and slavery that marred this movement in history. All of that is true. Yet at the same time many thousands of Spanish and Portuguese Catholics made a sincere effort to spread the Good News about Jesus among the peoples of the Americas.

By modern standards their missionary methods were faulty, just as Francis Xavier's were. Yet the fact remains that in the course of a very few years, millions of people turned from worshiping images and offering human sacrifices to becoming Christ's People . . . at least in name. The fact also remains that many of those early Catholic missionaries to the Americas were among the first people in all of history to speak up for basic human rights.

The most famous of them was a wealthy Spanish priest named Bartolomé de Las Casas (1474–1566). While living an easy life in the Caribbean, Las Casas gradually felt convicted of the wrongs being done by himself and other Spanish settlers. At the age of 48 he became a Dominican friar.

Back and forth across the Atlantic he sailed—sometimes persuading the king of Spain to make new laws protecting Native Americans, some-times leading the fight against those who broke the new laws in the New World. For his bold and tireless efforts in the name of Christ and humankind, Las Casas has been nicknamed The Apostle of the Indies.

A contemporary of Las Casas shared his passion for caring treatment of all people. Antonio de Montesinos was a Dominican friar in what is now the Dominican Republic. On December 25, 1511, he delivered a message that came as a real shocker to the wealthy Spanish owners of mines and plantations who were sitting in his congregation. His text was Matthew 3:3: "The voice of one crying in the wilderness" (KJV). A condensed version of his historic sermon is in the box on the following page.

On December 25, 1511, Antonio de Montesinos delivered this sermon based on Matthew 3:3:

I have climbed to this pulpit to let you know of your sins, for I am the voice of Christ crying in the desert of this island. You are in mortal sin because of the cruelty and tyranny you bring to bear upon these innocent people.

Tell me: By what right do you wage war against people who dwelt in peace and quiet on their own lands? By what justice do you keep them in such horrible servitude? Why do you oppress and exploit them, not even giving them enough to eat, not caring for them in their illnesses? They die—or rather, you kill them—so that you may extract more and more gold every day.

Are they not human? Have they no souls? Are you not required to love them as you love yourself? Be certain: In your present state you can no more be saved than the Moors or the Turks![6]

# LASTING RESULTS OF THE TWO REFORMATIONS

As the tumultuous century of the two Reformations moved toward its close, several important events gave signs of the future—some positive, some negative:

- *There were signs that the pressure of Muslim advance had been diminished—at least temporarily.* In 1571 the pope encouraged European Christians to send a fleet of ships that defeated a Turkish navy in the Mediterranean. During the later 1500s, Catholic missionaries succeeded in containing the spread of Islam from Indonesia into the Philippines.

- *There were signs of improved relations between Christ's People of different kinds.* In 1596 an agreement was signed between the Roman Catholic Church and many Eastern Orthodox Christians of Hungary, the Czech Republic, Poland, and the Ukraine: The Orthodox could keep their own ways of worshiping while recognizing the overall authority of the pope. In 1598 the king of France brought an end to conflicts between French Catholics and French Protestants. In 1599 the age-old Thomas Christians came into a closer fellowship with Portuguese Catholics in southern India.

- *There were also signs of trouble to come.* New anti-Christian rulers began to arise in Japan; new laws were passed against "devilish" foreign religions. Squabbles between Jesuit missionaries on the one hand and Dominican and Franciscan missionaries on the other did not help things, either.

What were the lasting results of events during the 1500s? Two results deserve special mention: the increase of Bible translations and the diversity among Christ's People around the globe.

## A Flood of New Bibles

The Protestant Reformers insisted that every Christian believer should have access to the written Word of God. That is why Martin Luther made his historic translation into everyday German. That is why William Tyndale bravely faced a martyr's death for translating the Scriptures in English.

Luther's German translation and the English-language versions prepared by Tyndale and others were by no means the only new Bibles of the Reformation period. A listing of years when other complete Bible translations first appeared in printed form is shown here.

Even Catholics got into the act. The adjacent list does not include parts of the Bible that were being translated into local languages by Roman Catholic missionaries all over the world. The Council of Trent had already ruled that the Latin Vulgate was the only official Bible translation, yet during the later 1500s Catholic exiles in France produced a Catholic version of the English Bible.

> ### Bibles in the Common Language[7]
>
> 1471 Italian
> 1478 Catalan (a language of Spain)
> 1522 Dutch
> 1530 French
> 1541 Swedish
> 1550 Danish
> 1553 Spanish
> 1561 Polish
> 1581 Slavonic
> 1584 Icelandic
> 1584 Slovenian
> 1588 Welsh
> 1590 Hungarian

## A Changing Map of the Christian World

Before Reformation times, virtually all of Europe was considered to be Christian—Orthodox Christian to the East and the Southeast, Roman Catholic Christian nearly everywhere else. After Reformation times, the map of Christian Europe was cut up into considerably more pieces.

Three areas in Europe were least affected by the Reformation: Russia and other Orthodox nations to the East; Spain, where Cardinal Jiménez had already carried out a reform of sorts before the Reformation proper ever got started; and Ireland, where Protestantism unfortunately came to be seen as a mark of the hated English and Scottish invaders.

We tend to think of France, Hungary, and Poland as countries with a long Catholic heritage. Yet at one time a majority of Hungarians were

Protestant, and there were strong Protestant minorities in France and Poland. We tend to think of Germany as the land of Luther; yet much of Germany stayed well within the Catholic camp.

Generally speaking, southern Europe eventually returned to the Catholic fold; northern Europe (except for Ireland) became Protestant. But even within Protestantism there were many divisions: Lutherans in Germany and Scandinavia; Presbyterians and Reformed in Switzerland, Scotland, and the Netherlands; Anglicans in England; Mennonites and other Anabaptists scattered almost everywhere. Many countries of Europe now had their own national church organizations: the Church of England, for example, which was Anglican or Episcopal; the Church of Scotland, which was Presbyterian; the Church of Sweden, which was Lutheran.

Most important of all among results of the two Reformations: In 1500, 95 percent of the world's Christians were all clustered in the continent of Europe. By 1600, Christians had spread far and wide— into Africa, many parts of Asia, and especially the Americas.

# KEY EVENTS

## 1500 TO 1600

*The events listed here are covered in chapters 8 and 9; the number following each event indicates the relevant chapter.*

In Rome, Michelangelo paints the Sistine Chapel; foundations are laid for a new St. Peter's; several Catholic leaders urge reform. (9)

Antonio de Montesinos protests mistreatment of Native Americans by settlers in the Caribbean. (9)

Martin Luther launches the Protestant Reformation in Germany; his *95 Theses* captivates Europe. (8)

In Switzerland, Ulrich Zwingli begins church reform. (8)

Luther refuses to recant before Emperor Charles V and others; he later translates the New Testament into everyday German. (8)

Pope Adrian VI tries but fails to reform the Roman Catholic Church from the inside. (9)

Anabaptists spread in Switzerland and Germany, in spite of persecution by Catholics and Protestants. (8)

William Tyndale translates and publishes the New Testament in everyday English; he dies a martyr. (8)

Luther and Zwingli meet but cannot fully agree on their beliefs. (8)

King Henry VIII becomes head of the Church of England; a Bible is placed in every English church. (8)

Catholics carry the Good News to many parts of the Americas; Bartolomé de Las Casas defends Native American rights. (9)

John Calvin publishes the most complete Protestant theology: *Institutes of the Christian Religion.* (8)

Pope Paul III approves Ignatius of Loyola's new Jesuit order; Francis Xavier and other missionaries go to many parts of the world. (9)

Some Anabaptists fall into extremism, recover under Menno Simons' wise leadership, and become known as Mennonites. (8)

The Council of Trent begins to correct abuses among Roman Catholic Christians and strengthens their opposition to Protestantism. (9)

In England, Archbishop Thomas Cranmer publishes *The Book of Common Prayer.* (8)

Queen Mary I tries to make England Catholic again; many Protestants take refuge with John Calvin in Geneva, Switzerland. (8)

John Knox leads the Reformation in Scotland. (8)

In Spain, Teresa of Avila and John of the Cross work to improve spiritual life among nuns and monks. (9)

In England, Queen Elizabeth I tries to find a "middle way" between Catholics and Protestants. (8)

In France, Catholics and Protestants fight wars. (8 & 9)

Navies from European Catholic countries combine to defeat a Muslim fleet in the Mediterranean. (9)

In Japan, Catholic missionaries have great success; in the Philippines, they stop the spread of Islam. (9)

Dutch Protestants successfully rebel against their Spanish Catholic rulers. (8)

In France, the king finally ends the fighting between Catholics and Protestants. (9)

Catholic missionaries experience success in Africa, the Americas, and many parts of Asia, but new Japanese rulers begin to oppose Christianity. (9)

Many Orthodox Christians in eastern Europe recognize the pope, without becoming Catholics. (9)

The Thomas Christians of India come into a close relationship with Roman Catholics. (9)

## OLIVER CROMWELL (1599–1658)

As the Puritan leader of the Parliamentary side in the Civil War,
he declared England a republic, or Commonwealth, in 1649.

# 10. A Time of Tumult
## (1600–1700)

**W**hat is the typical reaction to opposition, difficulty, or danger?

Psychologists tell us that human beings, like other living organisms when faced with a challenge, will usually react in one of two ways: *fight* or *flight*.

The 1600s were full of opposition, difficulty, and danger for Christ's People. Many of them took their stand to *fight* for what they believed was right. Many of them also took *flight* to a safer place.

During this century Europe was still the heart and center of Christianity, as it had been for more than a millennium. Yet by the beginning of the 1700s the situation had begun to change, because so many of Christ's People from Europe had moved to the Americas.

Christians are always in need of renewal and reform. The 1500s had brought the most far-reaching reforms yet seen, among both Protestants and Roman Catholics. The effects of those two Reformations continued during the 1600s—in art and music, in an increasing flood of new Bible translations (by Protestants and Catholics), and in the worldwide spread of Christianity. Yet Christians living during the 1600s still felt a need for further reform.

Thus the recurring themes among Christ's People three centuries ago were:

- Response of fight or flight.

- Increasing influence of Europe.

- Need for further reform.

# FIGHT OR FLIGHT

## Central Europe

One unintended side effect of the Reformation period was that government officials now had more control over religion than ever before. A king or queen, whether Catholic or Protestant, could decide which faith everyone in that realm must follow. The only exceptions were in Italy, where a strong pope could stay distanced from government interference, and in countries such as Scotland and the Netherlands where Protestants had overthrown Catholic rulers.

Since the mid-1500s an uneasy peace between Protestants and Catholics in central Europe had been maintained. This temporary truce ended in the first half of the 1600s with the coming of the Thirty Years' War.

More than one historian has said that this war started as a religious struggle with politics mixed in, but ended up as a political struggle with religion mixed in. The effect on ordinary people was devastating: Armies marched and countermarched across central Europe, killing and burning and stealing. In Germany, the main battleground, the population dropped from 16 million to 6 million. Plague and famine added to the misery.

To make matters worse, this long and bloody war settled very little. Much of northern Europe stayed Protestant; most of southern Europe stayed Catholic.

Gradually the idea began to dawn that religion might be an *individual* matter after all—that kings and queens did not necessarily have to make everybody follow the same faith. The pope was not even invited to the peace conference that brought the Thirty Years' War to an end. After more than 13 centuries, the old alliance between Christianity and government power, first forged by the Emperor Constantine, was at last beginning to break up.

In spite of the war, there was a new sense of freedom among European artists and musicians. During the 1600s great composers used their musical skills in worship: Catholics such as Monteverdi in Venice and Corelli in Rome, Protestants such as Pachelbel in Nuremberg and Purcell in London. A new development of those years was the oratorio, a religious music-drama retelling a story from the Bible.

Many hymns still being sung today were written during the 1600s. Martin Rinkart, a German pastor, not only suffered through the Thirty Years' War but also through an epidemic that killed thousands including his own wife. Somehow Rinkart found the faith and fortitude to write a hymn still known by Christians four centuries later, "Now Thank

We All Our God." (The adjacent sidebar lists other hymns from the 1600s.)

Jan Amos Comenius (1592–1672), a leader among Czech Christians, was one of Christ's People in central Europe who took flight after losing in the fight. Not only did these spiritual descendants of the martyred Jan Hus lose in battle with Catholic soldiers, they also lost property and loved ones: Comenius' house and his entire personal library were burned, and his young wife and two children died of the plague.

As he led his battered band of Hussites across the border into Poland, Comenius stopped first to pray, asking God to protect a "hidden seed" in their native land. (Chapter 11 tells how abundantly God would later answer that prayer.) For half a century Comenius ministered in exile—preaching, teaching, writing many books. He urged an end to the fighting; he called for religious liberty. After the burning of his house in Poland, the discouraged old man took flight again, living out his life in the Netherlands.

Comenius is most remembered as a pioneer of education among Christ's People. He was the first person ever to include pictures in schoolbooks for children. He knew all about learning step-by-step, about seizing the teachable moment. No wonder Comenius was invited to become the first president of Harvard in faraway North America!

(Chapter 11 tells how)

### Praise Hymns from the Tumult

"Praise to the Lord, the Almighty"
*Joachim Neander*

"Let All the World in Every Corner Sing"
*George Herbert*

"Praise God, from Whom All Blessings Flow"
*Thomas Ken*

"Fairest Lord Jesus" and "The First Noel"
*Unknown composers*

## England, Scotland, and Ireland

The Protestant Reformation in England began quite differently than on the continent of Europe. The king or queen, rather than the pope, became the earthly head of the Church of England. As to actual beliefs and ways of worshiping, initially it seemed as if nearly everything stayed the same. Changes were made later on, yet many English Christians began to feel that more changes were needed.

Two main groups continued to fight for what they thought was right: Puritans, who wanted to stay inside the Church of England while *purifying* it, and Separatists, who decided it was better to *separate* from the official government-sponsored church. Both groups mainly followed John Calvin's teachings.

What comes to mind when you see or hear the word "Puritan"? Thanks largely to a sharp-witted American newspaperman of the early

1900s, many people think of Puritans as joyless individuals who never had any fun and never wanted anybody else to have any fun either.

Nothing could be farther from the truth. The Westminster Catechism, written largely by Puritans, begins by stating, "The chief end of man is to glorify God and enjoy Him forever." Puritans enjoyed everyday things like swimming and skating, hunting and bowling (except, of course, on Sundays). They dressed in bright colors (except, of course, in church). They also painted their houses with bright hues. And they were known to take a nip of rum now and then.

Puritans had a hard time in England throughout the 1600s because of kings who wanted to be honored as God-given rulers. Since the king headed the Church of England, everyone had to be an Anglican. (To tell the truth, in secret some of those same kings would have liked it better if everyone had been a Catholic.)

Early in the 1600s, some Puritans met with King James I and presented their ideas for reform. He turned down all but one—a request for a new Bible translation. As a result, he became the English king whose name is most often mentioned by Christ's People today. The King James Bible was first printed in 1611. Initially many English Christians disliked it, preferring the Geneva Bible of 1560; but gradually the new version became popular—in part, because of its magnificent language. Even people who have never read the Bible quote the King James Version when they use such expressions as "my brother's keeper" (Genesis 4:9), "a drop in the bucket" (Isaiah 40:15), or "by the skin of my teeth" (Job 19:20). One unintended side effect of this translation's continuing popularity is that many Christians today still use old-fashioned language of the 1600s when they worship—for instance, saying "Thee" and "Thou" in prayer.

Unlike most Puritans, Separatists had already given up on the Church of England. They began taking flight to the Netherlands at first, and then in 1620, to the colonies of North America. By 1630 large groups of discouraged English Puritans began following the Separatist Pilgrims to Massachusetts. (See page 156 for more about these and other European Christians in America.)

Back in England matters were coming to a head. The son of King James I was even more determined than his father to have absolute rule over both England and Scotland. Finally a civil war broke out in 1642. Like the Thirty Years' War on the continent of Europe, it was not strictly speaking a war of religion; yet most Puritans and Separatists joined forces fighting against the king.

One of the most remarkable figures in Christian history came to the front during the English Civil War: Oliver Cromwell (1599–1658), a country gentleman with no rank or title but much conviction and influence. A gifted general, he led his pious and disciplined troops to victory. The king not only lost the war: In 1649 he lost his head as well. After that, representatives of the English and Scottish people ruled through Parliament. When this did not work out too well, Cromwell was made a virtual military dictator.

During Cromwell's administration, in Easter week of 1655, 5,000 French troops attacked Waldensian settlements in the Piedmont section of northern Italy. They looted, burned, tortured, raped, and killed without mercy. Children were dashed against rocks; bodies were cut to pieces. Christ's People in England were outraged (see the box on page 152). Cromwell sent letters to kings and dukes demanding an end to such outrageous persecution.

Puritans fared well as long as Cromwell was in control. When he died, things reversed. When the son of the beheaded king eventually came back from exile, Puritans began to be persecuted again—both in England and in Scotland.

Many Scottish Christians refused to recognize a human king as head of the church. Among them was Margaret Wilson who, with two teenage siblings, hid in a cave to avoid persecution. When captured, she was taken to the seashore, tied to a stake in the sand, and left to drown in the advancing tide. As Margaret began to choke in the waves, her captors jerked her head up and demanded, "Will you pray for the king of England?"

"I want everyone to be saved," she gasped.

"Then will you honor the king as head of the church?"

She shook her head. "I will not. I am one of Christ's children. Let me go!" And Margaret Wilson, 18 years old, died as a martyr in the sea.[1]

To avoid such treatment, more and more Christians gave up the fight and took flight to North America instead.

Late in the century came yet another revolution, bringing Protestant kings and queens to the throne of Great Britain. New laws gave religious freedom to nearly everybody.

During the course of that turbulent century of the 1600s, Christ's People in England, Scotland, and Ireland experienced several important new beginnings: new denominations, new classics of English literature, new understanding of divisions among Christians, and new religious rivalry.

**New Denominations:** From the English Puritans came the Congregationalists—so called because they believed each *congregation* should manage its own affairs. (Many settlers of New England were Congregationalists, as described later in this chapter.) From the English Separatists came the Quakers and the Baptists.

"Quaker" is actually a nickname, as "Christian" was at first; those who follow this way of worshiping prefer to be called Friends. Among their founders were George Fox (1624–1691) and Margaret Fell (1614–1702). Quakers were radical Separatists who rejected almost everything about traditional churches including baptism, the Lord's Supper, ministers, preaching, and hymn singing. In their meetings they would sit quietly, waiting for an inner voice to prompt someone, either a woman or a man, to stand up and speak a word from God.

"Baptist" was also a nickname at first, like "Anabaptist." Baptists agreed with Anabaptists in insisting that baptism is only for believers. They went even further than Anabaptists in deciding that the Bible teaches baptism by being immersed in water, not just being sprinkled with it. Two of the first Baptist leaders were John Smyth (1554–1612) and Thomas Helwys (1550–1616). Both of these brave pioneers experienced persecution: Smyth led his followers in escape to Amsterdam and Helwys died in an English prison. Today both are still honored by the name of a Baptist publishing house in America.

***New Classics of English Literature:*** John Bunyan (1628–1688) is the best-known Baptist of the period. He was a small-town repairer of pots and pans who preached on the side. While imprisoned for more than 12 years because of his beliefs, Bunyan began to write one of the greatest English classics: *Pilgrim's Progress.* Personal experience as a soldier and prisoner helped him paint vivid word pictures.

Another universal classic of the late 1600s was written by John Milton (1608–1674), who also suffered for the sake of Christ. While the Puritans were in control, Milton used his good education and writing talent to produce tracts on freedom. He also served as Oliver Cromwell's secretary. When it was no longer popular to be a Puritan in England and John Milton was elderly and blind, he dictated the great epic poem *Paradise Lost.*

Both of these towering works of literature present a Christian worldview. *Paradise Lost* goes back before the beginning of human history, showing God in charge of the universe. *Pilgrim's Progress* starts in the here and now, as ordinary people drop their burden

## "On the Late Massacre in Piedmont"

In response to the French massacre of Waldensians in Italy, John Milton penned a sonnet beginning with these words:

Avenge, O Lord, Thy slaughtered saints, whose bones

lie scattered on the Alpine mountains cold,

ev'n them who kept Thy truth so pure of old

when all our fathers worshiped stocks and stones.[2]

of sin at the cross and then go on pilgrimage through this world of sin, making their way toward the Celestial City.

**New Understanding of Divisions Among Christians:** Why must Christians be divided into so many groups? During the 1640s some believers assembled at Westminster to write a new catechism and new confession of faith. They also came up with these reasons for division among Christ's People: [3]

- All of us are limited; none of us can see the whole truth. (The pastor who preached a farewell sermon to the Pilgrims as they were about to leave for New England in 1620, said this: "The Lord has more truth yet to break forth from His Holy Word." [4])

- Just as all of us are limited as individuals, so are all of our churches limited; the true Church, with Christ as its Head, can never be represented fully by only one group of Christians.

- While agreeing on the more important matters, we may disagree on lesser points; each of us must follow what we believe the Bible teaches.

- If we disagree with others, this does not mean we oppose them; Christians can be divided in some ways and yet keep an overall unity.

To Christ's People of today, these four points seem sensible enough. To Christ's People of the 1640s, they were revolutionary. Yet out of these ideas today's situation has grown, with thousands of different Christian denominations all over the world.

**New Sense of Religious Rivalry:** When a revolution forced out the old king of England, he came back the next year at the head of an army, landing not in England but in Ireland. Scottish Protestants had settled in the northern part of Ireland; most of the Irish themselves were still strongly Catholic.

In 1690 at the Battle of the Boyne, the old king (James II) lost again to the new king (William III). That bitter conflict marked the beginning of a division in Irish society that has continued to this day. The news media usually report, "Protestants are fighting Catholics." Actually, it is descendants of the new king's followers who are fighting descendants of the old king's followers. (Sometimes it seems as if both sides have forgotten that they are supposed to be Christ's People.)

## Elsewhere in Europe

The Huguenots, French Protestants, prospered during the early 1600s. They worked in many different trades and professions, succeeding so well that there was a popular saying: "As rich as a Huguenot." They started five academies for the training of Protestant pastors. Yet as a minority group in Catholic France, they always felt a little uneasy.

The situation changed drastically when Louis XIV (1638–1715) became king. This powerful monarch was determined to strengthen national unity, with no one daring to question his rule. Through the years King Louis placed more and more restrictions on the Huguenots. Finally in 1685 he ordered them to become Catholics or else.

Usually when Christ's People in Europe lost the fight for what they believed, they could flee elsewhere. In France, though, the Huguenots were forbidden to leave; Protestants caught trying to escape were sent as slaves to row galleys in the French navy. Yet hundreds of thousands of French Protestants managed to get away; in the process some of them lost their wealth and others lost their lives. France became the weaker without their skills and energy.

As they made their flight to other countries, Huguenots adopted other ways. Many of them changed their names. For example, that famous rider of the American Revolution, Paul Revere, was actually descended from a Huguenot family named de Rivoire. Other famous Americans with French Protestant roots include Francis Marion, Alexander Hamilton, John James Audubon, and Theodore Roosevelt.

The Mennonites of Switzerland, Germany, and the Netherlands were spiritual descendants of the Anabaptists. As they too began to face new pressures, they *could not* fight back, since they believed that the Bible taught them to keep the peace at all costs. So in the later 1600s they began to make their flight to North America. Some of the Mennonites broke off into a separate movement, taking the name *Amish* after one of their leaders. Both groups began to settle in the new colony of Pennsylvania.

The Waldenses, that hardy group of Christ's People whose history stretches back even before the Reformation, were willing to fight for what they believed. Again and again they battled both French and Italian armies that tried to root them out of their strongholds in the high mountains. Finally in 1689 they achieved a measure of peace and freedom, partly because of changing political alliances in Europe and partly because of the Waldenses' own stubborn guerrilla resistance.

In Russia Christ's People also experienced a time of tumult. In 1598 the tsar died leaving no direct heirs. The Russian Orthodox Church became a center of national unity during this "Time of Troubles" as it was called. When a new tsar was finally crowned in 1613, he was the son of the head of the Russian Orthodox Church (and his father was the power behind the throne).

Later on in the 1600s Russian Orthodox Christians experienced a fight, mainly over differences in ways of worshiping. Some of them wanted to follow more "modern" practices such as singing "Alleluia" three times instead of twice or using three fingers rather than two in making the sign of the cross. Others (who came to be known as Old Believers) felt the old ways were good enough. The Old Believers suffered much persecution; Avvakum, their leader, was burned at the stake. All this infighting seriously weakened the Russian Orthodox Church by the end of the 1600s.

In spite of all their differences, there was one point on which all European Christians agreed: They must fight the empire of the Ottoman Turks. These fierce Muslim warriors once again invaded Europe in 1683 and came very close to capturing the city of Vienna. Unexpectedly a Polish army came to the rescue. The Turks took flight so quickly that they left their breakfasts behind in their tents; according to the story, this is how the Europeans first found out about croissants and coffee!

# EUROPEAN INFLUENCE GOES GLOBAL

Three centuries ago Europe was still by far the most important continent in the story of Christ's People. This situation was beginning to shift, however, because so many European Christians were moving to the Americas.

Not all of the newcomers in the Americas came from Europe, but all newcomers were influenced by Europe. Greedy Spanish and Portuguese settlers enslaved Native Americans for their mines and plantations. When too many Indians died, the settlers began importing captured Africans instead. If possible, these dark-skinned newcomers were treated even worse than the native tribes.

One earnest Jesuit stands out as a bright spot in the long and dismal story of African slavery in the Americas. Pedro Claver (1580–1654) labored for 44 years as a missionary to Africans in Colombia. He bought slaves who spoke several different African languages; then he made them his interpreters and treated them as his brothers. Claver and his colleagues met slave ships at the harbor and used familiar things to build a bridge to share the Good News of Christ. Giving the parched Africans a drink, they would tell of the Living Water. Showing a snake-skin, Claver would say that human beings also could leave their old lives behind.

Other Roman Catholic missionaries spread throughout Latin America and as far north as the areas of Florida, Georgia, Texas, New Mexico, and Arizona. Everywhere they went, tribal peoples learned at least a little about Jesus. Often the missionaries' work was hindered by settlers who only wanted quick riches. One way they tried to overcome this problem was by gathering Native Americans into new villages far from anyone else.

The most successful Christian villages were set up in that part of South America where Paraguay, Argentina, and Brazil meet. At one time as many as 150,000 Indians lived in these Christian settlements, where the missionaries could protect them from greedy outsiders.

Farther north, French Catholics also shared the Good News with many Native Canadians. One of the most notable missionaries was a Jesuit named Jean de Brébeuf (1593–1649); he tried to adapt the story of Jesus' birth so that the Huron Indians could understand and accept it (see the adjacent box). Unfortunately Brébeuf, along with two of his colleagues, was captured by tribal enemies, cruelly tortured, and burned alive.

Catholic outreach in Canada marked a new departure: Not only men but also women served there as missionaries. Dreams about Canada convinced a French Ursuline sister known as Mary of the Incarnation (1599–1672) that God was calling her to go. With five other Catholic teachers and nurses, she arrived at Montreal in 1639.

### An Unusual Christmas Hymn

Written in 1643 by Jean de Brébeuf, this hymn retold the Nativity story in ways the Indians could understand:

> Within a lodge of broken bark
> the tender Babe was found;
>
> a ragged robe of rabbit skin
> enwrapped His beauty round....
>
> The chiefs from far before
> Him knelt
>
> with gifts of fox and beaver
> pelt.[5]

The first permanent English colony in the New World was Jamestown, Virginia, in 1607. Many of its settlers behaved no better than most of the Hispanic settlers further south. They too enslaved Africans for personal gain. One notable exception was John Rolfe (1585–1622), a devout Christian. When he fell in love with the Indian princess Pocahontas (1595–1617), he prayed earnestly, asking God what to do. Finally he persuaded Pocahontas to become a believer, and they were married.

Most of the Pilgrims and Puritans who settled Massachusetts came with quite a different motivation from most of those who settled Virginia. These Congregationalists believed that God had given them the opportunity to set up a perfect Christian society in the New World. In an effort to do just that, they made many rules about church attendance and proper behavior.

They also believed that their good example would spread to others. William Bradford (1590–1657), governor and historian, once wrote: "Out of small beginnings greater things have been made by His hand that made all things of nothing . . . . As one small candle may light a thousand, so the light here kindled has shone unto many." [6] John Winthrop (1588–1649), another colonial governor in Massachusetts, put it this way: "The Lord will be our God and delight to dwell among us as His own people . . . for we must consider that we shall be as a city upon a hill, the eyes of all people are upon us." [7]

Unfortunately this sense of God's purpose led the Pilgrims and the Puritans to deny religious liberty to those who disagreed with them.

- Roger Williams (1603–1683) left Massachusetts to set up a free colony in Rhode Island; there he and Dr. John Clarke (1609–1676) started the first Baptist congregation in America.

- William Penn (1644–1718), a Quaker, founded Pennsylvania as a safe haven for Quakers, Mennonites, Lutherans, and other religious minority groups.

- Maryland was controlled at first by Catholics (who were then a persecuted minority), although in colonial times no more than one-fourth of its people were ever Catholic. Yet from this small beginning—along with Hispanic beginnings further south—has come the immense size and strength of the Roman Catholic Church in the United States.

Denial of freedom also extended to women at times. Anne Hutchinson (c.1591–1643) was a midwife who led Wednesday-evening Bible studies. At first only women attended, but soon many men were coming. The male authorities of church and state did not like this turn of events. They hauled Anne Hutchinson into court, accusing her of doing things "not comely in the sight of God, nor fitting for your sex."

In her own defense, Anne quoted Acts 18:26 (KJV), "Priscilla . . . expounded unto him [Apollos] the way of God" and Titus 2:3–4 (KJV), "The aged women . . . may teach."

When the judges demanded how she knew God was speaking to her, Anne asked, "How did Abraham know it was God telling him to sacrifice his son, since to do so would break the Sixth Commandment?" [8]

Anne Hutchinson and her family then took flight from Boston and found freedom in the colony of Rhode Island.

Cotton Mather (1663–1728) was another Bostonian who has been misunderstood. All the stereotypes about Puritans as joyless nitpickers seem to have settled on him. He has also been accused of being the one who burned the witches in Salem. Actually, Mather strongly disagreed with the way things were handled over in Salem. He stood united with other Boston ministers in saving even more people from being executed.

As a pastor, Cotton Mather visited from door to door and organized home groups for Bible study, prayer, and spiritual support. He urged his people to get smallpox shots and to treat African-Americans right. Out of concern for his fellow Bostonians, Mather also practiced prayer-walking. Several sample prayers are shown in the box below.

The Puritan settlers in New England felt a sense of responsibility for Native Americans living all around them. This concern led to the surprising fact that the first Bible ever printed in the Americas was in the language of an indigenous tribe in New England. The translation was made by John Eliot (1604–1690), a devoted missionary who served more than half a century. The Algonkian Bible was published in 1663. Sadly enough, wars between settlers and Indians almost wiped out Eliot's converts. Today Eliot's Bible translation is mainly an historical curiosity . . . although its word for a tribal leader, *mugwump*, is still sometimes used in North American English.

When Thomas Mayhew, Jr. (1621–1657), another New England missionary, died on an ocean voyage, his elderly father, Thomas Mayhew, Sr. (1593–1682), took up the task of sharing the Good News with American Indians. In fact four generations of Mayhews served as missionaries on the island of Martha's Vineyard while honoring the land titles and social structures of its inhabitants.

The Puritans had a great influence on the development of North America. Even with all their faults, most of their influence was positive. What a pity that many people today think of them only as killjoys and witch-burners!

## From a Puritan's Diary

In passing along the street, I have set myself to bless thousands of persons who never knew that I did it, with secret wishes after this manner sent unto Heaven for them. Upon the sight of:

*A tall man:* Lord, give that man high attainments in Christianity.

*A man carrying a burden:* Lord, help this man to carry a burdened soul unto his Lord-Redeemer.

*A man on horseback:* Lord, Thy creatures serve that man; help him to serve his Maker.

*Young people:* Lord, help them to remember their Creator in the days of their youth.

*A shopkeeper, busy in the shop:* Lord, let not the world cause that person to neglect the one thing that is needful.

*A man who going by me took no notice of me:* Lord, help that man to take a due notice of the Lord Jesus Christ.[9]

–Cotton Mather

# NEED FOR FURTHER REFORMATION

During the 1600s, many of Christ's People—both Protestant and Catholic—began to feel that the Reformation had not been complete or that another Reformation was still needed. Why did they feel this way? There were three reasons.

1. Among many Protestants, it had become *more important to believe the right teachings* than to believe on the Lord Jesus Christ.

2. Among many Catholics, it had become *more important to make people Catholics,* no matter how, than to lead them truly to become Christ's People.

3. Among both Protestants and Catholics, it had become *more important to be reasonable* than to be a Christian.

## Among Protestants

Back in the days of Luther, Zwingli, and Calvin, Protestants had been delighted to discover that they did not need to follow all the rituals and traditions of Roman Catholics. Instead, they could have a direct, personal relationship with God through the Lord Jesus Christ.

Gradually, though, the followers of Luther, Zwingli, and Calvin had come to develop their own rituals and traditions. They had written long statements of faith and even longer books of theology. To many Protestants, it had come to the point where the way to be a Christian was to believe the correct doctrine, whether or not you had any personal relationship with Jesus the Christ.

Of course there was a need for correct doctrine. A challenge to traditional Calvinist teachings arose from a Dutch pastor and theological professor named Jacob Arminius (1560–1609). As Arminius studied and taught the Bible, he began to believe that Calvin's doctrine of predestination could not possibly be right. The table on the next page shows several key differences between the views of Calvin and the views of Arminius; it also mentions which groups among Christ's People are likely to follow which teachings today.

Yet when all is said and done, a person can believe all of the right doctrines and still be far from salvation, unless he or she also has a personal relationship with God through believing on the Lord Jesus Christ. This is what many Protestants of three centuries ago seemed to be in danger of forgetting.

## Calvinist or Arminian—What's the Difference?

| The Views of **JOHN CALVIN** (held today by most Presbyterians, many Baptists, and many others) | The Views of **JACOB ARMINIUS** (held today by most Methodists and many others) |
| --- | --- |
| 1. Human beings are by nature spiritually dead; on their own, none of them will trust in Christ. | 1. In a spiritual sense, human beings on their own can do nothing good. |
| 2. If someone trusts in Christ, it is because God unconditionally chose that person. | 2. From the beginning God chose to save everyone who freely chooses to trust in Christ. |
| 3. In dying on the cross Christ provided atonement from sin only for those who would trust in him. | 3. Christ died on the cross for everyone, but his death redeemed only those who would trust in him. |
| 4. When God gives someone a new spiritual birth, that person cannot resist or reject God's grace. | 4. When God offers someone a new spiritual birth, that person has the choice of accepting or rejecting God's grace. |
| 5. Everyone who trusts in Christ will persevere, or continue faithful to him till the end. | 5. The Bible does not clearly state whether persons who trust in Christ can later lose their salvation. |

# Among Roman Catholics

Following the Reformation period, Roman Catholics put Protestants to shame by their evangelistic efforts worldwide. A famous Catholic leader of the 1600s even named world missions as one of several points proving why he believed Catholics were right and Protestants were wrong. (There were, of course, a few scattered efforts at outreach among Protestants such as the work of John Eliot and the Mayhews in colonial North America. In colonial Indonesia, Dutch Christians also brought some 140,000 people to Christ.)

This chapter has already told about widespread Catholic outreach in the Americas. On the continent of Africa, the results were more limited. An Angolan princess led many of her followers to become Christ's People. But in Mozambique on the other side of Africa, as well as on the huge island of Madagascar, Catholic missionaries made little impact.

Results also varied in Asia. When new rulers turned against Christianity in Japan, both Japanese Christians and Catholic missionaries died horrible deaths. They were crucified, burned alive, and tormented with Oriental methods such as the water torture.

Elsewhere in Asia there were significant gains for Christ's People:

- Virtually everyone in the Philippines came under the Christian banner, except for Muslims in the far south and a few tribal peoples here and there in the high mountains. By the early 1600s Catholic missionaries were already founding Christian universities in Manila.

- The French Jesuit Alexander de Rhodes (1591–1660) was a notable missionary to Asia. Not only did he succeed in bringing some 300,000 Vietnamese to Christ: He also put their difficult tonal language into alphabetic writing. Fortunately for Vietnamese believers, he chose to use everyday words, not high-flown literary expressions.

- The two most controversial Catholic mission fields in Asia during the 1600s were India and China. In India, the Italian Jesuit Roberto Nobili (1577–1656) followed the example of Matteo Ricci (1552–1610) in China by trying to reach the highest levels of society first. This approach brought some success but not as much as in China. Yet the question arose: How much can the Christian faith be adapted to fit the ideas and traditions of non-Christian nations? Of course there should be some adaptation; a good example of this is de Brébeuf's hymn that retold the Christmas story for Indians in Canada. But how much adaptation is too much?

Through the centuries many Catholics and many Protestants have made one of two opposite errors: Either they have insisted that new Christians must leave behind all of their old culture and customs, or else they have watered down the Good News about Jesus the Christ until it means next to nothing.

As the 1600s were drawing to a close, many thoughtful Catholics were beginning to wonder whether Jesuit missionaries in particular had done too much diluting. Some people were also beginning to feel that Jesuits would do almost anything to make someone a Catholic . . . even if in doing so they had to tell outright lies or otherwise act in ways morally unworthy of Christ's People.

## Among Catholics and Protestants

The third reason many Christians at this time felt the need for another Reformation might be stated this way: "Let's be *reasonable* about this." For some, logic and practicality took precedence over faith.

The century of the 1600s brought many advances in scientific thinking. Astronomers such as Johannes Kepler (1571–1630) and

Galileo Galilei (1564–1642) proved that the earth is not the center of the universe (although officials of the Inquisition later forced Galileo to deny his discoveries, thus starting a long struggle between certain Christians and certain scientists which has continued until today). Other scientists pioneered in physics, chemistry, and mathematics.

In 1687 Sir Isaac Newton (1642–1727) pulled all of these new discoveries together in an explanation of how the universe really works. For many people, there seemed to be no more good *reason* to believe in an all-powerful Creator-God; did not everything just run like clockwork, according to the laws of nature?

This emphasis on human knowledge, on what seemed reasonable to the human mind, carried over into religion. Some European Christians began to say that Jesus must have been only a great teacher; it was not reasonable to think that he could possibly have been the Son of God. (From this movement eventually came the Unitarian churches of today.) Other European Christians defended traditional beliefs, but they also took the approach of trying to prove how reasonable Christianity actually is. This was a hard sell when so many Christians had recently been killed by other Christians through war and persecution.

## ANOTHER REFORMATION? HOW?

There were diversified efforts toward more reform. Some were more successful and long lasting than others.

During the early 1600s seeds of reform began to blossom in unlikely places, such as among Eastern Orthodox Christians and other age-old traditions of the East. A reformer became the head of the church in Armenia; he sent monks out to teach, preach, settle arguments, improve public morals, and fight superstition.

Another reformer named Cyril Lukar (1572–1637) became head of the Greek Orthodox Church. He sent young Orthodox priests from Constantinople to study at Protestant schools in Europe. He gave the king of England one of the earliest known complete manuscripts of the Bible in Greek—a valuable tool for study and translation. He promoted a new confession of faith that included some Protestant beliefs. But Cyril Lukar turned out to be too far ahead of his time: Other Orthodox bishops strongly disagreed with him, and the Muslim sultan in Constantinople finally had him executed by strangling.

Cornelius Jansen (1585–1638) was a Dutch Catholic who became a university professor and then a bishop in Belgium. He felt that in their eagerness to make everybody a Catholic, Jesuits had watered down the gospel; they had cheapened the grace of God, saying in effect: "Sin all you want to, and if you confess and do penance, you are sure to be forgiven." In opposition to this "cheap grace," Jansen went back to the teachings of Augustine, 12 centuries before.

Jansen's teachings soon traveled to Port-Royal, a low marshy valley 16 miles from Paris where two remarkable brother-sister pairs promoted his ideas. Angélique Arnauld (1591–1661) was abbess of a Roman Catholic convent, while her brother Antoine Arnauld (1612–1694) was a professor of theology in Paris; he began to attack the Jesuits in print.

Not only Frenchwomen but also Frenchmen began to gather at Port-Royal. They were drawn there by the way *Jansenism* (as it was called) had brought the age-old teachings of Augustine up to date. One of those who came was a wealthy young woman named Jacqueline Pascal. Her brother Blaise Pascal (1623–1662) had at an early age become one of the leading scientists and mathematicians of Europe. Pascal was only 19 when he invented the first calculating machine, said to be the forerunner of the computer. He worked out the theory of probability and proved the existence of a vacuum. Some people say Pascal made the first wristwatch and set up the first bus route in Paris.

In 1654 this brilliant young man had a deep spiritual experience in which he came to know Jesus the Christ as personal Savior and Lord. He then joined his sister at Port-Royal and began to write articles opposing Jesuit teachings. When he died at the age of only 39, he left unfinished a masterful defense of the Christian faith against those who insisted, "Let's be reasonable about this." Pascal's notes were published after his death with the title *Pensées,* meaning thoughts. A few of Pascal's thoughts are shown in the adjacent box.

The Jansenist movement ran on collision course with the ambitious plans of the powerful King Louis XIV. He would allow no one to oppose Roman Catholicism. After many years

## Pascal's *Penses*

● What a vast distance there is between knowing God and loving Him!

● We come to know truth not only by reason, but still more so through our hearts.

● The heart has its reasons which the reason does not know.[10]

● Reason's last step is the recognition that there are an infinite number of things that go beyond it.[11]

● There is a God-shaped vacuum in the heart of every man, which cannot be filled by any created thing, but only by God the Creator, made known through Jesus Christ.[12]

of controversy, the convent and other buildings at Port-Royal were torn down; those who still followed Jansenist teachings had to take flight to the Netherlands.

Of all the movements toward a further Reformation that came out of the 1600s, the longest lasting was known as Pietism. The name of the movement comes from the title *Pious Desires*, written in 1675 by Philip Jacob Spener (1635–1705). Spener was a faithful Lutheran pastor in Germany who urged his flock to seek a personal relationship with Jesus, cultivating that relationship through Bible study, prayer, and small groups meeting in homes for mutual support. (When Dutch Christians picked up on the small-group idea, they used a new term: *huis kerk,* or house church.)

Spener gave strong encouragement to a young German university professor named August Hermann Francke (1663–1727). Soon Francke became the new leader of the Pietist movement. Another important figure among Pietists was Baroness Henrietta von Gersdorf (1656–1726), who offered her mountain estate as a retreat center.

This Pietist movement would keep on spreading; it would have a powerful effect on the coming century.

# KEY EVENTS
↝

## 1600 TO 1700

Baptists and Congregationalists begin to leave the Church of England; Puritans try to make changes from inside.

Jacob Arminius challenges the views of John Calvin.

In England, the King James Version of the Bible is published.

Christ's People in Japan are almost wiped out by intense persecution.

Catholics and Protestants fight a long, exhausting war on the European continent.

"Pilgrims" (Congregationalists) and Puritans begin migrating to North America; other Christians follow.

Eastern Orthodox leader Cyril Lukar, influenced by Protestantism, seeks reform but fails.

In Colombia, Pedro Claver ministers to African slaves; in Canada, Jean de Brébeuf, Marie of the Incarnation, and others minister to American Indians.

Persecuted Christians such as Roger Williams, John Clarke, Anne Hutchinson, and William Penn find religious freedom in Rhode Island and Pennsylvania.

Jan Amos Comenius flees persecution along with other Czech Christians; he prays for a "hidden seed" to remain in his native land.

The English Civil War leaves Puritans in control; they write the Westminster Confession of Faith.

Oliver Cromwell becomes military dictator of England; he opposes religious persecution.

Scientists discover how the universe really works; the Inquisition forces Galileo to deny his discoveries.

Cornelius Jansen and his followers oppose Jesuit practices by updating the teachings of Augustine.

Both Catholic and Protestant musicians and artists show a new sense of freedom in expressing their faith.

Strong emphasis on human reason leads to denial of Jesus' divinity; the great scientist Blaise Pascal and others defend the Christian faith.

Many of Christ's People suffer persecution—in Italy, England, Scotland, France, and North America.

Milton writes *Paradise Lost;* Bunyan writes *Pilgrim's Progress.*

Roman Catholic missionaries meet with success in Vietnam and the Philippines, but less so elsewhere.

John Eliot and the Mayhews (father and son) pioneer as Protestant missionaries to Native Americans.

Philip Jacob Spener writes *Pious Desires* and helps to launch the Pietist movement.

Russian Orthodox Christians divide into two groups; the "Old Believers" suffer persecution.

Muslim Turks once again invade central Europe.

Huguenots (French Protestants) are commanded to become Catholics; many escape to other countries.

Mennonites and Amish flee from persecution to North America; Waldenses, after much persecution earlier, are given a measure of freedom.

A revolution brings religious freedom to England and Scotland, but causes deep divisions in Ireland.

Cotton Mather and others work to build a perfect Christian society in New England.

In Germany, August Hermann Francke and the Baroness von Gersdorf join Spener in promoting Pietism.

## Susanna Wesley (1669–1742)

Many historians have called Susanna "the Mother of Methodism."

# 11. Disaster and Renewal
## (1700–1800)

Americans tend to have a positive image of the 1700s. That was the century of:

- The American Revolution, the Declaration of Independence, the Bill of Rights.
- Benjamin Franklin, George Washington, Paul Revere.
- American farmers daring to face the British army.
- Colonial soldiers suffering in the snows of Valley Forge.

Yet when it comes to exploring church history, an honest observer among Christ's People might declare much of that century a disaster area for several reasons. During the 1700s:

- European society had become top-heavy. While noble lords and ladies lived only for pleasure, ordinary people struggled to survive, feeling abandoned by Christian ministers who should have been caring for their welfare. French society erupted, causing a bloodbath that swept away both the national government and the established church.

- Those who considered human reason more important than Christian faith seemed to have the upper hand. For example, Thomas Jefferson was chief author of the Declaration of Independence. Like Benjamin Franklin and many other American patriots, Jefferson was not so much a Christian as a deist, believing in a Creator-God but not in a Father-God who loved us and sent Jesus to be our Savior. Some deists hoped that deism would unite all humankind, since in their view one religion was as good as another.

- Following two centuries of sending missionaries to five continents, Roman Catholic leaders made several bad decisions that caused a dire decline in world missions.

- Many Protestants became spiritually cold and indifferent; few of them thought about a world in need of the Good News about Jesus. Perhaps they were worn out after religious differences had kindled war and persecution throughout much of the two preceding centuries.

- Russian Orthodox Christians, also worn out by internal struggles, found themselves firmly under the thumb of the tsar. Greek Orthodox Christians, the same as in the previous century, were still firmly under the thumb of a Muslim sultan.

For Christ's People it appears that the 1700s might have been a complete disaster. However two things made positive contributions during this difficult time for Christians: new church music, and the *Pietist* movement.

# NEW CHURCH MUSIC

Chapters 9 and 10 tell how the period of the Reformation inspired new music among Christ's People both Protestant and Catholic. This trend increased dramatically during the 1700s.

Four of the greatest composers of all time were writing their music during the 1700s: Johann Sebastian Bach (1685–1750) and George Frederick Handel (1685–1759) during the first half of that century, Franz Josef Haydn (1732–1809) and Wolfgang Amadeus Mozart (1756–1791) during the last half of it. The first two were Protestants; the last two were Catholics. Even today's hymnbooks include familiar melodies composed by all four of them with words written by other Christians.

Bach was a staunch German Lutheran who devoted his life to family and church. He was strongly influenced by the hymn-singing tradition started by Martin Luther among churches in Germany. Simple chorales are scattered throughout his great compositions for soloists, choir, and orchestra. Hymn tunes also form the basis of many of his great works for organ. Historians have recently discovered Bach's own Bible, with handwritten markings showing that he read and studied it. Beside 1 Chronicles 25, which tells about music in the Temple, Bach wrote: "This chapter is the true foundation of all God-pleasing church music."[1]

Handel was also born in Germany but he spent much of his life in England as a composer and producer of operas and concerts. When his staged works stopped drawing big crowds, Handel turned to oratorios with texts taken from the Bible. Many of Christ's People in England thought it was not quite proper to sing Scripture verses from the stage like operatic arias. Therefore they would not attend Handel's performances; sometimes they would deliberately schedule church services at the same time. Although Handel had rather coarse manners and a thick accent, this big burly German musician had the soul of a true Christian. He testified that he felt he could "see all heaven before me—and the great God Himself" while writing the most famous of his many masterworks, the "Hallelujah Chorus" from the oratorio *Messiah*. [2]

Haydn followed the footsteps of Handel, both in finding new fame in England and in writing a great biblical oratorio, *The Creation*. At the beginning of each of his manuscripts Haydn would write *In Nomine Domini* (In the Lord's Name). At the end of each piece of music he would note *Laus Deo* (Praise God) or *Soli Deo Gloria* (Solely to the Glory of God).

Mozart, like Haydn, was an Austrian Catholic. His life followed a more worldly pattern than Haydn's or Bach's, yet he too wrote unforgettable music for Christian worship—music that is still being performed. For example, on September 11, 2002, when memorial services were held for victims of terrorist attacks on the World Trade Center one year earlier, massed choirs in many cities sang Mozart's last composition, *Requiem*, beginning: "Grant them eternal rest, O Lord; let perpetual light shine upon them."

The flood of new church music from this period was not limited to trained singers and instrumentalists. Compare a recent hymnbook with a hymnal of half a century ago and you may see that more hymns from the 1700s seem to be standing the test of time than hymns from the 1800s. No wonder many Christians call the 1700s "The Golden Age of Hymns." [3]

The box on page 170 lists only a few of the many great hymns that were written during this time. Isaac Watts (1674–1748), a short, sickly English parson and teacher, wrote hundreds of hymns. He also became famous as a writer of textbooks for various age levels. His work as a hymn-writer marked the beginning of a flood of new hymns that soon followed.

Charles Wesley (1707–1788) has earned the title of the greatest Christian hymn-writer with thousands of hymns to his credit. A later section in this chapter tells more about how he worked with his brother, John Wesley to bring about a great change in England.

One of the most unusual hymn-writing teams linked John Newton (1725–1807) with William Cowper (1731–1800). Newton had been the rough-and-ready captain of a slave ship but later became a noted Anglican pastor. He never quite got over his sense of awe that Jesus

## The Golden Age of Hymns

### Isaac Watts
O God, Our Help in Ages Past

Jesus Shall Reign

Am I a Soldier of the Cross?

Come, We That Love the Lord

Alas, and Did My Savior Bleed?

I Sing the Mighty Power of God

When I Survey the Wondrous Cross

Joy to the World!

### Charles Wesley
Hark, the Herald Angels Sing

Christ the Lord Is Risen Today

Love Divine, All Loves Excelling

And Can It Be That I Should Gain

Jesus, Lover of My Soul

O for a Thousand Tongues to Sing

Rejoice, the Lord Is King

Soldiers of Christ, Arise

### Newton and Cowper
Amazing Grace

Glorious Things of Thee Are Spoken

How Sweet the Name of Jesus Sounds

God Moves in a Mysterious Way

O for a Closer Walk with God

There Is a Fountain Filled with Blood

### Lesser-known Hymn Writers
Guide Me, O Thou Great Jehovah

All Hail the Power of Jesus' Name

Blest Be the Tie That Binds

Come, Thou Almighty King

How Firm a Foundation, Ye Saints of the Lord

Rock of Ages, Cleft for Me

---

would not only save a person like himself but would even call him into Christian ministry. Millions of people all over the world have echoed Newton's emotions as they sing "Amazing Grace."

Even if William Cowper had never written a single hymn, he would still be remembered in English literary history as a poet. When he met John Newton, however, Cowper was suffering from depression that bordered on mental illness. As spiritual therapy Pastor Newton suggested that Cowper help him prepare a new collection of hymns. Texts written by both of these unlikely collaborators are still being sung today.

# THE PIETIST MOVEMENT

Chapter 10 tells how Pietism first arose among German Christians in the later 1600s. During the next century this movement spread in all directions with good results such as inspiring the flood of new hymns just mentioned. It also laid firm foundations for even better things to come.

# Hard Times for Historic Churches

At the beginning of the 1700s one of the unintended side effects of the Reformation continued: National governments were tightening their control in matters of religion. This was not a good time for the historic churches of Europe.

## Orthodox

In Russia, Tsar Peter I, also known as Peter the Great (1672–1725), held Orthodox Christians firmly under his control. When the head of the Russian Orthodox Church died in 1700, Tsar Peter refused to name a successor. Instead, he set up a ruling board of church leaders whose members he could hire or fire at will. His royal successors confiscated all churches and monasteries and made them government property; they also limited the number of monks and nuns.

Under such circumstances it seems rather amazing that earnest Orthodox Christians experienced a measure of deepening spiritual vitality. They also succeeded in carrying the Good News about Jesus to many new areas: along the valley of the Volga River in Russia, into the steppes near the Ural Mountains between Asia and Europe, across the vast sweep of Siberia, even into the Aleutian Islands and Alaska.

Tikhon Zadonsky (1724–1783) was a Russian Orthodox bishop of great wisdom and humility who has been immortalized as the character Father Zosima in Fyodor Dostoevsky's famous *The Brothers Karamazov*. "The kingdom of heaven has sent a letter to you!" said Bishop Tikhon. "Whenever you read the Gospel, Christ Himself is speaking to you."[4]

Cyril Vasilyevitch Suchanov (1741–1814) was a layman who devoted his life to sharing the Good News with nomadic tribes in Siberia. Suchanov believed that deeds spoke louder than words: He reduced all his possessions to what he could carry in one traveling bag and then spent years among the nomads. After a time he was able to build a church; he then settled new believers around it and gave them their first lessons in farming and other useful skills. Yet even this Orthodox outreach movement was under strict government control: Many Russian tribal peoples chose to become Christians so they could receive a tax break.

In some ways Greek Orthodox Christians had more freedom under the rule of Turkish Muslim sultans than Russian Orthodox Christians had under the rule of tsars. Yet there was always a threat of martyrdom for any Greek Orthodox leader who tried too hard to spread the gospel. Kosmas the Aetolian (1714–1779) became known as "the Greek John Wesley." Like Wesley in England (see page 176 in this chapter), he crisscrossed his native land, preaching the Good News to huge crowds and inspiring a religious and cultural revival among

Greek Orthodox Christians. Yet like many other devout believers under the rule of Ottoman Turk sultans, Kosmas was martyred.

### Catholics

The 1700s brought no better times for Catholic Christians than for Orthodox Christians. During the 1500s and 1600s Roman Catholics, spearheaded by Jesuit missionaries, had taken the Good News about Jesus to five continents. Yet many Catholic leaders had become distrustful of the Jesuits and thought they had gone too far in adapting the Christian faith to native customs. Kings and governors also felt uneasy because Jesuits reported directly to the pope.

During the mid-1700s Jesuits were banned by one European nation after another. Finally in 1773 Catholic rulers of Europe forced a weak-kneed pope to eliminate the Jesuit order. The results were disastrous—in Asia, in Africa, and perhaps worst of all in South America where the Jesuits' work was swept away by unsympathetic officials and greedy settlers. The Indians of Paraguay, who had been protected in Jesuit villages, were made slaves.

Other factors also worked against Catholic missions during the 1700s:

- A large percentage of Catholic missionaries had been Spanish or Portuguese. Since Spain and Portugal were no longer the great world powers they had once been, the supply of new recruits was drying up.

- The slave trade in Africa, along with shifting locations of African tribes, brought ruin to Catholic missions there.

- Catholic leaders in Rome decided all worship services must be held in Latin and allowed no adaptations in language or procedure. This caused an angry Chinese emperor to order Catholic missionaries out of his realm; he also began persecuting local believers. Much the same thing happened in India.

There were a few bright spots: A Roman Catholic majority in the Philippines, a strong Roman Catholic minority in Vietnam, and pockets of faithful Catholics here and there across Asia and Africa. There was also a stubborn little Franciscan friar named Junípero Serra (1713–1784) who led the way in planting Catholic missions along the coast of California.

Nowhere was Catholicism thought to be stronger than in France, the most populous country of Europe. Yet France in the 1700s was like a tall tree with a rotten or hollow trunk. The king and his nobles, along with cardinals and bishops, held much of the land and most of the money. More than 80 percent of the French were lowly peasants.

France became a fertile field for growth of the idea that human reason is more important than religious faith. When anger and discontent among the common people was mixed with anti-religious ideas among opinion-makers, the result was an explosion. The French Revolution swept away the king and his family, the nobles, the cardinals, and the bishops. Many lost their heads at the guillotine; thousands of Catholic priests went into exile. Churches were made government property; some of them were even used as stables. At the high altar in the great Notre Dame Cathedral of Paris, an opera singer was enthroned as "the goddess of reason." By the end of the century the pope himself was being held a prisoner in France.

### Protestants

Protestant countries of Europe were not much better off in the 1700s than Catholic countries. If you happened to be born in Scandinavia or northern Germany, this meant you were a Lutheran. If you were born in Scotland, you were assumed to be a Presbyterian. If you were born in England, then you were an Anglican. Whether or not you had a personal relationship with God through Jesus the Christ had little to do with the matter.

The upper and middle classes in English society enjoyed wealth and pleasure. Many of them, including many Christian ministers, had become deists, believing in a Creator-God but not really believing in Jesus as Lord and Savior. To this group God was like a divine watchmaker who had wound the watch and then left it to run on its own. If the upper and middle classes were enjoying a comfortable life, then this must be a part of God's plan from the beginning.

For the lower classes in England life seemed hopeless. They suffered from miserable working conditions, drunkenness, gambling, child labor, and many other social evils. Both adults and children could get the death penalty for any of 160 crimes, down to stealing a lady's handkerchief or catching a rabbit on a gentleman's estate. Every six weeks mass hangings drew crowds of curious onlookers. Many Anglican pastors accepted government pay but never bothered to shepherd their flocks; instead they hired underpaid assistants to do it for them.

With conditions similar to Catholic France, Protestant England seemed ripe for a violent revolution. Yet it never happened. Why?

# Pietists to the Rescue

The influence of the Pietist movement spread from Germany to many other areas. It became so important for Christ's People that some church historians even called it "a second Protestant Reformation."[5] Several aspects of Pietism made this movement important.

1. Pietism stressed that true belief in Jesus involves being born again—a spiritual new birth or regeneration. All recent evangelical movements, revivals, and evangelistic appeals to make a personal decision for Christ can be traced back to Pietism. According to Pietists, *the way to change the world for the better is to change the people in the world, one person at a time.*

2. Pietism marked the beginnings of what we now call the *parachurch* movement. Those early German Pietists were faithful Lutherans; they never left their church or tried to start another. Instead, they started new Christian agencies and activities within or across denominational lines. These new organizations usually had only one main purpose such as caring for the needy in society, getting the Bible to people in a language they could understand, or spreading the Good News to distant lands.

3. Pietists had no intention of starting new denominations, yet this happened. The *Moravians* and the *Methodists* grew out of the Pietist movement. In later centuries still other new denominations would grow out of the Methodist movement.

4. Pietism gave new strength and purpose to older existing groups of Christ's People such as Lutherans, Presbyterians, Anglicans, Congregationalists, and Baptists.

When Philip Jacob Spener (1635–1705) helped start a new university at Halle near Berlin and used his influence to bring August Hermann Francke (1663–1727) to teach there, he never dreamed how far-reaching the effects would be. The adjacent box gives a partial list of the new Christian agencies and activities Francke started or promoted during his years at Halle.

One of the Pietists' partnerships in world missions grew out of the concern felt by King Frederick IV (1671–1730) for his small Danish colony in India. When he found no missionary candidates in Denmark, he turned to Francke for help. Two young graduates from Francke's school at Halle were immediately sent out. One of them, Bartholomaus Ziegenbalg, was only 23 years old when he reached India in 1706. Before dying at the age of 36, Ziegenbalg had succeeded in translating all of the New Testament and much of the Old into the Tamil language. Many other dedicated Christians were also sent out through this Danish-Halle Mission. Notable among them were Hans Egede and his son Paul Egede, who served in Greenland.

A similar mission partnership was established with an Anglican agency called the *Society for Promoting Christian Knowledge,* or *SPCK.* For many years faithful German Pietist missionaries worked in British-ruled India. The most famous of these was Christian Friedrich Schwartz

(1726–1798), who served in southern India for 48 years without a break.

Through mission partnerships such as these and through other means the influence of Pietism continued to spread. Sometimes even human evil helped to promote its growth: When Sweden lost an important battle to Russia in 1709, Swedish prisoners of war were sent to Siberia. In that cold and distant place, homesick Swedes began to spread the new ideas of Pietism.

### Zinzendorf and the Moravians

An American magazine article about Count Nikolaus Ludwig von Zinzendorf (1700–1760) was entitled "The Rich Young Ruler Who Said Yes."[6] That is a fitting description. In contrast to the rich young ruler who came to Jesus and then "went away sorrowful: for he had great possessions" (Matthew 19:22, KJV), Count Zinzendorf devoted his great wealth, his influence, even his very life to Jesus.

Young "Lutz" (as he was called) lost his father when he was very young. After his mother remarried, he was raised by his Pietist grandmother, the Baroness Henrietta von Gersdorf (1656–1726). When he was ten years old he was sent to Francke's school in Halle.

While Zinzendorf was still in his early 20s, persecuted Christians from what is now the Czech Republic were turning up on his estate in Germany. Although a Lutheran, he gave these refugees from a different tradition a place of safety and their numbers began to grow. From a book by Jan Amos Comenius (1592–1672), Zinzendorf learned that these believers were descendants of the Hussite Christians; they were the "hidden seed" for whom Comenius had prayed so earnestly a century before (see page 149).

Gradually he gave more and more of his time and attention to these people. Since many of them came from the area known as Moravia, they began to be called Moravians. God's Holy Spirit gave

Zinzendorf and the Moravians a new sense of oneness and a new desire to serve. Beginning in 1727, they pledged themselves as a community to take turns praying around the clock. Believe it or not, this 24/7 prayer meeting continued for over a hundred years!

In 1731 Count Zinzendorf attended the coronation of a new king in Denmark. There he met a dark-skinned believer from the West Indies and two Christians from Greenland—living fruits of the work of the Danish-Halle Mission. Zinzendorf recalled how as a teenager in Francke's school he had heard exciting stories from Ziegenbalg in India.

Back home with his Moravian friends, Zinzendorf urged them to make world missions their passion. The results were amazing. The very next year, 1732, the first Moravian missionaries set sail for the West Indies. Of the first 29 workers 22 soon died. Even so there were always ready recruits to fill the empty places. Within ten years the little Moravian community of only 600 had sent 70 missionaries to 10 different countries.

These early Moravian missionaries were ordinary people, not highly educated or specially trained. Most of them were craftsmen—potters, carpenters, even gravediggers! They worked with their hands to support their ministries. Willing to live and die among those with whom they shared the Good News, they were usually sent to remote places or to neglected people groups. One of them, David Zeisberger (1721–1808), set a seeming world record by serving among North American Indians for 63 years. The simple, eager spirit of these early Moravians echoes through the words of a man who was asked whether he was ready to go to Labrador: "Yes, tomorrow, if I am only given a pair of shoes." [7]

Moravians not only sent and supported missionaries: They also migrated to other lands, taking with them their strong Pietistic faith. Count Zinzendorf himself named Bethlehem, Pennsylvania, which was founded as a Moravian colony. Another notable Moravian settlement is Old Salem, now a part of Winston-Salem, North Carolina. To this day Moravians continue to emphasize outreach and ministry. Besides their own accomplishments, they have influenced and inspired many Christians of other groups.

### Wesley and the Methodists

From Zinzendorf and the Moravians on the European mainland, a direct line of Pietist influence runs to Wesley and the Methodists in the British Isles. John Wesley (1703–1791), the son of an Anglican pastor, had a most remarkable mother. Although Susanna Wesley (1669–1742) was a busy pastor's wife with 11 children, she made time every week to counsel individually with each one.

When her grown sons John and Charles asked what she thought about their becoming missionaries, Susanna replied, "If I had 20 sons,

John Wesley (1703-1791),
founder of the Methodist Movement

Charles Wesley (1707-1788),
greatest of all hymn writers

I should rejoice if they were all so employed, though I should never see them [any] more." [8] When John had doubts about letting a layman preach, Susanna said, "John, he is as surely called to preach as you are." [9] Many historians have called Susanna "the Mother of Methodism"; author Elsie Harrison even named her biography of John Wesley *Son to Susanna.* [10]

Young John did well in school and at Oxford University, where he became a member of a Christian students' club started by his younger brother Charles Wesley (1707–1788). In place of the deism that was then so popular in England, the students' club emphasized *methodical* Bible study and holy living. Other students teased them and called them "Bible-Moths," "Holy Club," and "Methodists." Only one of the three nicknames stuck.

During the 1730s both John and Charles Wesley went as missionaries to the English colony of Georgia in North America. On the ship crossing the stormy Atlantic, John was struck by the calm faith of a group of Moravian Christians. After the Wesleys' mission in Georgia produced no spiritual fruit, the two brothers returned to England, where John sought out a young Moravian pastor. Through this and other influences from Pietism, both John and Charles experienced spiritual rebirth—only three days apart. For the first time in their lives the Wesleys felt a personal assurance of salvation in Jesus the Christ.

John Wesley was so much impressed by Pietism that he even visited Germany to meet with Count Zinzendorf and other Moravians. Coming back home again, he realized what a sad state his native land was in. Along with his brother and a few friends, he began preaching and witnessing wherever he could. Charles Wesley experienced a remarkable ministry among condemned prisoners on Death Row in London. When John Wesley was refused permission to speak in the church where his father had been pastor, he preached outdoors standing on his father's tombstone.

Wealthy nobles and comfortable clergymen were outraged. In those days "enthusiasm" was a bad word among traditional Christians. The Wesleys' opponents encouraged rowdies to heckle them and break up their meetings. Yet nothing could stop this new moving of God's Holy Spirit.

Charles Wesley's greatest contribution to the beginning of the Methodist movement was in writing thousands of hymns; what would Christmas be without his "Hark, the Herald Angels Sing" or Easter without his "Christ the Lord Is Risen Today"? In this, too, he followed the example of earlier hymn writers among the Pietists.

John Wesley was the tireless preacher and organizer of the Methodist movement. "I look upon the world as my parish," he declared. [11] During his long life he preached 40,000 sermons and rode on horseback a quarter of a million miles—ten times around the world. Usually he let the horse set its own pace while he read or studied for his next sermon. He was constantly writing: some 5,000 different religious tracts, pamphlets, and letters.

In promoting his "Methodist societies," John Wesley never intended to leave the Church of England. Yet more and more he and his coworkers, on both sides of the Atlantic, felt forced by circumstances to go their own way. Many outstanding Christians of other groups were also strongly influenced by Wesley, such as the previously mentioned Anglicans John Newton and William Cowper. In Wales a brave schoolteacher named Howell Harris (1714–1773) spread the Good News. In Scotland William McCulloch and others prepared the way for the evangelistic preaching of George Whitefield. Even in faraway Greece an Eastern Orthodox evangelist was nicknamed "the Greek John Wesley" (see page 171 in this chapter).

As a result of Wesley's long ministry, England was transformed. Not only had tens of thousands found faith in Christ; not only had hundreds of churches been touched by Pietism so that the Good News was again being preached: More than that, English society itself had been changed. It is not overstating the case to say that John Wesley and his friends saved England from a bloody revolution like the one that devastated France during that same period of history.

# Whitefield and the Great Awakening

At Oxford University Charles Wesley made friends with a poor, cross-eyed student who had to wait on tables in order to pay his tuition fees. George Whitefield (1714–1770) later became an earnest believer and a strong supporter of the Wesleys. After reading a book by Francke, he felt drawn even further into the Pietist movement.

As a teenager Whitefield had been stage-struck. As a mature Christian he came to see how many social evils were tied to the theater of his day. Yet he never quite left behind some of what he had learned during his play-acting days. He developed a great booming voice that could be heard by 30,000 people at once. He made dramatic gestures; he used heart-tugging sermon illustrations. All in all, he became one of the most remarkable preachers of all time.

Whitefield's preaching went beyond England as he traveled to Ireland, the Netherlands, and Bermuda. He made more than a dozen evangelistic tours into Scotland. Seven times he sailed across the Atlantic to North America, where he preached in public squares, at horse races, and anywhere a crowd might gather. Before the American Revolution, Whitefield was probably the only person besides England's King George III who had instant name recognition throughout the colonies from Maine to Georgia. It is estimated that as many as 80 percent of American colonists heard him preach at least once.

George Whitefield did not try to run a one-man show. In fact, before he ever preached in America, others were already calling the colonists to a personal faith in Christ. Among Whitefield's forerunners were a Dutch Reformed pastor named Theodorus Frelinghuysen (1692–1747), a Presbyterian pastor named Gilbert Tennent (1703–1764), and most importantly, a Congregational pastor, theologian, and university president named Jonathan Edwards (1703–1758).

Yet it was Whitefield's preaching campaigns that breathed new life into this *Great Awakening,* as North American Christians began to call it. This great spiritual movement had remarkable results. Martha Stearns Marshall (born 1726) was among the many people influenced by it. She joined her brother Shubal Stearns and her husband Daniel Marshall in preaching the Good News about Jesus. Some of her fellow Baptists felt that God may have called her brother and her husband to preach, but surely He had not called a mere woman. Martha Marshall never listened to them. She preached all through the backwoods of colonial Virginia and North Carolina and she would not stop preaching even when she was jailed while three months' pregnant.

Whitefield did not try to pull people away from their own faith communities; a true parachurch minister, he encouraged them to stay in their individual churches and to make a difference by staying. Benjamin Franklin (1706–1790) was a deist rather than a true Christian; yet he was so impressed by Whitefield's preaching that the two of them became good friends. Franklin gladly published Whitefield's sermons; Whitefield became quite skillful in working the mass media of his day.

In later years Whitefield and the Wesleys drifted apart, mainly because Whitefield was a Calvinist while the Wesleys held to Arminian beliefs. (See the box on page 160 for a reminder as to the differences.) Yet when George Whitefield died, Charles Wesley wrote a poetic tribute and John Wesley preached the funeral.

Whitefield had shared Christ with blacks as well as whites. As a result, Phillis Wheatley's (c. 1753–1784) first published poem mourned his death. Born in Gambia, West Africa, Phillis was stolen from her parents at the age of seven and brought as a slave to America. Fortunately her Bostonian master and mistress encouraged her to learn reading, writing, and the Good News about Jesus the Christ. While still in her teens Phillis Wheatley became a well-known poet; Christians in England helped publish some of her works. The adjacent box highlights the poetic words she put into Whitefield's mouth.

> **George Whitefield's Appeal[12]**
> **(According to Phillis Wheatley)**
>
> Take Him, ye Africans, He longs
>    for you!
> Impartial Savior is His title due;
> Washed in the fountain of redeeming
>    blood,
> You shall be sons, and kings, and
>    priests to God!

# NEW FREEDOM FOR CHRIST'S PEOPLE

At the turn of the century in 1800, things were looking better for Christ's People than they had a hundred years before.

This chapter has barely mentioned the most important event of the 1700s according to secular history books: The founding of the United States of America. Deism probably had as much to do with that famous beginning as Christianity did; the Declaration of Independence uses such deist terms as "nature's god" and "divine providence."

Yet Christ's People found much to give thanks for in their new climate of freedom. America was the first nation where the choice of religion was completely left up to the individual. Christians who prospered most in an independent America were those who had never at any time been sponsored or controlled by any government: Methodists and Baptists, for instance.

Isaac Backus (1724–1806) was brought up believing that everyone in his native Connecticut ought to go to the Congregational Church. His feelings began to change during the Great Awakening when as a 17-year-old youth he first experienced a personal assurance of salvation in Christ. Continuing to study the Bible, Backus felt forced by his convictions to become a Baptist. Yet he still had to go on paying taxes to support the Congregational Church. Before, during, and after the American Revolution, Isaac Backus led the fight for religious liberty. Thanks to him and others like him, there is no government-supported or government-controlled church anywhere in the United States of America.

George Liele (c.1751–1828) was a freedom fighter of a different kind. Born a slave in the colonial Deep South, he attended church with his master. (Many such interracial churches were among the positive results of the Great Awakening.) Experiencing spiritual rebirth in 1773, Liele began preaching the Good News in Georgia and South Carolina. His master knew a good thing when he saw it, so he set Liele free.

Like many other African-Americans, George Liele favored the British side during the American Revolution because the British had gone much farther toward ending human slavery than the Americans had. Leaving Georgia with retreating British troops, Liele sailed for Jamaica. There he worked as a farmer and a teamster while preaching on the side. By 1784 Liele had started a Baptist church in Kingston, the capital of Jamaica. By the end of the 1700s his church had 500 members including a few whites.

Not only is George Liele remembered today as the founder of the large and prosperous Baptist Union of Jamaica: His earlier ministry in North America also bore fruit in unexpected ways. Andrew Bryan, one of George Liele's first converts, later moved to Savannah, Georgia, and started what was probably the first independent black congregation in America. David George, one of George Liele's early co-workers in South Carolina, later became a missionary to Nova Scotia in Canada and to Sierra Leone in western Africa.

Thanks to the contributions of great composers such as Bach and Handel, Christians centuries later enjoy a rich musical heritage. Thanks to the tireless preaching of John Wesley, George Whitefield, and others, England was saved from France's bloody fate. By two centuries ago Christ's People in England had been aroused to minister to the poor and needy in their midst. They had begun to set up relief agencies, to reform the prison system, to offer free medical care, and to help people who had no jobs. The first Sunday school was started in 1769 by Hannah Ball, a Methodist. Around 1780, Robert Raikes (1735–1811), a Church of England layman, took up the Sunday school movement and made it popular, ministering especially to children from poor families. John Wesley's last letter, written only four days before his death at age 88, encouraged a fellow believer to continue the fight against human slavery.

Most importantly, by 1800 more and more of Christ's People were becoming concerned about their responsibility for spreading the Good News all around the globe. A humble shoe repairman and part-time preacher in England cried, "See what these Moravians have done! Can we not follow their example?"[13] Spurred on by Pietist pioneers, William Carey (1761–1834) and his fellow Baptists started a new missionary society in 1792. Similar agencies soon followed during those exciting years just two centuries ago. The Pietist movement was well on its way toward spreading its blessings all around the world!

# KEY EVENTS

## 1700 TO 1800

Near Berlin August Hermann Francke builds a Pietist center for social ministries and world outreach; with Danish and British Christians he sends missionaries to several countries.

Isaac Watts and others write new hymns; Bach and Handel compose great Christian music.

National governments across Europe tighten their controls over religion, notably in Russia and Greece.

Susanna Wesley, an Anglican pastor's wife, nurtures her sons John and Charles in biblical truth.

Human reason is increasingly considered more important than Christian faith.

Many Europeans and Americans (even clergy) become deists, believing in a Creator-God but not in a Father-God who sent Jesus.

Persecuted descendants of Hussite Christians find a safe haven with Count Zinzendorf; they become known as Moravians, and send out many missionaries.

Frelinghuysen, Tennent, Edwards, and others foster the beginning of a Great Awakening of religious faith in the North American colonies.

Influenced by Moravians, John and Charles Wesley experience spiritual rebirth; they begin preaching and witnessing wherever they can.

George Whitefield furthers the Great Awakening through preaching tours in England, Scotland, the Netherlands, Ireland, Bermuda, and North America.

Junípero Serra and others establish Roman Catholic missions along the coast of California.

Preachers such as Martha Marshall and Isaac Backus spread the Good News in eastern North America.

The Jesuit order is banned; this along with other factors causes a disastrous decline in Roman Catholic missions worldwide.

Eastern Orthodox Christians such as Kosmas the Aetolian in Greece, along with Tikhon Zadonsky and Cyril V. Suchanov in Russia, spread the Good News.

Phillis Wheatley, an African-American in colonial Boston, writes Christian poetry.

John Wesley organizes and promotes the Methodist movement; his brother Charles Wesley writes thousands of new hymns.

English society is transformed by the influence of Whitefield, the Wesleys, and their friends.

American independence opens new opportunities for Christ's people to spread the Good News; Isaac Backus and others fight for complete religious liberty.

John Newton and William Cowper write new hymns; Haydn and Mozart compose great Christian music.

Hannah Ball (a Methodist) and Robert Raikes (an Anglican) start the first Sunday schools.

George Liele, an African-American, preaches in North America and Jamaica; Andrew Bryan starts the first independent black church in America.

The French Revolution sweeps away the national government, the upper classes, and the established church.

Influenced by Moravians and others, William Carey leads his fellow Baptists to found a new privately-supported missionary society; many other agencies for world outreach soon follow.

## WILLIAM CAREY (1761–1834)

With his fellow English believers, Carey pioneered a
Baptist society for world missions in 1792.

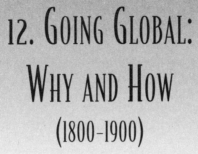

# 12. GOING GLOBAL:
# WHY AND HOW
# (1800-1900)

The great church historian Kenneth Scott Latourette named the 1800s "The Great Century." Why does that century deserve such a name? Because that was when Christianity became a world religion— the first truly worldwide religion in all of history.

From the beginning Christ's People tried to spread beyond the Middle Eastern lands of their origin. They won many tribes and nations to Christ. They established beachheads in distant lands. Yet for 1500 years Christianity was centered on the one continent of Europe (plus a few areas near Europe or areas settled by Europeans).

By one century ago that situation had changed dramatically: Christ's People had reached every continent and almost every country. In 1800 a part or all of the Scriptures had been translated into only 67 languages; by 1900 there were complete Bibles in 100 languages and parts of the Bible in 400 more. Whole populations had become Christians in the islands of the Pacific. Millions in Africa and hundreds of thousands in Asia had become Christ's People.

## REASONS FOR WORLDWIDE GROWTH

After 18 centuries of being largely contained within a fairly small area, why and how did it happen that during the next 100 years Christ's People managed to share their faith in almost every part of globe?

Because Christians had a strong home base in Europe and North America, they were able to focus their attention on other peoples and other lands. By the end of the 1800s Christ's People had significantly strengthened that home base. This is such an important reason for the explosive worldwide growth of Christianity during the 1800s that it will be explored separately in the next chapter.

This chapter will deal with four other factors that contributed to the spread of the Gospel: voluntary societies, relative world peace, technological and communication advances, and European dominance worldwide.

## Voluntary Societies

By 1900 many voluntary societies were carrying out worldwide Christian outreach. Some of these were missionary societies of a particular denomination or group of Christians; others were interdenominational. Some targeted specific tasks such as translating and circulating the Scriptures, ministering to the sick, or sharing the Good News with women in areas where women rarely appeared in public.

William Carey (1761–1834) and his fellow English believers led the way by establishing a Baptist society for world missions in 1792. Other British missionary societies soon followed in 1795 and 1799, along with the first of the world's Bible societies in 1804. The society movement soon spread to other countries as shown in the adjacent box.

Note that these were *voluntary* societies. No king decreed their creation; no tax money was channeled to support them; no members of religious orders were commanded to go out as missionaries. Latourette, the church historian referred to at the beginning of this chapter, summed up this century well:

| The Spread of Volunteer Societies | |
| --- | --- |
| United States | 1810 |
| Switzerland | 1815 |
| Denmark | 1821 |
| France | 1822 |
| Germany | 1824 |
| Sweden | 1835 |
| Norway | 1842 |

> Never before had Christianity or any other religion had so many individuals giving full time to the propagation of the faith. Never had so many hundreds of thousands contributed voluntarily of their means to assist the spread of Christianity or any other religion.[1]

All of these new societies could well be considered a further outgrowth of the Pietist movement. Chapter 11 described how during the 1700s the warm spiritual devotion of Pietism had caused Moravians and other Christians to go out as missionaries to many lands. Yet this was nothing as compared to what happened in the following century.

An important and often overlooked fact is that until the 1800s, world missions were mainly male dominated. Of course there had been exceptions such as Lioba in the 700s (see chapter 3) or Marie of the Incarnation in the 1600s (see chapter 9). Yet almost all Roman Catholic missionaries had been single men. Some of the Protestant missionaries had been married, but wives had not generally been given the same status as husbands.

That all changed during the 1800s. Heroic missionary wives went out all over the world to serve alongside their husbands. Few have been more celebrated than an unlikely trio whose biographies were published at Boston in 1860 within one book: *The Three Mrs. Judsons.*[2] This unusual title reflects the sad fact that missionaries' lives were often cut short by disease and poor medical care. Furthermore, the dangers of childbearing often caused missionary wives to die younger than missionary men.

Ann Hasseltine Judson (1789–1826) pioneered in Myanmar (Burma) alongside her husband, Adoniram Judson. She kept him alive during a brutal imprisonment by caring for his needs and badgering hostile officials. Her busy pen reported all the gory details for eager readers back home in Massachusetts. Ann bore several children but none survived early childhood. Her own death plunged Adoniram into deep depression for which the hard work of Bible translation seemed to be the best cure.

Ann Hasseltine Judson (1789-1826), missionary Adoniram Judson's first wife

Sarah Hall Boardman Judson (1803–1845) was still a teenager when she wrote a poem about the death of a pioneer missionary in Myanmar. This attracted the attention of young George Boardman who was bound for Myanmar himself. Soon they were married and went out to serve together. They helped launch a large movement toward Christ among the Karen peoples. Sarah's biography of Ann Judson aroused strong missionary support back home. After George Boardman died, Sarah continued serving alone. When the senior missionary, Dr. Judson, finished the Myanmarese translation of the New Testament, Sarah wrote him a letter of thanks and congratulation. Once again her pen led her to a husband: She and Adoniram Judson enjoyed 11 years of busy family life and joint ministries before her early death.

Emily Chubbuck Judson (1817–1854) met the grieving widower Adoniram Judson when he took his only home assignment (then called furlough) during 38 years of missionary service. At that time Emily was already well established as a popular writer. A few months later she sailed for Myanmar as Adoniram's third wife. Emily followed a unique family tradition by writing a warmly sympathetic biography of the woman who preceded her as Mrs. Judson. She also cared for Sarah Judson's motherless children, as well as a child of her own.

Even a mere listing of all the notable missionary wives would be too long for a book of this type. As revolutionary as this group of women was, many unmarried women even more broke with tradition by volunteering and serving on the mission field. In fact, during the 1800s a majority of Protestant missionaries were single women. Besides the undoubted call of God, foreign missions offered a new outlet for gifted and determined females, a way for them to make a difference in life.

Many of these bold singles did not fit the stereotype of the proper Victorian lady missionary. Lottie Moon (1840–1912) was brought up to be genteel, but she was a natural rebel. Parents and teachers in old Virginia almost despaired of ever making this petite miss act prim and proper. After several years of teaching school, Lottie Moon sailed for China in 1873. There, too, she chafed under restrictions. Finally she struck out on her own, spreading the Good News from village to town as few had ever dared to do. She took her private daily devotions very seriously and read from the New Testament in the original Greek language.

Giving to world missions increased greatly when Lottie Moon encouraged Baptist women back home to take up a special collection at Christmas time. This Lottie Moon Offering is still gathered every year and millions upon millions of dollars have gone to world missions as a result. Lottie Moon herself died from eating too little so she could share her food with starving Chinese.

Mary Slessor (1848–1915) never was refined in the first place. A red-haired Scottish mill-hand, she sometimes slept in the street to escape her drunken father. By reading as she worked her mill machinery, Mary educated herself enough to serve as a missionary—first among gangs of tough-talking boys in city slums, then among cannibals in Nigeria. She was one of the first to realize how unsuitable Victorian clothing was for the tropics: Other missionaries were scandalized when she went barefoot, dressed only in light cottons, and even climbed trees.

Along with spreading the Good News about Jesus, Mary Slessor bravely fought against evil. Her blue eyes especially blazed with anger over the custom of killing twin babies because they were considered bad luck. She rescued many a black twin, sometimes bringing them up as her own. Once when a panther tried to eat one of her babies, she attacked the beast with a flaming log. Another time she fought off an angry hippopotamus with pots and pans. Mary Slessor later proved to be so adept at defusing tribal conflicts that she was made the first woman magistrate in the British Empire.

Did all of these missionaries, whether male and female, serve with pure, unmixed motives? Did all of them use good missionary methods?

Of course not. It is reported that one German Christian went out to see whether it could possibly be true that there was no winter in Indonesia even though Genesis 8:22 seemed to promise just the opposite.[3] Like all the rest of Christ's People, missionaries of the 1800s were ordinary sinful men and women. Therefore their work was a mixture of wise, effective means and foolish, insensitive means. The chart below offers a balance sheet as to what missionaries did wrong and what they did right.

Once again, Kenneth Scott Latourette gives the best summary: "When all that can be said in criticism of the missionaries has been said, however, and it is not a little, the fact remains . . . that for sheer altruism and heroic faith here is one of the bright pages in the history of the race."[4]

## A Balance Sheet for Missionaries of the 1800s[5]

### What They Did WRONG

- Adopted a paternalistic, superior attitude.

- Held narrow views of other ways of worshiping.

- Failed to distinguish between the Christian faith and their own home culture.

- Exported their own denominations along with their basic Christian beliefs.

- Slow to surrender control/let new Christians become church leaders.

- Used monetary gifts unwisely.

- Identified too closely with foreign governments and with the colonial system.

### What They Did RIGHT

- Loved, helped, protected those they served.

- Tried to preserve the best of other cultures.

- Brought different cultures/peoples closer together.

- Learned/translated the Bible into many new languages.

- Recognized the potential of people once considered "backward" or "uncivilized."

- Introduced modern science/education through their schools, presses, and hospitals.

- Facilitated social/political reforms while planting new churches worldwide.

## Relative World Peace

By 1900 the world had been enjoying almost 100 uninterrupted years of relative peace. With no threat from hostile armies or navies, Christ's People had unhindered access to most parts of the world.

Of course there were still wars; it may be especially hard for North Americans to think of the 1800s as a century of peace because the bloodiest war in American history was fought during the 1860s. Yet exploring church history on a worldwide scale reveals that most years of that century was peaceful. There was no widespread, devastating conflict like the Thirty Years' War of the 1600s or the Napoleonic Wars of the early 1800s.

Furthermore, non-Christian cultures and civilizations were relatively weak or quiet during the 1800s; in those years they were not mounting many challenges to the spread of Christianity. China and other countries with strong Buddhist backgrounds had been hemmed in and intimidated by European colonial powers. The Ottoman Turkish Empire, once the strongest Muslim nation in the world, was now nicknamed "The Sick Man of Europe"; it had lost all of its land possessions in southeastern Europe except a small ring of territory around Constantinople. India was split up among various Muslim and Hindu rulers and was largely under the control of the British.

## Technological Advances

By 1900 humankind had experienced an explosion of remarkable technological advances. Strange as it seems, the Emperor Napoleon had no faster means of transportation or communication at his command than the Emperor Augustus had had 18 centuries earlier. Then during the 1800s came a great burst of new sources of energy and new ways to use them—first steam, then electricity. Transportation was revolutionized. This century saw the first steamships, the first steam railroads, even the first motorcars. Christ's People could travel farther and faster than ever before.

Means of communication were also vastly improved. The first half of the century brought the telegraph; the last half brought the telephone. Modernized machines could churn out more Bibles, more Christian books, more textiles and other objects useful in worldwide trade.

## European Dominance Worldwide

By 1900 European peoples had achieved worldwide dominance, with one person in every three being of European descent. In past centuries Europe had been relatively weak on the world scene, its people wasted by disease and divisions. A third of all Europeans died of the plague in the mid-1300s; almost two-thirds of all Germans died during the Thirty Years' War in the mid-1600s.

By contrast, Europeans in the 1800s were strong, numerous, and relatively at peace with one another. They had built up powerful nation-states with large populations and prosperous economies. They were in a good position to spread out all over the world. And Christianity was the dominant religion among these dominant European peoples.

*A question worth considering:* Did the cross follow the flag, or did the flag follow the cross?

Both. In many cases European missionaries entered foreign lands only after European powers had set up trading posts or colonies there. This did not necessarily mean that Christ's People approved of colonization (as a matter of fact colonial governments often tried to keep missionaries out). It was a simple matter of practicality: European-style law and order offered greater protection for everyone, missionaries included.

Yet in some cases it was missionaries who led the way and colonial officials who followed. This was notably true of the great explorer David Livingstone (see chapter 13). It was not so much that Livingstone wanted British rule in Africa, but he was willing to do almost anything to stop the slave trade that brought captivity and death to so many Africans.

Historians argue as to whether colonization caused more good or more harm for the peoples of Africa, Asia, and the islands of the sea. Law and order, modern science, and education must be balanced against destruction of age-old cultures and lifestyles. It is not surprising that many Asians and Africans see the worldwide expansion of Christianity as just one more aspect of European imperialism.

Yet in recent years many national leaders in the Third World have realized that they can no longer blame their troubles on colonial mistakes of the past. Some of those same leaders have openly expressed appreciation for all that was done for their people in the past by missionaries of European descent.

# CHALLENGES TO WORLDWIDE GROWTH

Christianity had to face many challenges in achieving its new status as the first global religion. These were inter-related and included: socio-economic, political, scientific, philosophical and theological, and literary and artistic challenges. How did Christ's People respond?

The Industrial Revolution brought great wealth to the nations of Europe, allowing much social and economic change. The making of money and the consumption of goods seemed to take on a life of its own, without reference to religion or human welfare. The new wealth was held by only a few; industrialism brought misery to many. Charles Dickens (1812–1870) quite accurately described the results of this economic upheaval in his novels (for example, *Oliver Twist*, *David Copperfield*, and *A Christmas Carol*).

Even though the 1800s were relatively peaceful, those were years of continuing political revolution. The various peoples of Europe were turning against traditional rulers; they were seeking freedom and democracy. During the later 1800s both Germany and Italy forged national unity after having been split into many smaller countries. In each case national unification was strongly tied to limiting the power of government-sponsored religion—Lutheranism in Germany, Catholicism in Italy.

The more human beings understood how things worked scientifically, the less need they felt for an all-wise God. The greatest challenge for Christ's People of this period was the publication in 1859 of *The Origin of Species* by Charles Darwin (1809–1882). The new reasoning included thoughts like: *If human beings are the result of a process of evolution, if humans and apes share common ancestors, then what happens to the biblical account of creation?* Some Christians welcomed Darwin's theory, believing they could make it fit with biblical faith; others fought diligently against the very idea of evolution. The struggle continues today.

During the 1800s many people embraced an exalted view of the individual, a glorification of humankind standing tall in princely grandeur. Theologians taught that experiencing God in one's inner self was more important than formulating confessions of faith. This emphasis on feelings took many forms: Church buildings were erected in conscious imitation of Gothic cathedrals from a simpler age. Newer hymns and gospel songs tended to be saturated with sentiment. Women were thought to be more emotional than men; from this came a tendency to excuse men for their misdeeds while expecting women to be pious churchgoers. (Look around next Sunday: Are there still more females than males in your church?)

Christian scholars of the 1800s applied the methods of historical and literary criticism to the Scriptures. Many of them became convinced that the Bible had gone through much more revision than previously thought. Some even came to believe that the New Testament was a reflection of the way Christ's People wanted to believe things must have been at the beginning—more of a literary creation than an historical record. New biographies featured Jesus more as a loving Teacher than as a dying and risen Savior. Poets such as Byron and Shelley, composers such as Beethoven and Wagner used their art to popularize the ideal of humankind reigning supreme, freed from the shackles of old-fashioned Christian beliefs.

# HISTORIC FAITHS: SURVIVAL AND RENEWAL

How did Christ's People face up to these daunting challenges? How could they achieve worldwide expansion while at the same time warding off attacks at their very foundations? The rest of this chapter offers some answers; it tells how several old historic faiths not only survived but even experienced renewal during the 1800s.

## Roman Catholics

At the beginning of the 1800s the Roman Catholic Church seemed to be weak and perhaps close to extinction. The pope had died in French captivity. It was months before the cardinals dared to elect a successor, and even then they had to meet in Venice instead of Rome.

Yet many ordinary folks among Christ's People in France still looked to the pope for leadership. The French Revolution had swept away the old structure of Catholicism in France with all its abuses and corruption. When French Catholics longed for a sense of certainty in their faith, they tended to look over the mountains toward the Roman pope.

The Emperor Napoleon (1769–1821) was a smart enough politician to sense this grassroots yearning, so in 1801 he came to terms with the new pope. Later he and the pope would disagree again, and once more the pope would become a captive in France. Napoleon should have been smart enough to realize that making a martyr arouses sympathy: After the great French Emperor himself had been bundled off into exile, Pope Pius VII (1740–1823) returned in triumph to Rome.

One of the first things the pope did in Rome was to reestablish the Jesuit order. Once more Jesuits and other Catholic missionaries spread out all over the world. Notable among them were Cardinal Lavigerie (1825–1892), who sent his Arab-robed White Fathers (later joined by the White Sisters) into many parts of Africa, and Father Damien (1840–1889), whose statue was placed in the United States Capitol by the state of Hawaii in honor of his sacrificial ministry among victims of leprosy (Hansen's disease). Like the new Protestant societies, both old and new Catholic orders also sent out a flood of single women during the 1800s. A majority of Catholic missionaries during "The Great Century" were French.

The newly planted Roman Catholic communities, like the older Roman Catholic communities back in Europe, were strong enough to withstand persecution: 70,000 Indochinese Catholics died for their faith in 1850; 25,000 Korean Catholics were martyred in 1866; another 100,000 Indochinese Catholics became martyrs in 1885.

Migration to North America greatly increased the strength of Roman Catholics there. In 1830 there were only half a million Catholics in the United States; by 1860 there were 4.5 million. This great migration came first from Ireland, then from Italy and southern Germany, and still later from eastern Europe. In Maryland Elizabeth Ann Seton (1774–1821), a young widow with five children, started one of the first of what would become a vast network of Catholic schools in America.

During the 1800s Roman Catholics also experienced renewal in music and literature. The devout Anton Bruckner (1824–1896) wrote long symphonies, musical settings of the Catholic mass, and other sacred music. Josef Mohr (1792–1848) and Franz Gruber (1787–1863), a humble village priest and his choirmaster in the mountains of Austria, together composed the all-time favorite Christmas carol, "Silent Night." Later in the century two noted Catholic poets emerged: Gerard Manley Hopkins (1844–1889), a Jesuit missionary in the slums of Liverpool, and Francis Thompson (1859–1907), who wrote his Christian testimony in the form of a haunting ballad entitled "The Hound of Heaven."

Several characteristics of Catholics during the 1800s were not really new but were given new importance. One characteristic has already been mentioned: stronger ties to the pope. Consecutive reigns of two able and long-lived popes spanned the last half of the 1800s; this strengthened a worldwide tendency to turn to the pope for guidance and authority. Further reinforcement came from an announcement in 1870 that the pope is infallible; that is, when he speaks officially on matters of doctrine, the Holy Spirit keeps him from making any mistake.

Other newly emphasized characteristics of Catholic piety during the 1800s were an increasing use of rosaries as prayer guides, an even stronger reverence for the Virgin Mary, and a renewed devotion to the Sacred Heart of Jesus. Religious pilgrimages had almost stopped, but with new destinations such as Lourdes in France, many Roman Catholics became pilgrims once again.

Thus the historic faith of Roman Catholicism, which had seemed about to fade away two centuries ago, not only survived but also experienced renewal during the 1800s. By a century ago it was strong and growing in many lands.

Yet all was not well with the Roman Catholic Church in 1900. In facing the many challenges already mentioned, Catholic leaders tended toward a fortress mentality. The earlier of the two strong Catholic leaders mentioned above, Pope Pius IX (1792–1878), started out as a reformer but the pace of change so overtook him that he retreated to his headquarters in the Vatican and sent out decrees condemning almost everything that might be considered new or modern. His successors as popes were a bit more open, but Roman Catholics of a century ago were still showing a worldwide tendency to circle the wagons, ready to fight all comers who suggested any kind of change.

## Eastern Orthodox

Two centuries ago the Eastern Orthodox Church, like the Roman Catholic Church, seemed to be in a bad way. Yet Orthodox Christians also experienced survival and renewal during the 1800s.

As the empire of the Ottoman Turks weakened, Christ's People in southeastern Europe enjoyed a new freedom. In Serbia, Bulgaria, Romania, and Greece they set up their own nationwide Eastern Orthodox organizations, free of control from Constantinople.

Tsars and tsaritsas, who controlled religious affairs in Russia, were strongly influenced by new ideas sweeping Europe. The effects of this were either positive or negative depending on the ruler's personal religious bent. Catherine the Great (1729–1796) proclaimed religious freedom throughout Russia; many minority groups, feeling they had been pressured to become Christians, promptly went back to Islam. But one of Catherine's successors encouraged the beginning of the Russian Bible Society; another successor released Russia's landless serfs.

Russian spirituality deepened during the 1800s; the number of Orthodox monasteries doubled. After two decades as a religious hermit, Seraphim of Sarov (1759–1833) felt that God had called him to offer himself as a Christian counselor. "The Holy Spirit fills with joy whatever He touches," said Seraphim.[6] Sometimes hundreds sought his counsel in a single day. Among those deeply touched by Seraphim was Fyodor Dostoevsky (1821–1881), whose great novels *Crime and Punishment* and *The Brothers Karamazov* stress the human need for God.

One of the most remarkable individuals in all of Eastern Orthodox history is John Veniaminov (1797–1879), born the son of a church sexton in Siberia. As a young man he became a missionary to the Aleutian Islands, then to the mainland of Alaska. Later he started Orthodox mission work (or helped others to do so) in Japan, on the island of Sitka (now part of Alaska), and in many parts of his native Siberia. His retirement to a monastery was short-lived: Orthodox leaders called the 70-year-old Veniaminov to become the most important archbishop in Moscow. There he served for another decade, encouraging all Orthodox Christians to support evangelism.

*A question worth considering:* Why has the Orthodox faith not spread as widely as Catholicism or Protestantism?

At least part of the answer comes from history and geography. For many centuries Orthodox Christians have been either under the control of Muslim rulers or hedged about on nearly every side by Muslim states.

## Other Historic Faiths

As Catholic, Orthodox, and Protestant missionaries spread all over the world during the 1800s, they came into contact with other historic Christian faith communities. Sometimes this renewed contact helped; sometimes it did not.

Take the Thomas Christians of southern India, for instance. Missionaries encouraged them to study the Scriptures in their own language so they would base their beliefs and practices on biblical teachings. Yet this renewed contact with Christ's People from foreign cultures also resulted in splitting the ancient faith community into several parts. One part of it stayed Roman Catholic, as it had been since the late 1500s. One part became Anglican. Another part stayed true to its Indian roots while setting up a new and reformed church structure. Christ's People in this last group are generally known as the Mar Thoma Christians.

A similar situation developed in Egypt, where the Coptic Church had been holding its own since ancient times. Early missionaries tried with little success to move members of this faith toward renewal and reform. Later missionaries drew modern-minded Coptics toward becoming Presbyterians.

Much the same thing happened in Turkey, Lebanon, Syria, Palestine, and other parts of the Middle East. Remnants of historic faith communities were sometimes helped and sometimes hindered by the coming of Christ's People from foreign lands.

Somewhat different was the situation south of Egypt, where the Ethiopian Orthodox Church still claimed millions of members. When missionaries arrived there in the 1800s, they found that the Ethiopian way of worshiping seemed to have taken about as much from Old Testament Jewish practices as from New Testament Christianity. Yet neither Catholics nor Protestants had much success in influencing Christ's People in Ethiopia.

One of the most remarkable encounters between Christians of the 1800s and ancient faith communities came when an officer in the British army first found out about the Waldensian movement. General John Charles Beckwith (1789–1862) had lost a leg at the Battle of Waterloo, Napoleon's final defeat. Finding a book about the Waldenses, he decided to go to the mountains of northern Italy and pay them a visit. The visit lasted 30 years! At his own expense General Beckwith built new schools and churches; he sent promising young Waldenses to cities in Switzerland for advanced study.

## Neglected or Secret Believers

The most poignant encounters experienced by missionaries of the 1800s were with groups of long-neglected or secret believers.

When Joseph Kam (1769–1833) arrived in 1814 as a Dutch Reformed missionary in the Moluccas (or Spice Islands of Indonesia), he was greeted by a strange procession. In front marched several old women, wearing black dresses that looked a little like the robes worn by Portuguese priests two and a half centuries before. Each woman was singing as she held a psalm-book in her hands, but neither tune nor text made much sense. Kam noticed that some of the women were holding their books upside down. Later he learned that not a one of them could read!

On another island Kam found that all of the Christians gathered on Christmas Day to wail and mourn. Somehow they thought that Jesus died on December 25. Then on New Year's Day they all went to church again and celebrated Jesus' resurrection day!

Fortunately Joseph Kam was a stouthearted seafarer. For many years he sailed from island to island, bringing Moluccans back to a clearer understanding and truer faith in Jesus the Christ.

Even more touching was an event much later in the 1800s when a group of Japanese women timidly approached a Catholic missionary. They began asking questions that seemed to be about the Virgin Mary and the great "king of the doctrine," their name for the pope. These women turned out to be representatives of thousands of secret believers who had stayed faithful through more than two centuries of persecution and isolation.

About half of these underground village Christians became convinced that the missionaries were authentic believers, so they became Roman Catholics. The other half continued worshiping in their own unique way—as some 30,000 on a few islands still do today, totally separate from all other Christians in Japan or anywhere else.

Chapter 13 continues to explore the great worldwide expansion of Christ's People that took place during the 1800s.

# KEY EVENTS
ॐ

## 1800 TO 1900

*The events listed here are covered in chapters 12 and 13; the number following each event indicates the relevant chapter.*

Christ's People in Europe and North America start many voluntary societies—for world missions, for Bible translation, and for other ministries. (12)

Circuit riders and camp meetings help spread the Good News in North America. (13)

The pope is freed from captivity in France; he reestablishes the Jesuit order. (12)

European peoples begin to gain dominance in many parts of the world. (12)

William Wilberforce and other European Christians lead in banning slavery and urging other reforms. (13)

William Carey and two friends, the "Serampore Trio," are among many Protestant and Catholic missionaries sent out all over the world. (13)

Charles G. Finney and others encourage spiritual renewal movements in North America and in Europe. (13)

Robert and Mary Moffat, David Livingstone, and others lead in spreading the Good News in Africa. (13)

Seraphim of Sarov, John Veniaminov, and others lead the Russian Orthodox Church toward renewal and expansion. (12)

Pressures from European nations cause the opening of China, Japan, and Korea to outside influences; many missionaries enter Asia, with varying success. (13)

Christian opposition to slavery splits several American denominations and helps bring on the Civil War. (13)

Charles Darwin's *The Origin of Species* challenges Christians' understanding of human history. (12)

Many women, single and married, are sent out as missionaries. (12)

Christ's People in Madagascar increase fourfold during 25 years of intense persecution. (13)

Henri Dunant, Florence Nightingale, Catherine and William Booth, and many other Christians lead the way in bringing about reforms in society. (13)

Sheldon Jackson and many others spread the Good News in western North America, including Alaska. (13)

New denominations arise among Christ's People: the Christian Church (Disciples of Christ), Seventh-Day Adventists, Salvation Army, Plymouth Brethren, and various Holiness groups. (13)

D. L. Moody evangelizes in America and Europe; he starts Christian schools and other ministries. (13)

Led by strong popes, the Roman Catholic Church experiences renewal and worldwide expansion, yet tends toward a fortress mentality in opposing change. (12)

Bishop Crowther and Chief Khama lead their fellow Africans to follow Jesus the Christ. (13)

Christian look-alikes arise in America: Shakers, Mormons, Jehovah's Witnesses, Christian Science. (13)

Ludwig Nommensen leads a people movement to Christ in Indonesia; whole populations become Christians on other islands of the sea. (13)

Hudson Taylor pioneers in spreading the Good News into the interior of China. (13)

As prime minister of England, the devoutly Christian William E. Gladstone urges many reforms. (13)

Many of Christ's People die as martyrs in many parts of the world. (12 & 13)

Christianity has become the first world religion; one-third of all the world's people are Christians. (12 & 13)

**WILLIAM BOOTH (1829–1912)**

With his wife Catherine, he founded the Salvation Army in
London to aid the poor.

# 13. Going Global:
# Where and When
# (1800-1900)

Through the centuries various individuals and groups among Christ's People have often found themselves disagreeing in terms like these:

- *We mustn't expend all our effort and energy on ourselves, on our own city [or area or country]; we must reach out to the rest of the world!*

- *Not so fast! How can we reach out to the rest of the world unless we build up our own church [or denomination or movement] into a strong home base?*

Christians of the 1800s knew that both sides in this timeless argument have a point. It is both/and, not either/or.

The previous chapter listed five reasons for the explosive world-wide growth of Christianity during the 1800s. This chapter explores the first of those five reasons in greater depth.

## BASE FOR WORLDWIDE OUTREACH

A major factor enabling Christianity to go global was its strong home base in Europe and places such as North America where many European descendants lived. This strengthening of Christ's People came about as Christians responded to social and economic changes. They felt compelled to share with others everywhere the same Good News that had transformed them.

# Europe

As Europe became industrialized, every aspect of society was impacted. Since England was the world's first industrialized economy, English Christians were often the first to respond to the socio-economic challenges of the Industrial Revolution.

## Socio-economic Reforms

Chapter 11 tells about societal and church reforms that grew out of the ministries of George Whitefield and the Wesley brothers during the 1700s. This reform movement gained greater strength in the 1800s.

Several prominent English reformers south of London lived in the village of Clapham, so that they were sometimes nicknamed "the Clapham Sect." Actually they did not start a new sect or denomination; they were all faithful Anglicans. William Wilberforce (1759–1833), a member of Parliament, was an outstanding member of this group who took a stand against slavery. He would not let poor health or powerful opposition stop his campaign to end human bondage. In 1814 he and his friends gathered a million signatures on anti-slavery petitions, representing 10 percent of the total population of England. Just three days before Wilberforce died, slavery was finally outlawed throughout the British Empire.

Others who fought against gambling, pornography, inhumane working conditions, child labor, hellish prisons, and filthy hospitals continued the struggle for socio-economic reform.

Florence Nightingale (1820–1910) faced stiff family opposition when she announced that God was calling her to be a nurse. In those days no proper English lady would think of taking up such lowly work; to find out how to do it, she had to go to a Pietist center in Germany.

At her own expense she equipped a corps of nurses and sailed to southern Russia, where too many British soldiers had been dying needlessly in the Crimean War. Within a few months "The Lady of the Lamp" (so nicknamed because of the lamp she carried while making rounds in the evenings) reduced the hospital death rate from 42 percent to 3 percent. Though she suffered from poor health throughout much of her long life, Florence Nightingale continuously wrote reports and petitions aimed at improving care of the sick and wounded.

Other notable examples of Christian reformers of the 1800s include prime ministers of two countries:

- William Ewart Gladstone (1809–1898) of Great Britain considered politics to be a "most blessed calling."[1] Between 1868 and 1894 he was called on to lead his country four separate times.

- Abraham Kuyper (1837–1920) of the Netherlands pastored large Dutch Reformed churches and started a Christian university before entering politics. As prime minister he changed Dutch colonial policy in the East Indies to the great advantage of the Indonesians. Like many other Christians before and since, Kuyper was strongly influenced by reading Augustine's classic, *The City of God.*

## New Movements

New movements within established denominations also strengthened the home base of Christ's People. There were a variety of movements—too numerous to mention them all.

One European religious awakening was named the *réveil* (meaning reveille or wake-up call). It began in French-speaking areas of Switzerland and quickly spread across the continent:

- One leader of the *réveil* was César Malan (1787–1864), a Swiss preacher and hymn writer. In a counseling session Malan advised Charlotte Elliott (1789–1871) to come to Jesus just as she was; Elliott later wrote the familiar hymn, "Just As I Am, Without One Plea."

- Henri Dunant (1828–1910), son of a wealthy Swiss family, was deeply influenced by the *réveil.* Concerned about the condition of wounded soldiers and prisoners of war, he led in founding the International Red Cross in 1863. He also led in the calling of an international meeting in 1864 that adopted the Geneva Convention for protection of prisoners of war.

- Hans Neilsen Hauge (1771–1824) was the first in a succession of Christian laymen whose preaching brought new spiritual life to Norway.

- In Denmark Søren Kierkegaard (1813–1855) warned that God is too big to be boxed up within our little systems, whether doctrinal or political.

- In England the preaching of the independent (and not ordained) Baptist Charles Haddon Spurgeon (1834–1892) brought new life in Jesus to many. Taking quite a different approach, leaders of the Oxford Movement tried to renew a sense of wonder and majesty in Anglican worship services.

## New Denominations

Some of the reform and renewal movements among Christ's People of the 1800s resulted in new denominations. Abraham Kuyper, the prime minister of the Netherlands already mentioned above, led a split from the traditional Dutch Reformed Church.

One of the best-known new denominations is the Salvation Army, largely coming out of the Methodists. Catherine Booth (1829–1890) and William Booth (1829–1912) were its co-founders. Many may immediately think of bell-ringers collecting money in a Christmas kettle, but this is only a tiny part of what the Salvation Army does. Conducting rescue missions in the slums, fighting against child sexual abuse and other practices that endanger bodies and souls, establishing homes for orphans and old folks, starting canteens that minister to soldiers on active duty—these are just a few of the Salvation Army's many accomplishments.

Catherine Booth was generally considered the better preacher of the two co-founders. Yet a man once challenged her: "Paul said to the Corinthians it is a shame for women to speak in the church." She answered him: "Oh yes, so he did; but in the first place this is not a church, and in the second place I am not a Corinthian; besides [she continued, looking at the man's wife], Paul said in the same epistle that it was good for the unmarried to remain so." [2]

Another new group of Christians emerged in England during the 1800s that was harder to classify. They claimed to reject all denominations, all creeds, and all specialized ministers, anything that might cause divisions among Christ's People. Most of their congregations recognized no organization past the local church level. Yet this movement did in fact result in several new denominations.

An outstanding leader in this hard-to-classify movement was John Nelson Darby (1800–1882), formerly an Anglican clergyman in Ireland. Because Darby's ministry centered in and around Plymouth, one nickname for this group is the Plymouth Brethren. Other famous members of the Brethren movement were George Müller (1805–1898) and Thomas Barnardo (1845–1905), whose faith-based children's homes saved many orphaned boys and girls from death . . . or worse.

Darby made preaching tours to France, Germany, Switzerland, Canada, and the United States. One of his teachings became especially popular: *dispensationalism.* Darby divided all human history into dispensations or eras. Based on his study of the Book of Revelation, he taught that Jesus would return to earth and set up a thousand-year reign or millennium. Darby's views were built into the *Scofield Reference Bible,* a study tool used by many of Christ's People for the past century. These same views form the background for a series of novels that became immensely popular during the 1990s, the *"Left Behind"* books by Jerry Jenkins and Tim LaHaye.

### Authors, Artists, Musicians
Christ's People with artistic talents also helped to strengthen the Christian home base in Europe during the 1800s.

- The composer Felix Mendelssohn (1809–1847) was born into a Jewish family but became a follower of Jesus the Christ. Drawing on Lutheran heritage in his native Germany, Mendelssohn used the tune of Martin Luther's "A Mighty Fortress Is Our God" in his *Reformation Symphony*. He also wrote two still-popular biblical oratorios: *Elijah* and *St. Paul*.

- Leaders of the Oxford Movement (already mentioned on page 203), in their effort to bring back an atmosphere of awe and reverence in worship, translated many ancient Christian hymns from Greek and Latin.

- Cecil Frances Alexander (1823–1895), an Irish pastor's wife, wrote simple hymn texts to help children understand major Christian doctrines: for the Creation, "All Things Bright and Beautiful"; for the Nativity, "Once in Royal David's City"; for the Crucifixion, "There Is a Green Hill Far Away."

- Popular songbooks and brass bands organized by the Salvation Army brought the Good News in musical form to millions of people.

- Some of Charles Dickens's best-selling novels were mentioned in chapter 12. It is not as well known that he also wrote *Life of Our Lord* and that *A Christmas Carol* is but one of his many Christmas stories.

- Marian Evans, another Victorian novelist who wrote under the name of George Eliot (1819–1880), turned away from Christian faith and Christian morality. Yet in her fiction she drew sympathetic word-portraits of Christians such as Dinah Morris, a Methodist preacher who is a leading character in *Adam Bede*.

- There were also Europeans in the visual arts who combined romantic imagination with Christian devotion. Among them were the German painter Caspar-David Friedrich (1774–1840) and the English artist William Blake (1757–1827), who was both a poet and an illustrator.

## North America

Was North America a part of Christianity's strong home base? Many Americans tend to think of the United States as having been a Christian nation from the start, yet historical facts show that at the beginning of the 1800s hardly one American in ten was a church member. The percentage of church membership was much higher in Canada, in part because so many Canadians were Catholics of French descent. On the American frontier, tough-talking settlers were more likely to be engaged in fighting, gambling, horse-racing, and hard drinking than in going to church.

Francis Asbury (1745–1816) was one of the first to try to change this situation. Sent as a Methodist missionary to North America, he soon realized that a new system was needed to overcome vast distances between frontier settlements. So Asbury became the first *circuit rider*—a minister serving congregations in several different places. He enlisted many young Methodists for this difficult task; each of them had to meet only the four basic qualifications listed in the adjacent box.

Timothy Dwight (1752–1817) was another Christian who wanted to change the situation in America but he used prayer rather than preaching. Dwight, an Ivy League college president like his famous grandfather Jonathan Edwards, saw his prayers answered when half of the students at Yale professed faith in Christ. On another New England campus, a rainstorm drove students at an outdoor prayer meeting to take refuge under a haystack. There they pledged themselves to work and pray toward spreading the Good News to foreign lands.

## Qualifications for a Circuit Rider [3]

1. Are you truly one of Christ's People?

2. Do you know our Methodist rules and keep them?

3. Can you preach acceptably?

4. Do you have a horse?

As this moving of God's Spirit reached the frontier, it took on a new form: the *camp meeting.* Tens of thousands of men, women, and children would gather around a backwoods church-house and stay for days, camping out while hearing sermons from preachers of different denominations. Those who were spiritually born again sometimes danced, shouted, or fell to the ground.

The more educated Presbyterians scoffed at such goings-on. Other Presbyterians joined with Methodists and Baptists in reaping a harvest from these revival meetings. The new movement became known as the *Second Great Awakening,* like the first one in the days of Jonathan Edwards many years before.

The results of those years of spiritual ferment were truly amazing: By the mid-1800s there were already 1.5 million Methodists in the United States, plus a million Baptists and hundreds of thousands in other churches. As often happens when there is a new touch of the Spirit, several new denominations also appeared:

- Presbyterians who liked camp meetings more than they liked strict Calvinism broke off and became Cumberland Presbyterians.

- Several new groups refused at first to answer to any name except "Christian," just as they refused to follow any creed except the Bible; from this movement came today's Christian Church, also called Disciples of Christ.

- Many of Christ's People got all excited because they thought Christ's promised Second Coming, or *Advent,* would happen sometime in the 1840s; after much disappointment and regrouping, the Seventh-Day Adventists came out of this movement.

- Much later in the 1800s, certain Methodists began to stress the doctrine of "Holiness," feeling that many Christians had become too worldly; this movement resulted in The Church of the Nazarene and other Holiness groups.

- A Canadian-born pastor named A. B. Simpson (1843–1919) founded The Christian and Missionary Alliance, a parachurch organization at first but later a denomination in its own right.

The Second Great Awakening continued to spread through the ministry of Charles G. Finney (1792–1875). A New York lawyer, Finney began using his courtroom skills in the pulpit. Before, during, and after his years as pastor of several large city churches and president of a college in Ohio, he conducted countless evangelistic meetings. Finney was one of the first to teach that a revival could be worked up as well as prayed down. Some half a million people professed faith in Christ as a result of his preaching. Along with his eagerness for evangelism, Finney also strongly supported the rights of women and African-Americans.

The unjust practice of human slavery ate like a cancer in the soul of America. In 1800 the percentage of black Americans who were Christians was no higher than it was among white Americans. Some African-Americans, like some Native Americans, rejected Christianity as "the white man's religion." Others found in Christ a new hope for liberty. Many blacks as well as many whites came to Christ during the Second Great Awakening.

- Richard Allen (1760–1831), born a slave, founded the African Methodist Episcopal (AME) Church, the first major independent black denomination.

- Lott Cary (c.1780–1828) earned freedom for himself and his family by hard work. Feeling called as a missionary, he sailed for Liberia with other freed slaves. There he became pastor, doctor, teacher, and finally acting governor of the struggling colony. Cary died while fighting those who were still trying to take Africans as slaves.

- In the Deep South slaves announced their secret church meetings by singing "Steal Away to Jesus" or "Let Us Break Bread Together." Many of their spirituals echoed the story of the Exodus, when Moses led God's people to freedom.

- In the northern states there were many African-American preachers of righteousness. Among them was a woman who called herself Sojourner Truth (c.1797–1883), the name she felt God had given her after she was freed. She also felt that God had called her to "travel up and down the land showing people their sins" [4]—especially the sin of slavery but sometimes also the sin of looking down on a woman. Once a man tried to humble her with this outburst: "Old woman, I don't care any more for your talk than I do for the bite of a flea!" "Perhaps not," Sojourner answered, "but, Lord willing, I'll keep you scratching." [5] Another time someone challenged her: "Suppose there is no heaven. What will you say if you never get there?" In a twinkling Sojourner replied, "Why, I'll say 'Bless the Lord! I had a good time thinking I would!'" [6]

Sojourner Truth (c. 1797–1883), orator and abolitionist

- Abraham Lincoln (1809–1865), the President who freed the slaves, never became a church member, yet he showed great spiritual depth. Recent writers have even called him one of America's leading theologians. [7] In a famous speech Lincoln wondered aloud whether the terrible loss of life and property in the Civil War might well have been God's punishment on those who had dared to enslave their fellow human beings.

Before the Civil War, slavery had already divided several white denominations, South from North. After the Civil War, more and more freed slaves established their own churches. African-American congregations often became the backbone of African-American communities. Taken as a whole, Christianity has influenced the history of black Americans at least as much as it has the history of white Americans.

How about Native Americans? Greedy settlers repeatedly forced American Indians to move or killed them. Humanly speaking, it is thanks to a few exceptional Christians that any significant number of Native Americans have ever become Christ's People.

The Delawares were the tribe that made a treaty with William Penn so that persecuted Quakers could live in peace. This tribe turned to Christ when Moravian missionaries came to live among them. In times of war the Delawares were often advocates for peace. Yet when Charles Journeycake (1817–1894) became the Delawares' last high chief, his tribe,

EXPLORING CHURCH HISTORY

like most of the other Indian tribes, had fallen on hard times. Even so, Chief Journeycake, pastor as well as tribal leader, could see the hand of God in human history: Read his moving words in the adjacent box.

During the mid-1800s a Third Great Awakening began in Canada with the preaching of a Methodist lay-leader named Phoebe Palmer (1807–1874), assisted by her husband, a medical doctor. The movement soon spread to the United States. As a well-known pastor in New York City was leading 3,000 people in a noonday revival service held in a theater, he was interrupted by singing from an overflow prayer meeting at a bar next door. The pastor stopped preaching and offered a prayer of thanks that such a thing could happen.

The ripple effect from this Third Great Awakening continued to be felt for many years. One major aspect left out of secular accounts of this period of history, including Ken Burns's nine-hour documentary *The Civil War*, was the fact that there were genuine spiritual revivals in many army camps on both sides of the conflict. Another continuing effect was the work of the YMCA (Young Men's Christian Association). At the time of its founding everyone knew what the "C" stood for. Through its ministries many young men in American cities were set on the right path in life.

A veteran of both the YMCA and service to soldiers during the Civil War was Dwight L. Moody (1837–1899). Starting out as a shoe-clerk with little formal education, Moody proved to be an effective public speaker and organizer of effective follow-up. He succeeded Finney as the most successful

Dwight L. Moody (1837–1899), evangelist and founder of Christian schools

mass evangelist of the later 1800s. On both sides of the Atlantic he called people by the millions to turn from their sins and commit their lives to Christ. At the same time he helped spread the Good News by starting a mission Sunday school that grew into a great church, as well as Christian schools for both men and women.

Ira D. Sankey (1840–1908) was an associate of Moody. Sankey was one of many who introduced Christ's People to contemporary Christian music of the 1800s. Some of these gospel songs he wrote himself; more often he popularized the work of others such as the blind hymn-writer Fanny J. Crosby (1820–1915), author of "Blessed Assurance," "To God Be the Glory," and thousands more.

As Americans followed wagon trails westward, Christ's People went with them. A Methodist preacher in Arizona compared the desert heat to what sinners might expect in the world to come. A frontier evangelist, preaching in a saloon, used the figures on a deck of cards as object lessons.

Among those who won the West for Christ, none was more colorful than a five-foot-four-inch fireball named Sheldon Jackson (1834–1909). During half a century as a missionary he logged nearly a million miles (with no interstates) while organizing the first Presbyterian churches in Arizona, Utah, Wyoming, Montana, and Alaska. He started 53 schools in Alaska, many of them for Native Americans. He founded two newspapers and a college. When support from his own denomination was not enough, he raised money wherever he could, either from private donors or from part-time work as a government agent.

In such a vast land with so many different kinds of settlers, it is not surprising that the United States became the birthplace of several Christian look-alikes. One group that came out of the Quakers were the Shakers, who taught that God is both Father and Mother and that the original human sin was sexual intercourse. Living in strict sexual abstinence, the Shakers—before they died out—left as their heritage many beautiful handcrafts and a hauntingly lovely song: "Simple Gifts" (the tune of which has also been matched with a modern hymn text, "Lord of the Dance").

Another group that achieved remarkable growth were the Latter-Day Saints or Mormons. They claimed to be Christians but adopted several strange teachings. (For example: The American Indians are descended from the Old Testament Israelites. An unmarried woman cannot hope for full salvation, but a man may rescue her through marriage . . . even if he already has another wife.) In addition to using the Scriptures, they also study the Book of Mormon written by Joseph Smith. After suffering much persecution during their first years in the eastern United States, the Latter-Day Saints made a heroic trek to Utah, which they hoped was so far away that no one would bother them.

Still other groups arose later in the 1800s: The Christian Science movement emphasized health and healing. Jehovah's Witnesses, like the first Adventists, started out with predictions of Christ's Second Coming. Like Mormons, they interpreted the Scriptures in their own special way, even insisting that all Bible translations except theirs were wrong.

Throughout the 1800s American Christians were using their God-given talents in many fields. The Moravians of Pennsylvania and North Carolina kept alive a remarkable tradition by composing and performing music for many instruments. Lowell Mason (1792–1872) brought better music to churches and schools across the nation. The devout Quaker John Greenleaf Whittier (1807–1892) wrote some of America's finest poetry, including hymns such as "Dear Lord and Father of Mankind."

Nathaniel Hawthorne (1804–1864) wrote highly-praised stories (such as *The Scarlet Letter*) based on traditions of Christ's People in early New England. Yet more Americans read popular Christian novels, especially these two:

- *Uncle Tom's Cabin,* written in 1851–1852 by Harriet Beecher Stowe (1811–1896), aroused Americans' sympathy for those held in slavery.

- *In His Steps,* written in 1896 by Charles Sheldon (1857–1946), a Congregational minister in Kansas, became a runaway best-seller by posing a simple question: "What would Jesus do?"

## Europeans Elsewhere

Christ's People in Europe and North America formed the strong home base for the worldwide expansion of Christianity during the 1800s. Yet there were also Christians of European descent elsewhere.

Settlers from the Netherlands took the Dutch Reformed Church to South Africa, while settlers from England took the Anglican Church and other denominations there. Most of those who settled in Australia and New Zealand were from the British Isles, and many of them were Christ's People.

The largest concentration of Christians of European descent was in Central and South America. Settlers from Spain, Portugal, and elsewhere mingled with Indians and Africans. During the early 1800s the peoples of Latin America were bucking a worldwide trend: Just when European nations were starting new colonies in Asia and Africa, Latin American colonies were winning their freedom from European powers.

Freedom in South America, like freedom in North America a generation earlier (1776), did not necessarily bring progress for Christ's People. Most Roman Catholics of Latin America showed so little spiritual life during the 1800s that one book of church history refers to them as

"A Church Asleep."[9] It is understandable that Protestants from North America started mission work in South and Central America during the later 1800s. By a century ago perhaps half a million Latin Americans had become Protestant Christians.

*A question worth considering:* Should Christ's People of one type send missionaries to countries where there are already many who claim to be Christ's People of another type?

This is a question that cuts both ways. During the 1800s Roman Catholic missionaries moved into parts of Africa and the South Pacific where there were already strong Protestant communities. And, as just mentioned above, during the 1800s Protestant missionaries moved into areas where almost everybody claimed to be a Roman Catholic.

Actually Roman Catholics themselves have come to realize that Latin America is still a mission field. A Catholic church historian has identified four kinds of Catholics living there: formal Catholics, nominal Catholics, cultural Catholics, and folk Catholics.[10] At one time about half of all Roman Catholic foreign missionaries from the United States were serving in South and Central America.

# RESULTS OF WORLDWIDE OUTREACH

Moving out from their strong home base, Christ's People achieved worldwide outreach during the 1800s. This outreach included Asia, the islands of the seas, and Africa.

## Asia

Long before this point in history there were believers in southern Asia—first the Thomas Christians of India, then those converted by earlier Catholic and Protestant missionaries. A new chapter in the story of Christ's People in India began with the arrival of William Carey (1761–1834) and two of his colleagues, known collectively as the "Serampore Trio."

Carey himself was the most famous of the three. A largely self-taught cobbler who preached on the side, he challenged his fellow Baptists to launch out into world missions. Yet during his early years in India he accomplished little until he was joined by the rest of the team. After that Carey led the way in a remarkable program of translating, printing, and circulating the Scriptures in many Asian languages.

It was William Ward (1769–1823) who supervised the printing of all those many different translations. He also preached, wrote, and did translation work himself. Some people considered him the best preacher of the three. Certainly he became a sterling role model and mentor for William Carey's rambunctious sons, whose mother had become mentally ill.

Joshua Marshman (1768–1837) and his wife ran three schools: a free school for children of India and two fee schools for English children in India. In this and other ways he became the principal fund-raiser for the team. He, too, was active in preaching and translating.

By present-day standards the famed Serampore Trio should have been called the Serampore Quartet, for Hannah Marshman (1767–1847) was an able member of the team. Ann Hasseltine Judson, a younger missionary to Asia, judged that Mrs. Marshman did "more good than half the ministers in America." [11]

Throughout the 1800s many kinds of Christians arrived in India. Along with Indian people whose lives they influenced, these brave pioneers became the spiritual ancestors of the 25 million Christians living in India today.

- Henry Martyn (1781–1812) was actually a British army chaplain but his real desire was to bring India to Christ. Upon arrival in India he wrote in his journal: "Now let me burn out for God!" [12] Before his death less than seven years later, he had made Bible translations into three of the major languages of Asia—versions that are still useful today.

- Reginald Heber (1783–1826), Anglican bishop of Calcutta, wrote "Holy, Holy, Holy" and many other hymns, including one he wrote in 1819 that is displayed in the adjacent box.

- Alexander Duff (1806–1878), a Presbyterian, took a new approach. He experienced some success in trying to educate and influence the upper classes in India but greater success as an eloquent speaker and promoter of missions back home in Scotland.

- Lars Olsen Skrefsrud (1840–1910), who found Christ while doing time in a Norwegian jail, took an opposite tack from Alexander Duff: He faithfully shared the Good News with thousands of simple tribal peoples in the hills of India.

> ### A Missionary Hymn of 1819 [13]
>
> Shall we, whose souls are lighted
> with wisdom from on high,
> shall we to men benighted
> the lamp of life deny?
> Salvation! O salvation!
> The joyful sound proclaim,
> till earth's remotest nation
> has learned Messiah's name.
> –Reginald Heber

• Narayan Vaman Tilak (1861–1919), from the highest caste in India's social system, believed Christianity was dangerous for India . . . until one day on a train he read Matthew 5 and changed his mind. After that he wrote hundreds of hymns in his own Marathi language.

Four million Christians live in Myanmar today, but most of them are not the majority Bama (or Burmese) people. One of the most important things ever done by the pioneer missionary Adoniram Judson (1788–1850) was witnessing to Ko Tha Byu (c.1778–1840), a former murderer and gang leader who became the founding father of Christ's People among the Karen tribes.

In neighboring Thailand and Malaysia the situation is similar to Myanmar in that many of the Christians are not members of the majority population; they are ethnic Chinese rather than Thai or Malay, and there are not as many of them proportionally as in Myanmar.

Rather different is the situation in Indochina (Vietnam, Cambodia, Laos), where there has been a strong minority of Roman Catholics since the 1600s. In fact it was persecution of Christians there that caused France to step in during the later 1800s and claim Indochina as its colony.

Turning from southern to eastern Asia, the great nation of China still seemed as hard to reach in 1800 as it had been centuries earlier. The first Protestant missionary to China, Robert Morrison (1782–1834), never got beyond the edges of the mainland. Yet he made his mark through translating the Bible into Chinese and compiling a six-volume Chinese dictionary.

A disgraceful event partially opened the door into China. To its continuing shame, Great Britain went to war in 1839 with the aim of forcing Chinese to buy the hard drug opium from British India. After Britain won the Opium War, foreigners could safely land on the coast of China. Christ's People were quick to take advantage of the situation. A steady stream of missionaries arrived from Europe and North America; a steady trickle of Chinese became Christians.

A few years later there occurred yet another of those tantalizing might-have-beens that mark the history of Christ's People in Asia. During the 1840s several influential Chinese showed great interest in Christianity, yet never claimed to be Christians. Instead, they recruited a liberation army and sparked what came to be known as the Taiping Rebellion.

During those years a foreign imperial family from Manchuria ruled the native Chinese. Leaders of the Taiping Rebellion announced three goals: driving out the Manchu rulers, stopping the use of opium, and destroying idols. They also claimed to observe the Ten Commandments and to pray in the name of Father, Son, and Holy Spirit.

For 15 years this unusual revolutionary movement controlled much of China. What if their understanding of Christianity had been more complete? What if they had acted more in the spirit of Jesus rather than ruthlessly killing their enemies? Would there have been a great Chinese movement toward Christ during the mid-1800s?

With the help of an English general, the armies of the Manchu emperor eventually wiped out the Taiping Rebellion, and everything pretty much went back to what it had been before.

A major change came with the arrival in Shanghai of J. Hudson Taylor (1832–1905). A young Englishman with little education or experience and even less money, he set out to revolutionize missions in China. Three major convictions marked Taylor's work:

Hudson Taylor (1832-1905), missionary to China

- Too many missionaries were clustered along the coast (so Taylor struck out for the interior).

- Missionaries were too much separated from the Chinese (so Taylor urged colleagues to follow his example in wearing a pigtail and Chinese clothing).

- God would supply all the money needed (so Taylor never asked for financial aid).

With the help of his wife and several friends, Taylor set up the China Inland Mission (CIM). By a century ago the CIM had sent hundreds more missionaries to China than any other sending agency. After his first wife died, Taylor married one of the single women in the group and continued his work. Others followed CIM's example and worked in the interior. By a century ago there were close to half a million Christians in China.

Both Japan and Korea were like China before the Opium War in that they were closed to foreigners. History books tell how Commodore Matthew Perry sailed his American warships into Tokyo Harbor in 1853 and virtually forced Japan at gunpoint to open itself up for international trade and communications. It was almost 30 years later before a new treaty opened the way into Korea.

A remarkable figure in Japanese Christianity is Shimeta Niishima, known in America as Joseph Hardy Neesima (1843–1890). Yearning to learn more about foreigners and their ways, he became a Japanese language teacher for a Russian Orthodox missionary. Stowing away on a ship (it was still illegal for Japanese to go abroad), he eventually reached America where kind friends led him to Christ and helped him get an education.

Like Alexander Duff in India, Neesima believed that the best way to reach the proud Japanese was through education. He gathered enough support to go back to his homeland, where he started what became a great Christian university. Other missionaries started schools of various types in Japan; some of these campuses experienced remarkable spiritual awakenings.

By a century ago the number of Christ's People in Japan was in the tens of thousands. There were also a similar number of Christians in Korea.

## Islands of the Seas

The two largest islands in the Indian Ocean are Sri Lanka and Madagascar. Different in language, culture, and history, they were also quite different in their response to Christianity during the 1800s.

Although Sri Lanka is just off the coast of India, it is not a Hindu country like India. Instead it has a long history of Buddhism. Like the Buddhist majority peoples of Myanmar and Thailand, the Buddhist majority of Sri Lanka have been slow to respond to the Good News about Jesus.

The people of Madagascar are Malayo-Polynesian, like most of the peoples of Indonesia and the Pacific. Their response to Christianity was also slow when the first Protestant missionaries from England arrived in 1818. The king of Madagascar was friendly enough though he did not become a believer, but he was succeeded in 1835 by a queen who launched a fierce persecution. Christ's People in Madagascar were fined, flogged, tortured with boiling water, thrown over cliffs, burned alive, and buried alive.

After the wicked queen had died in 1861, surviving Christians crept out of their caves and jungle hideouts. Amazingly it turned out that the number of believers had increased four times during a quarter-century of persecution! A major reason was that these brave believers already had the New Testament in their own Malagasy language. When they could not obtain printed copies, they wrote out the Scriptures by hand. It is no wonder that almost half of the people of Madagascar are Christians today.

The 13,000 islands of Indonesia stretch like a bridge from the Indian Ocean into the Pacific. Nearly all Indonesians are Malayo-Polynesians but of many different types. By the 1800s a very refined and artistic culture (with a thin Muslim overlay) had already developed on the island of Java. At the same time there were still savage cannibal tribes in parts of Sumatra and Kalimantan (or Borneo).

A key figure in spreading the Good News on the island of Java was Kiayi Paulus Tosari (1812–1881). As a boy he was fascinated by Javanese shadow-puppet shows. As a man he wrote Christian poems, using the same style of verses as those chanted during intermissions in the ancient folk dramas. Today more people on Java have come to Christ than in any other place where Islam is the strong majority religion.

On the island of Sumatra, Ludwig Ingwer Nommensen (1834–1918) was a major figure in spreading the gospel. Born on a Danish island, he was sent to Indonesia by a German missionary society. At first Dutch colonial officials would not let him make contact with the fierce Batak tribes who had killed and eaten two earlier missionaries. At last Nommensen reached the interior and began his great work. Bravely facing many dangers, he stuck to his mission for more than half a century. The result? A great movement of people to Christ. By a century ago the total of Batak Christians had already increased to six figures; today they number in the millions.

Even more striking were the results when missionaries began to reach other Malayo-Polynesian tribes on smaller islands of the Pacific. Again some of the first missionaries were clubbed to death or shot with arrows; many others died of tropical diseases. Yet the outcome was overwhelming: On island after island the population became more than 90 percent Christian.

It is worth noting that many of these devout islanders then went as missionaries to other islands. Christians from Australia carried the Good News to the Maori tribes of New Zealand. The patient teacher Ruatoka (1846–1903) and his faithful wife Tungane (c.1850–c.1900) were among dozens of Rarotongans (Cook Islanders) who carried the Good News to fierce bushy-haired natives in the dense jungles of Papua New Guinea.

# Africa

The northern tier of nations in Africa has been strongly Muslim for many centuries. During the 1800s Christ's People learned to bypass this barrier by entering Africa from the West, the South, and the East.

Unfortunately western Africa soon became known as "the white man's grave." Tropical diseases killed off many members of missionary families during the 1800s. Quite typical is the fact that 53 missionaries died within the first 20 years of Anglican missions in western Africa. An historical marker on a busy street in Raleigh commemorates

Melville B. Cox (1799–1833), who went from North Carolina as a pioneer Methodist missionary. The plaque records Cox's dying words four months after his arrival: "Let a thousand fall before Africa be given up."

Sierra Leone was unique in having been set up by British believers as a homeland for freed slaves. A generation later, American Christians followed suit by establishing Liberia further south in western Africa. Both of these new countries played key roles in spreading the Good News.

Nigeria is the largest nation in western Africa and the most populous nation in all of Africa. It has also become the scene of some of the most heroic efforts by Christ's People to share the Good News with Africans.

Samuel Adjai Crowther (c.1807–1891) was captured by slave-traders as a teenage boy. Set free by the crew of a British warship, he landed in Sierra Leone, where he became a Christian and got a good education. Later he also studied in England, finally being given a doctor's degree. Sent back to his native Nigeria as a missionary, he was delighted to be reunited with his mother and his sisters; they were among the first new believers he baptized. Later Dr. Crowther became the first African bishop of the Anglican Church; along with his son he pioneered for Christ in eastern Nigeria, where people had been honoring iguanas and boa constrictors as sacred animals.

Robert Moffat (1795–1883) and Mary Smith Moffat (1795–1871) were outstanding among Christ's People who entered Africa from the South. The Moffats boldly pushed farther into the interior than missionaries had gone before. One of the many Africans they met and influenced was Khama Boikano (c.1830–1923). This leader almost failed to succeed his father as paramount chief in Botswana because as a Christian he refused to take more than one wife. For more than half a century Chief Khama fought to protect his people against sorcery, slavery, thievery, wife buying, alcohol abuse, and the trickery of greedy white settlers.

As great as the Moffats were, during their own lifetimes they saw their fame eclipsed by that of their son-in-law, David Livingstone (1813–1873). Livingstone was more of an explorer than a missionary; he traced the route of the mighty Zambezi River and named Victoria Falls after his queen. Yet his explorations opened the way for other Christians to follow. In a letter to those who supported him back home, Livingstone asked this striking question: "Can the love of Christ not carry the missionary where the slave trade carries the trader?" [14]

In the early 1870s Dr. Livingstone stayed deep in the jungle for such a long time that many people feared he was dead. Henry M. Stanley (1841–1904), a British-American newspaper reporter, became famous by leading an expedition to find the missing missionary. Influenced by Livingstone, Stanley himself became a noted explorer and a missionary of sorts. His writings encouraged many more missionaries to sail for Africa.

Stanley also played a role among Christ's People who entered Africa from the East. For many years missionary work in eastern Africa was slow and hard because of Muslim sultans and Arab slave-traders along the coast. It was only when the missionaries leapfrogged over Kenya and Tanzania into the beautiful highlands of Uganda that a real Christian movement began.

A Ugandan chief welcomed the missionaries; many of his people became Christians. Trouble came when a teenage son succeeded him; several earnest young believers were roasted over a slow fire. But—as had happened again and again in Europe so many centuries before—Christ's People kept on growing even as they took two steps forward and one step back.

A remarkable feature of the Christian movement in Uganda was the way these new believers quickly took responsibility for sharing the Good News with their neighbors. The Ugandans had often been at war with nearby tribes. Yet they boldly went as missionaries, even to the shy and dangerous pygmy peoples of the forest.

By a century ago there were 9 million Christians in Africa; this was one-tenth of the total population of the continent. (By the year 2000 almost one-half of all Africans, or 360 million people, would be Christians.)

# THE GREAT CENTURY

The Great Century—truly the century of the 1800s lived up to the name it was given! During nearly a hundred years of relative peace and prosperity Christ's People spread the Good News over almost all of planet earth. By one century ago more than a third of the world's people were Christians. Almost one Christian out of every five was not a white-skinned person of European descent. Surely a bright future lay just ahead!

Of course there were a few clouds on the horizon as the 1800s drew to a close. Non-Christian nations and religions were becoming more aggressive:

- In 1895 Turkish Muslims slaughtered 300,000 Armenian Christians.
- During the Boxer Rebellion of 1900, followers of the Manchu dowager empress killed 50,000 Christians—both Catholic and Protestant, both foreign missionaries and native Chinese believers.

- At the Chicago World's Fair in 1893, many people listened when an eloquent young Hindu scholar called for all religions to be recognized as valid ways to God, without anyone ever being encouraged to change his or her way of worshiping.

- It also seemed that more and more people—especially in Russia—were paying attention to the wild-eyed radical ideas of two Germans who had taken refuge in England: Karl Marx (1818–1883) and Friedrich Engels (1820–1895). Communism was the name some people gave to these new notions.

Yet by and large Christ's People were filled with optimism a century ago. Since the years of the 1800s had turned out to be so great, surely the years of the 1900s would be greater still . . . wouldn't they?

# KEY EVENTS

## 1800 TO 1900

*The events listed here are covered in chapters 12 and 13; the number following each event indicates the relevant chapter.*

Christ's People in Europe and North America start many voluntary societies—for world missions, for Bible translation, and for other ministries. (12)

Circuit riders and camp meetings help spread the Good News in North America. (13)

The pope is freed from captivity in France; he reestablishes the Jesuit order. (12)

European peoples begin to gain dominance in many parts of the world. (12)

William Wilberforce and other European Christians lead in banning slavery and urging other reforms. (13)

William Carey and two friends, the "Serampore Trio," are among many Protestant and Catholic missionaries sent out all over the world. (13)

Charles G. Finney and others encourage spiritual renewal movements in North America and in Europe. (13)

Robert and Mary Moffat, David Livingstone, and others lead in spreading the Good News in Africa. (13)

Seraphim of Sarov, John Veniaminov, and others lead the Russian Orthodox Church toward renewal and expansion. (12)

Pressures from European nations cause the opening of China, Japan, and Korea to outside influences; many missionaries enter Asia, with varying success. (13)

Christian opposition to slavery splits several American denominations and helps bring on the Civil War. (13)

Charles Darwin's *The Origin of Species* challenges Christians' understanding of human history. (12)

Many women, single and married, are sent out as missionaries. (12)

Christ's People in Madagascar increase fourfold during 25 years of intense persecution. (13)

Henri Dunant, Florence Nightingale, Catherine and William Booth, and many other Christians lead the way in bringing about reforms in society. (13)

Sheldon Jackson and many others spread the Good News in western North America, including Alaska. (13)

New denominations arise among Christ's People: the Christian Church (Disciples of Christ), Seventh-Day Adventists, Salvation Army, Plymouth Brethren, and various Holiness groups. (13)

D. L. Moody evangelizes in America and Europe; he starts Christian schools and other ministries. (13)

Led by strong popes, the Roman Catholic Church experiences renewal and worldwide expansion, yet tends toward a fortress mentality in opposing change. (12)

Bishop Crowther and Chief Khama lead their fellow Africans to follow Jesus the Christ. (13)

Christian look-alikes arise in America: Shakers, Mormons, Jehovah's Witnesses, Christian Science. (13)

Ludwig Nommensen leads a people movement to Christ in Indonesia; whole populations become Christians on other islands of the sea. (13)

Hudson Taylor pioneers in spreading the Good News into the interior of China. (13)

As prime minister of England, the devoutly Christian William E. Gladstone urges many reforms. (13)

Many of Christ's People die as martyrs in many parts of the world. (12 & 13)

Christianity has become the first world religion; one-third of all the world's people are Christians. (12 & 13)

**CORRIE TEN BOOM (1892–1983)**

This Dutch Christian aided Jews during World War II and recalled
her story in *THE HIDING PLACE*.

# 14. ADVANCE AND RETREAT
## (1900-1950)

Hig_h optimism: That was the hallmark of Christ's People in the
early 1900s. John R. Mott, a dynamic young Christian leader strongly
influenced by Dwight L. Moody, was busily recruiting thousands of
university students to go abroad as missionaries. Their motto? *The
Evangelization of the World in This Generation!*[1] Not that they thought
they could finish the job within their own lifetimes: Rather, they resolved
that everyone of their generation anywhere in the world would have an
opportunity to hear the Good News.

Christ's People were indeed advancing around the globe. During
1904–1905 a new spiritual awakening swept out of Wales. By far the
majority of Canadians claimed to be Christians. Church membership
in the United States had climbed from 15.5 percent in 1850 to 35.7
percent in 1900; by 1910, it was 43.5 percent. There were 30,000
Eastern Orthodox Christians in Japan and 100,000 Lutherans in
Indonesia. Catholics claimed a million members in Indochina; both
Catholics and Protestants were growing fast in Africa.

Many Christians were working together to improve society.
City pastors such as Washington Gladden (1836–1918), Walter
Rauschenbusch (1861–1918), and Frank Mason North (1850–1935)
led the way in what came to be known as the *social gospel movement.*
Books by Rauschenbusch set forth the movement's ideals; hymns such
as Gladden's "O Master, Let Me Walk with Thee" and North's "Where
Cross the Crowded Ways of Life" expressed a renewed concern for
human needs. John D. Rockefeller (1839–1937), a faithful Baptist who
had become a multi-millionaire by questionable means, was donating
much of his wealth to Christian causes.

Modern technology offered new opportunities for Christ's People of the early 1900s. First automobiles, then airplanes became common. Long-distance telephone calls were still something special when the wireless telephone, an early form of radio, also became available.

Events of the early 1900s continued to fuel Christian optimism:

- 1910: a great worldwide meeting of Christians assembled at Edinburgh, Scotland. Representatives came not only from historic Christian strongholds such as Europe and North America but also from Asia, Africa, and islands of the seas. With 45,000 missionaries already on the job, the Edinburgh conference set a goal of three times that many by mid-century.

- 1911: Chinese freedom fighters overthrew the old Manchu empire. Sun Yatsen (1866–1925), leader of the new China, was a Christian; so was his associate, Chiang Kaishek (1887–1975).

- 1912: V. S. Azariah (1874–1945), a young, internationally respected Christian leader, became the first non-European Anglican bishop in India, symbolizing a growing maturity among Christ's People worldwide.

- 1913: Christian outreach gained further momentum when Albert Schweitzer (1875–1965), famous both as a theologian and a musician, left this outstanding double career and went as a medical missionary to Cameroon in the jungles of Africa. (In mid-century Schweitzer would be awarded the Nobel Peace Prize.)

Not surprisingly Christ's People began using an optimistic reference to the 1900s—a phrase that even became the name of a new magazine: *The Christian Century*.

## WHAT HAPPENED?

The overall high optimism of the early 1900s got a jolt when the *Titanic*, a new ocean liner considered unsinkable, struck an iceberg and went down in the Atlantic. In 1914 growing nationalism in Europe triggered World War I.

Although the United States sent a million soldiers to Europe in 1917–1918, American losses were light compared to those suffered by England, France, and Germany. Young men who would have become the next generation of leaders among Christ's People died on bloody battlefields. Even worse, it was professing Christian fighting professing Christian once again: Turkey was the only major non-Christian nation on either side in the conflict.

Many died besides those who fell in battle. Turkish Muslims used the war as an excuse to increase genocide against historic Christian communities in Armenia. Between one million and two million Armenian Christians were massacred, plus many more were driven away into other areas.

The stresses of wartime brought down the tsar of Russia in 1917. During the confusion that followed, Communists gained control of the government while killing their enemies by the hundreds of thousands.

During 1918–1919 a worldwide epidemic of influenza proved to be nearly as bad as the Black Death of the plague-stricken 1300s. Some 20 million people died.

Woodrow Wilson, the idealistic American president, called for fighting a "war to end all wars" in order to "make the world safe for democracy," but it did not turn out that way. Harsh terms for the losers left many postwar Germans feeling angry and disillusioned.

Racism was a bitter fact of life during the first half of the 1900s. It took many forms: rigid separation between races in many areas; separate but (un)equal schools; mobs of hooded vigilantes, lynchings, and denial of the right to vote, especially in the American South; colonialism and (white) imperialism in Africa and Asia.

During the 1920s and 1930s many countries of "Christian" Europe fell under the control of dictators. Totalitarian rulers in Portugal, Italy, and Spain came to terms with the Roman Catholic Church. In Germany, Adolf Hitler (1889–1945) got the support of many Christians at first because he was an anti-Communist who never smoked or drank; he opposed pornography and other social evils, while calling for a revival of historic German values. Soon though, Hitler showed his true colors by persecuting not only Jews but also Christians. One of his lieutenants boasted, "We shall not rest until we have rooted out Christianity."[2]

Meanwhile Communists had combined Russia, Ukraine, and several other countries into the Union of Soviet Socialist Republics. Little about it, however, resembled a republic: Instead it was a dictatorship, especially after Joseph Stalin (1879–1953) took over. No one knows the actual number of people who starved to death or were killed outright as Stalin and his followers drove to establish full control; some say 20 million, some same 60 million.

Communists especially targeted the Russian Orthodox Church as a remnant of the old tsarist regime. Some 200,000 Christian leaders were killed—shot, scalped, strangled, crucified, or frozen into columns of ice. Millions of ordinary Christians also died for their faith; 40,000 church buildings were destroyed; all monasteries were shut down. Said Stalin, "The [Communist] Party cannot be neutral towards religion; it conducts an anti-religious struggle against all and any prejudices."[3]

Arnold Toynbee (1889–1975), one of the greatest historians of the 1900s, suggested that Christianity and all other major religions had been replaced by three new systems of belief: nationalism, Communism, and individualism.[4]

- It was nationalism that made possible the rise of dictators in several countries.

- It was Communism that brought drastic changes (along with death and destruction) to Russia and its neighbors in eastern Europe and central Asia.

- It was individualism that caused many Europeans, as well as many people in other areas, to turn away from historic ways of worshiping. *If I as an individual have become the most important thing in life, then why do I need a god or a religion?*

This tendency toward secularism affected many parts of the world. Hu Shih (1891–1962), a popular Chinese ambassador to the United States, declared that the Chinese would be the first people to "outgrow" religion, as if religion were merely an early stage in human development.[5] Uruguay in South America changed its calendar: Christmas became "Family Day" while Easter became "Tourist Day." The largest newspaper in the Uruguayan capital began printing "God" without a capital letter. Many people in Brazil turned from Roman Catholicism to various forms of occultism, spiritism, or animism. Many people in the United States seemed bent on nothing but the pursuit of pleasure; when the sale of liquor was banned, murderous mobs set up criminal networks to keep alcohol flowing.

Beginning in 1929, a worldwide financial depression put many people out of work. When you cannot feed your family, how can you give generously through your church? Sad stories were told of missionaries coming back home for lack of support or of new mission volunteers with no money to send them.

Some people were beginning to wonder about missionaries anyway. Protestants in several denominations had become increasingly influenced by liberalism and modernism. They viewed the Bible as a collection of parables and ethical teachings rather than the record of God's self-revelation to humankind. They downplayed the need to turn away from sin and make a life-commitment to Jesus the Christ. Some Christian leaders began to call for missionaries to come back home since other world religions were equally valid as ways of finding God.

Even Albert Schweitzer, the missionary doctor in Africa, felt that Jesus had been mistaken in hoping for the kingdom of God to come on earth during his lifetime. Rudolf Bultmann (1884–1976) was one of many theological scholars who urged that the Bible needed to be demythologized.

As if all of this were not bad enough, the specter of war still threatened. Japan's invasion of China in 1931 grew into a full-scale war by 1937.

World War II, the worst conflict in human history, came to Europe in 1939 and to America in 1941. If World War I was a disaster, World War II was a catastrophe. Not only military forces but also civilian populations were targeted. From 1939 to 1945 wholesale destruction became common: homes, schools, churches. Once again many of Christ's People—especially those of the younger generation—became victims. Missionaries were put in prison or forced to leave many countries of the world.

Just as Muslim Turkey had used World War I as an excuse for increasing genocide against Armenian Christians, so Nazi Germany used World War II as an excuse for stepping up its campaign of genocide against Jews. Between 1939 and 1945 Germany and its allies slaughtered 6 million Jews, plus significant numbers of Christians.

The aftermath of war often breeds violent change. During and just after World War I, Russia and many smaller countries were taken over by Communists. During and just after World War II, Communists also took control of many other countries: nearly all of eastern Europe, the northern halves of both Korea and Vietnam, and finally China, the most populous nation in the world. Missionaries were forced to leave; some of them were martyred, along with local believers.

Everywhere Communists gained control, Christ's People suffered persecution. More Christians died for their faith during the 1900s than in any previous century.[6] Furthermore, by half a century ago there were more non-Christians living on planet earth than there had been when Jesus the Christ died and rose again—even more than there had been in 1900.[7]

In June of 1950 Communist forces from North Korea invaded South Korea. Indeed, by that time Communists seemed poised to take over many more areas—in Asia, in Europe, in Africa, even in some parts of the Americas. People began to speak of an Iron Curtain and a Bamboo Curtain that had divided Communist countries from the rest of the world; they spoke of a long-lasting Cold War against the Communists, with no end in sight.

So much for all those high hopes about "the Christian century."

When things turned so disastrously bad between 1900 and 1950, what did Christ's People do about it?

The rest of this chapter gives a series of answers to that question.

## THEY STOOD STRONG AGAINST TYRANNY

Martin Niemöller (1892–1984) was a naval hero of World War I who became a pastor in Germany. Speaking out against the tyranny of Hitler and other Nazis, he suffered eight years of imprisonment for his boldness.

After being set free at the end of World War II, he often warned other Christians with these chilling words:

> First they came for the socialists, and I did not speak out because I was not a socialist. Then they came for the trade unionists, and I did not speak out because I was not a trade unionist. Then they came for the Jews, and I did not speak out because I was not a Jew. Then they came for me, and there was no one left to speak for me.[8]

There is more than one way to stand strong against tyranny. A Dutch Christian named Corrie ten Boom (1892–1983) along with her father and sister did it quietly by hiding persecuted Jews in their home. Eventually they were caught and thrown into one of the infamous Nazi concentration camps where her father and sister died. Released by clerical error one week before she was due to be executed, Corrie later narrated her experiences in a best-selling book, *The Hiding Place.*

Dietrich Bonhoeffer (1906–1945) was a German pastor and professor of theology who could have escaped the Nazis by taking a teaching position in America. Instead, he chose to stay and fight. After he was no longer allowed to preach, teach, or publish, he became a secret agent, trying to bring down Hitler's dictatorship. When he helped a group of Jews escape into Switzerland, he was caught, imprisoned, and finally hanged only a few days before the end of World War II in Europe.

Bonhoeffer's writings, both before and during his years in prison (such as *The Cost of Discipleship*), have been challenging Christ's People for more than half a century now. The adjacent box gives a few samples.

It was not only Europeans who stood strong against the tyranny of their times: Nee Tosheng, known outside China as Watchman Nee (1903–1972), was a noted preacher and Bible teacher who started a new denomination of Christians. Like Bonhoeffer, he too could have stayed away in safety when Communists took over his native land at mid-century. Instead he went back home to face almost certain imprisonment. While in prison he became famous, as his writings were smuggled out from behind the Bamboo Curtain.

## Hard Sayings

- When Christ calls a man, he bids him come and die.

- Cheap grace is the deadly enemy of our church. We are fighting today for costly grace. Such grace is *costly* because it costs one's life; it is *grace* because it leads to the only true life. Above all, it is *costly* because it cost God the life of his Son; it is *grace* because God did not reckon his Son too dear a price to pay for our life.

- The church was silent when it should have cried out. Only those who cry out for the Jews may sing Gregorian chant.[9]

–*Dietrich Bonhoeffer*

Sohn Yang-Won (1902–1950) grew up in a Korea that had been taken over by Japan. While still a schoolboy he suffered beatings because he would not bow to a picture of the emperor. While serving as pastor of a leper colony he was thrown into prison. Near the end of World War II he was set free.

Pastor Sohn had brought up his children to be sturdy believers like their father. When Communists began to infiltrate South Korea in the late 1940s, two of his sons were killed for refusing to deny Jesus. At the murder trial, Korean authorities were amazed when Pastor Sohn asked that one of the killers be spared. The young man turned out to be more confused than Communist; after being released into the custody of Pastor Sohn, he soon became a believer and even a seminary student.

Then war broke out again. When North Korea invaded South Korea in 1950, Pastor Sohn could have escaped but chose to stay. After being taken prisoner he tried to share the Good News with his guards till they beat his mouth with rifle butts; then they shot him.

The former Communist youth leader came home to preach Pastor Sohn's funeral. "I stand here today like another Saul of Tarsus," he said to an overflow crowd in the church at the leper colony. "Once I persecuted Christians; now I proclaim the Good News. And you . . ." His voice broke as he looked down into the coffin: "You saved my life!" [10]

# THEY FOUGHT FOR PEACE

Woodrow Wilson (1856–1924), son of a Presbyterian pastor and himself a devout Christian, was the American president during World War I. He believed it was possible to stop wars in the future by fighting a "just war" in the present. After the battles were over, he led in establishing the League of Nations as a forum for world peace, . . . only to see his allies insist on harsh terms that left the defeated Germans feeling angry and bitter, and then to see his own fellow Americans refuse to join the League.

No one fought harder for peace and democracy in postwar Europe than a Protestant named Tomás Masaryk (1850–1937), founder and first president of Czechoslovakia (now divided into the Czech Republic and Slovakia). Another Christian who worked tirelessly against social conditions that breed war was an American Catholic labor activist named Dorothy Day (1897–1980); she opened homeless shelters known as "houses of hospitality."

Toyohiko Kagawa (1888–1960) was of noble Japanese descent, but his mother was a mistress rather than a wife. When both parents died he endured a miserable childhood. Coming to Christ in his teens, he felt a special closeness to those who suffer. While preparing himself for Christian service, he chose to live in the slums, ministering to the dregs of society. Even when his lifestyle brought on long-term health problems, he did not turn away from needy people.

Kagawa became well-known through his writings, both prose and poetry. This gave him leverage to fight for causes he believed in: fair treatment for laborers, low-cost housing, and an end to all wars. It was this pacifism that most often got him into trouble, as his native country began to attack its neighbors. Yet with all of his campaigns for reform and social action, Kagawa never stopped sharing the Good News. The adjacent box displays a stanza from one of his poems.

## A Fighter for Peace

Fervent the vow I swore to fight,
   nor falter,

Fight with a faith not flickering
   nor dim;

God is my Father; in my heart an altar

Glows with the sacrifice I offer Him."

*—Toyohiko Kagawa*

The dream of peace on earth did not die with the failure of the League of Nations. It was mainly Christians who led in founding the United Nations after World War II—Christians such as John Foster Dulles (1888–1959) of the United States, Charles Malik (1906–1987) of Lebanon, and Dag Hammarskjöld (1905–1961) of Sweden.

During the 1930s and 1940s America's first lady Eleanor Roosevelt (1884–1962) fought against injustices in society that make wars more likely. In 1948 she and her coworkers persuaded the United Nations to adopt the Universal Declaration of Human Rights. After World War I, and even more so after World War II, Christ's People led the way in doing more to meet the needs of war victims than had ever been done before in all of human history.

John Foster Dulles and his associates made sure that the peace treaty with Japan after World War II had a different effect from the peace treaty with Germany after World War I; the US-Japan treaty gave that defeated nation an opportunity to recover. Yet Dulles was a realist: When Communists threatened free peoples in many parts of the world, he led in building up defense forces ready for action whenever needed and in putting policies in place to contain the spread of Communism.

# THEY STARTED NEW MOVEMENTS

Some of the new movements among Christ's People during the early 1900s arose in some of the oldest Christian communities. The Zoë Brotherhood, true to the meaning of its name, brought new "Life" to the Greek Orthodox Church. Sunday schools and Bible study became more common among the Coptic Christians of Egypt. The emperor of Ethiopia encouraged better education among ministers in the Ethiopian Orthodox Church.

### Neo-Orthodoxy

During the early years of the 1900s many of Christ's People in Europe and North America became more and more concerned about liberalism and modernism in their midst. *If the Bible can no longer be trusted, then what's the use of believing it? If other religions are as valid as Christianity, then what's the use of being a Christian?*

One of several new movements to combat liberalism and modernism came to be known as Neo-Orthodoxy. This movement had nothing to do with Eastern Orthodox Christians; rather, that same Greek word was used as a way of re-emphasizing the need to worship God in the *right way.*

In 1919 Karl Barth (1886–1968), a Swiss Protestant pastor and professor, published a book of theology that started turning many of Christ's People back toward a stronger belief in the Bible. Barth also joined with other German-language believers such as Niemöller and Bonhoeffer in speaking out against the tyranny of Hitler and the Nazis. As a result he was forced to move from Europe to North America.

Many other writers, teachers, and theologians also contributed to the Neo-Orthodox movement. Notable among them were two brothers born in a Missouri parsonage:

- Reinhold Niebuhr (1893–1971) became a pastor like his father, as well as a professor of theology who wrote influential books about Christians in human society. His most famous words form a well-known prayer: "Lord, give us serenity to accept what cannot be changed, courage to change what should be changed, and wisdom to distinguish the one from the other."[12]

- H. Richard Niebuhr (1894–1962) also wrote forcefully, especially about the relationship between Christ and human culture. He once described liberal theology in these mocking words: "A God without wrath brought men without sin into a kingdom without judgment through . . . a Christ without a cross."

### Fundamentalism

A more widespread movement that arose in opposition to modernism and liberalism was Fundamentalism. Its name comes from a short list of beliefs first formulated in 1895 and then widely circulated through a series of publications entitled *The Fundamentals:*[13]

1. Jesus the Son of God is uniquely divine.

2. Jesus was born of a virgin.

3. Jesus took our place in dying as a sacrifice for sin.

4. Jesus will come to earth again.

5. The Bible in its original form is *inerrant;* that is, it contains no errors.

Besides these basic beliefs, most Fundamentalists also held to high standards of Christian morality. Often this has led to nit picking: Opposition to alcohol abuse becomes opposition to all drinking (and all smoking as well). Opposition to gambling becomes opposition to all games that use cards or dice. Opposition to indecent performances becomes opposition to all dancing, all movies, and all plays.

One of the Christian leaders most often attacked by Fundamentalists was Harry Emerson Fosdick (1878–1969), a respected author and distinguished pastor of the famous interdenominational Riverside Church in New York City. In fact, one of the things Fundamentalists seemed to do best was to attack those they did not agree with. Not too surprisingly, they often attacked each other. Each of these leading Fundamentalists of the early 1900s was "fundamentally" different from the others:

- Curtis Lee Laws (1868–1946) coined the term Fundamentalist in a 1920 editorial; for many years he was editor of an influential (and independent) publication, the *Watchman-Examiner.*

- Billy Sunday (1862–1935) was a former pro baseball player who led colorful evangelistic campaigns all across North America; often he attacked liberals and modernists from the pulpit.

- W. B. Riley (1861–1947) was a dignified pastor and seminary president who nevertheless did not flinch from firing faculty members and splitting denominations in order to get rid of liberalism and modernism.

- J. Frank Norris (1877–1952) called himself "the Texas Cyclone"; he fought his opponents through dramatic preaching, bitter name-calling, and once even through drawing a pistol and killing a man.

- J. Gresham Machen (1881–1937) refused to be called a Fundamentalist, yet he upheld Fundamentalist principles; a respected Bible scholar and author, he started a new seminary and a new denomination to support his conservative views.

The Fundamentalist movement got a lot of publicity in 1925 when a high school faculty member in Tennessee was tried for breaking a state law against teaching evolution. The trial became a media circus, with famous Americans as members of both legal teams. Unfortunately most press reports gave the impression that Fundamentalists were know-nothings with their heads in the sand. (Have you ever seen *Inherit the Wind,* a play and film based on this historic case?)

## Pentecostalism

An even more important Christian movement than Fundamentalism or Neo-Orthodoxy is Pentecostalism. In fact many church historians regard Pentecostalism as the single most important new movement among Christ's People within the past century. Unlike the other two movements, Pentecostalism did not arise as a protest against modernism and liberalism. Rather, it grew out of various Holiness groups during the later 1800s, along with movements throughout Christian history that have emphasized gifts of the Spirit. The name of the movement comes from the account in Acts 2 about the Day of *Pentecost*, when the Holy Spirit came upon Christ's People and enabled them to speak in other languages. For many Pentecostal Christians this *speaking in tongues* is viewed as a sure sign of God's blessing.

The early Pentecostal movement had many leaders, but none more important than an African-American named William J. Seymour (1870–1922). In the spring of 1906, Seymour began holding evangelistic services at an abandoned church building on Azusa Street in Los Angeles. The results were spectacular: People turned from their sins while shouting, singing, dancing, falling down in ecstasy, and speaking in unknown tongues. The meetings would start at mid-morning and sometimes go far into the night.

Yet Seymour urged the joyful new believers: "Don't go out of here talking about tongues: Talk about Jesus." [14] Indeed, the most notable characteristic of genuine Pentecostal Christians, then and now, is a contagious joy in Jesus—Jesus the Savior, Jesus the Christ, Jesus the King whose triumphant return is expected soon.

The Azusa Street revival rapidly became big news. People traveled great distances to see what was going on. Some came to scoff but stayed to pray. The series of meetings continued for weeks, then months, then nearly three years.

An unusual aspect of the Pentecostal movement in its early days was the lack of distinction between black and white or male and female. Canadian-born Aimee Semple McPherson (1890–1944) seemed an unlikely candidate for the founder of a new denomination among Christ's People. A high-school dropout, then a teenage widow when her young missionary husband died in Hong Kong, she felt the call of God during a near-death experience.

Starting in 1919, Aimee McPherson became famous through Pentecostal revival meetings in many cities. She proved to have great gifts both as a preacher and as a channel of divine healing. People fondly called her "Sister". She wore theatrical costumes; sometimes she would zoom in on a motorcycle with lights flashing as she warned sinners to "Stop!" on their way to hell.

In 1923 "Sister" dedicated Angelus Temple in Los Angeles; it could hold 5,300 worshipers. She started a free lunchroom for the poor, a radio ministry, a Bible school, a monthly magazine. In red-light districts she witnessed to drunks, gamblers, and prostitutes; once she walked into a bar and got the crowd's attention by playing "Jesus, Lover of My Soul" on the piano. From Aimee McPherson's ministry came The International Church of the Foursquare Gospel, a Pentecostal denomination with 2 million members.

As the 1900s wore on, pressures in society caused the Pentecostal movement to become more like other Christian groups in separating the races and in giving more leadership positions to men. Yet this did not mean failure to grow. Quite the contrary, huge predominantly black Pentecostal denominations arose, as well as huge largely white Pentecostal denominations—not to mention the many Latinos who also became Pentecostal Christians. Pentecostalism spread to all parts of the United States, to Europe, Latin America, Asia, and Africa. Two of the biggest Pentecostal denominations in the United States today are the Church of God in Christ and the Assemblies of God.

### New Denominations

Clearly these new movements, both Fundamentalism and Pentecostalism, resulted in many new denominations. During the 1920s and 1930s Fundamentalists in America forced splits among both Presbyterians and Baptists. Other factors caused The Churches of Christ to split off from the Christian Church (Disciples of Christ). Pentecostals went even further than Fundamentalists in their tendency to divide into different groups.

These new groups in North America were only a few among many new denominations all over the world. Protestants were not the only ones suffering divisions: Catholics started breakaway groups in the Philippines, in China, and in several countries of Europe. As already mentioned, Watchman Nee started a new denomination in China. Nowhere, however, did more new denominations spring up during the 1900s than in Africa.

William Wadé Harris (1853–1929), like Aimee Semple McPherson, seemed an unlikely candidate for the founder of a new denomination among Christ's People. He was a political prisoner already nearing age 60 when he heard the call of God. Leaving his native Liberia in western Africa, he began to walk through the neighboring countries of Ghana and Côte d'Ivoire (Ivory Coast), calling men and women to turn from their sins. Barefoot he walked, wearing a long white robe and carrying a Bible in one hand and a bamboo cross in the other.

"There is only one God!" he thundered. "Throw away your charms and your idols! There is only one Savior, who died on a cross that looked like this; turn to him and be saved!" [15] People began calling him "The Prophet". And they did turn to Christ, by the tens of thousands.

Harris's ministry was brief—less than two years before colonial officials put a stop to it. One historian wrote ███ never has there been another case in modern times "of such multitudes being brought to God in so short a time by the preaching of a single man." [16] Some of his converts were gathered into existing churches; others are still known today as "Harris Christians."

Most African "prophets" of the early 1900s are well-known in Africa but little known elsewhere: Simon Kimbangu (1889–1951) of Congo, for instance, or Sampson Oppong (c.1884–1965) of Ghana, or Joseph Babalola (1904–1959) of Nigeria, or Simeon Nsibambi (1897–1978) of Uganda, or Isaiah Shembe (1870–1935) among the Zulus of South Africa. By and large the new denominations they founded are strongly based on the Bible (as interpreted by the founders). The size of these new denominations often startles non-African observers: Some of them have millions of members. For example, there are more Kimbanguist Christians in Africa than there are Presbyterians in the Church of Scotland or Episcopalians in the United States.

Some of these independent African churches have been classified as *Ethiopian:* They stress that their leaders must be dark-skinned, like Ethiopians; they also follow many Old Testament practices as the Ethiopian Orthodox do. Others have been identified as *Zionist:* They focus on a "Zion" of their own on earth as a foretaste of the heavenly Zion yet to come; they also stress spiritual gifts and follow many African traditions.

Some church historians have compared these African independent churches to Anabaptists of the 1500s, because they have sprung up in many different forms and have sometimes gone to extremes. Still another name used for these groups is *"prophet-healing"* churches. Whatever name they go by, it is clear that the Good News of Jesus the Christ has found a home in the hearts and minds of many Africans.

## THEY TRIED TO GET TOGETHER

At the same time Christ's People were splitting into many different denominations, they were also trying hard to get together. Many Christians felt convicted by a phrase Jesus used in prayer: "Neither pray I for these alone, but for them also which shall believe on me through their word; *that they all may be one"* (John 17:20–21, KJV, emphasis added).

In the United States several denominations that had divided over slavery before the Civil War got back together during the first half of the 1900s. As the children and grandchildren of newcomers to America became more at home in the English language, similar churches that had grown up out of different ethnic groups found they could unite. For one example, the Evangelical and Reformed Church (which was itself the result of an earlier merger) joined with the Congregational Christian Church to form the United Church of Christ. Church union went even farther and faster in Canada, where most Presbyterians, Methodists, and Congregationalists joined in 1925 to form the United Church of Canada.

In 1940 government pressure caused most Protestant Christians in Japan to merge into a denomination usually referred to by a part of its Japanese name, the Kyodan. In 1947 the Church of South India brought together Methodists, Presbyterians, Anglicans, and Congregationalists. A similar union in 1948 formed the United Church of Christ in the Philippines.

Church mergers were not the only ways Christ's People tried to get together. They often worked in harmony through parachurch organizations—seeking to reach young men, for instance, through the YMCA and young women through the YWCA. They also teamed up to fight against social evils such as alcohol abuse.

The most wide-ranging effort to bring unity among Christians in the 1900s became known as the *ecumenical movement.* The word *ecumenical* comes from a Greek word meaning "household," a reference to the "household of faith" mentioned in the New Testament (see Galatians 6:10). One of the outstanding leaders in this movement was an American named John R. Mott (1865–1955), who in his youth had recruited missionaries from many denominations and as an adult had organized the great world-wide conference of Christ's People held at Edinburgh in 1910.

Growing out of that ground-breaking meeting in Scotland, further efforts toward cooperation and unity developed simultaneously along three tracks:

- Beliefs and church structures
- Lifestyle and ministries
- World missions

By 1937 even Eastern Orthodox Christian were joining with many types of Protestants in seeking ways to respond to Jesus' prayer for unity.

# THEY DEVELOPED NEW MINISTRIES

During the 1900s Christ's People tried to be on the cutting edge in using new communication media. The first Christian radio program was broadcast in 1924. An outstanding center of radio ministry soon followed in 1931: HCJB at Quito, Equador (its call letters stand for "Heralding Christ Jesus' Blessings"). The first Christian telecast aired in 1940.

One of the first Roman Catholics to realize the possibilities of radio ministry was Charles Coughlin (1891–1979), a priest who urged radical reforms in American society. A less controversial Catholic media star of both radio and television was the widely respected and immensely popular Bishop Fulton J. Sheen (1895–1979).

Poor health forced Joy Ridderhof (1903–1984), a Friends/Quaker missionary, to come back home. As she was recuperating in Los Angeles, she wished for some way of having her voice back in Honduras to speak with Christ's People there and to encourage them in their faith. Out of this yearning she launched a new ministry in 1939 that later became known as Gospel Recordings. Today native speakers all over the world are speaking and singing the Word of God onto tapes and records for people who have little or no other means of hearing the Good News.

Other new approaches besides state-of-the-art communication media were also being developed among Christ's People during the first half of the 1900s. Christians began to realize as never before the importance of youth ministries. In the early 1930s a California blue-collar worker named Dawson Trotman (1906–1956) began his emphasis on one-on-one mentoring and discipleship; because he and his friends often worked with young sailors, the worldwide organization that later grew out of their ministries became known as The Navigators.

Many denominations developed their own youth organizations, complete with discipleship training, area-wide rallies, summer camps, and Bible conferences. Along with this emphasis on youth, many Bible institutes and Bible colleges were established. Some of these became accredited institutions of higher learning; all of them became major sources for Christian ministers and missionaries.

Some of those new mission volunteers turned their eyes toward Latin America; previously more Protestant missionaries had gone to Asia or Africa. After all, weren't most Latin Americans supposed to be Roman Catholic Christians? Yet reports kept filtering out about tribes in the interior of Latin America—tribes that knew nothing about Jesus.

Such reports encouraged the founding in 1942 of the New Tribes Mission. This new sending agency got off to a rocky start when savage tribes in Bolivia killed five men from their first group of missionaries. Yet the survivors boldly persisted and eventually saw the first of many unreached tribal peoples turn to Christ.

Caring for the needy is nothing new among Christ's People; neither is translating the Bible. Yet Pandita Ramabai of India and W. Cameron Townsend of the United States developed new approaches to these age-old ministries.

Pandita Ramabai (1858–1922) was more fortunate than most young widows in her native India. Little girls were often promised in marriage and then blamed when their husbands died young; they were forced to become slaves . . . or worse. Ramabai came from the highest caste in the Hindu system; *Pandita* is actually a title given to her, meaning "Great Woman Scholar." When this famous and learned Hindu became one of Christ's People, she set up a home for child widows, supported by sale of her writings and by financial help from friends in Asia, Europe, and America. Later she took in orphans, boys as well as girls; then children with physical impairments; then young unmarried mothers. The home grew into a whole village with its own farm and workshops; she called it *Mukti:* "Liberation." The adjacent box shows how Pandita Ramabai described her life work.

W. Cameron Townsend (1896–1982), an earnest young Presbyterian from California, went to Guatemala in 1917 as a Bible salesman. Soon he discovered a basic problem: All of his Bibles were in Spanish, the national language; yet once he got out among Indian tribes, his intended customers knew little or no Spanish. An Indian challenged him one day: "If your God is so smart, why hasn't he learned our language?" [18]

> ### Sweeping Away Hindrances
>
> Christ gives different gifts to different people: prophets, preachers, teachers. Since I have become a Christian, Christ has given me the gift of being a sweeper. I want to sweep India clean of all that has hindered the spread of the gospel among women. [17]
>
> *–Pandita Ramabai*

For 13 years Townsend labored to learn that tribe's language. He had a terrible time because it did not seem to fit with any of the tenses or parts of speech he was used to. After he had at last completed a New Testament in the tribal language, he realized there were other tribes with little-known languages all over the world—languages that had never even been put into writing.

In 1934 Townsend founded Wycliffe Bible Translators, named after a pioneer translator of the English Bible. During Townsend's lifetime the new organization grew until it was sending out more missionaries than any other agency. Townsend called on skilled linguists to train translators for their specialized tasks. Hundreds of New Testaments were prepared in the languages of minority groups; yet thousands more still waited to be done.

# THEY DEDICATED THEIR TALENTS

As in previous centuries, gifted men and women of the 1900s dedicated their talents to Jesus the Christ. Two outstanding Christian authors in England became best known, strangely enough, as writers of detective stories: Lord Peter Wimsey was the fictional creation of the Anglican

Dorothy L. Sayers (1893–1957), while Father Brown was the brainchild of the Roman Catholic G. K. Chesterton (1874–1936). Sayers also authored religious dramas and works of theology. Chesterton wrote so much in defense of Christianity, and in so many different literary forms, that he has been nick-named "defender of the faith." (See the adjacent box.)

In the United States, Sinclair Lewis (1885–1951) caricatured a revivalist preacher in his novel *Elmer Gantry*. By contrast, two other American novelists presented honest yet sympathetic portraits of Christian ministers: a Protestant in *A Simple Honorable Man* by Conrad Richter (1890–1968) and a Catholic in *Death Comes for the Archbishop* by Willa Cather (1873–1957).

> ## Chesterton, Defender of the Faith
>
> - Where there is anything there is God.
>
> - You cannot evade the issue of God. Whether you talk about pigs or the binomial theory, you are still talking about Him.
>
> - The riddles of God are more satisfying than the solutions of man.[19]

Theologians of the 1900s have already been mentioned in this chapter—theologians who took widely differing views but were alike in using their literary skills: Bonhoeffer, Barth, and Schweitzer in Europe, along with Rauschenbusch, Fosdick, Laws, Machen, and the Niebuhr brothers in America. Noted Christian writers of Asia included Nee in China, Ramabai in India, and Kagawa in Japan. Pearl S. Buck (1892–1973), who grew up as the child of missionaries in China, won Pulitzer (1932 for *The Good Earth*) and Nobel prizes for her novels that tried to help outsiders understand Chinese culture. Charles Williams (1886–1945) used Christian themes in his science fiction books.

Professional writers also teamed up with Christians whose unusual life stories deserved to be told, such as Corrie ten Boom of the Netherlands, and Gladys Aylward (1902–1970), a humble English housemaid with little education and a learning disability who felt God calling her to go as a missionary to China. Turned down by a sending agency, she saved her meager wages and bought a railway ticket across Europe and Siberia. Arriving in China after a long and harrowing journey, she faced many hardships there. During World War II she shepherded a hundred Chinese orphans over the mountains to safety in Thailand. Gladys Aylward became famous with the publication of her biography, *The Small Woman* (later made into a film, *The Inn of the Sixth Happiness*).

Christ's People of the early 1900s kept on obeying the psalmist's call to "Sing unto the Lord a new song" (Psalm 96:1, KJV). Two among the many hymn writers of the new century were mentioned near the beginning of this chapter. In 1913 George Bennard (1873–1958), a traveling evangelist, wrote both words and music for "The Old Rugged Cross"; a record-breaking 20 million copies were sold in the next 30 years.

Two remarkable talents combined to honor God and the co-founder of the Salvation Army when the classical composer Charles Ives (1874–1954) wrote stirring orchestral and choral music for the poem "General William Booth Enters into Heaven" by Vachel Lindsey (1879–1931). Lindsey often took long walking tours, swapping rhymes for food and lodging. Ives, who ran a large insurance firm on weekdays and played the organ at church on Sundays, used familiar hymn tunes in his symphonies and chamber music.

# THEY KEPT ON SPREADING THE GOOD NEWS

In the face of catastrophic events during the first half of the 1900s, Christ's People kept right on spreading the Good News about Jesus the Christ. Kenneth Scott Latourette, the church historian who called the 1800s "The Great Century," wrote about Christianity after 1914 and entitled his work *Advance Through Storm.*[20]

There were many outstanding heralds of this advance through storm. The missionary careers of Lottie Moon in China and Mary Slessor in Nigeria (see chapter 12) continued well into the early 1900s. Lilias Trotter (1853–1928), gifted artist and writer as well as missionary, served for decades in Algeria. Irish-born Amy Carmichael (1867–1951) carried on a dual ministry for 55 years, protecting children at risk in India while building mission support back home through her 35 books. Yet another notable missionary was the Canadian Jonathan Goforth (1859–1936), who survived near-martyrdom in 1900 to lead tens of thousands to Christ through evangelistic tours in China, Korea, and Manchuria.

The number of Roman Catholic missionaries doubled during the first half of the 1900s to a total of more than 42,000. By mid-century there were also more than 34,000 Protestant missionaries.

The many faithful believers on continents outside Europe and America were even more important than missionaries in the continuing spread of Christianity during the early 1900s. Chief Khama (see chapter 13) continued to stand up for Jesus in Botswana till his death in 1923. Simeoni Nsibambi was one of several preachers through whom a spiritual awakening spread during the 1930s and 1940s from Uganda into Kenya, Tanzania, Rwanda, and other parts of eastern Africa.

This chapter has already mentioned Sohn Yang-Won and his family in Korea, as well as Pandita Ramabai and Bishop V. S. Azariah in India. Still another notable Asian Christian of the early 1900s was

Dr. John Sung (1901–1944), who led evangelistic campaigns with remarkable success in China, Taiwan, the Philippines, Malaysia, Thailand, and Indonesia.

During the first half of the 1900s the number of Roman Catholics in the United States nearly doubled. Worldwide, the grand total of Christ's People doubled from about half a billion in 1900 to about a billion in 1950, even though during those same years many Christians died as victims of war, plague, and persecution. By half a century ago there were already organized Christian congregations in every country of the world except Afghanistan, Saudi Arabia, and Tibet.

# THEY HAD HOPES FOR THE FUTURE

During the war years of 1939–1945 many of Christ's People—like nearly everybody else who was not too young or too old—served in the armed forces in parts of the world they had never seen or even dreamed of. Some of them realized, as never before, that the whole world needed to hear the Good News about Jesus the Christ. They came back home after the war and started doing something about it. Both the number of Christian missionaries and the number of organizations sending out missionaries took a great leap forward in the years just after the end of World War II.

For example, Betty Greene (1920–1997) and Jim Truxton, both of them former military pilots, started Mission Aviation Fellowship (MAF) in 1945. In 1948 John Broger, another war veteran, launched the Far Eastern Broadcasting Company (FEBC), a powerful Christian radio station in Manila, Philippines; a few years later Paul Freed founded Trans World Radio (TWR). A former Dutch army commando who used the name Brother Andrew (1928–    ) became well known for smuggling in Bibles and otherwise working to help Christians suffering under Communist rule.

As the twentieth century neared its mid-point, several events gave renewed hope for the future. In 1947 the discovery of the Dead Sea Scrolls, a collection of ancient manuscripts, gave new proof that the Bible as we know it is trustworthy. The founding of the state of Israel in 1948 was seen by many of Christ's People as a fulfillment of biblical prophecy.

Christians were also continuing their efforts in response to Jesus' prayer, "that they all may be one." John R. Mott, now a Christian elder statesman, lived long enough to help conduct the founding meeting of the World Council of Churches in 1948. Catholics did not join with Protestants and Orthodox Christians in this ecumenical organization, but the 32 new cardinals appointed by the pope in 1945 did include several from outside Europe and North America.

Many organizations involved in translating and circulating the Scriptures combined in 1946 to form the United Bible Societies, with regional offices in Kenya, Singapore, and Mexico. In 1800 only 67 of the world's language groups had had any part of the Scriptures in their own language. By 1900 that number had jumped to 523; by 1950 it had reached 1,043.

As always throughout church history, Christ's People of 50 years ago were placing their hopes on the younger generation of Christians. In 1946 InterVarsity Christian Fellowship held the first in a notable series of youth meetings for world missions that later became known as the Urbana conferences. During the late 1940s a widespread youth revival movement involved many earnest believers; outstanding among them was a tall young preacher with a soft Southern accent.

Billy Graham (1918– ), as a young preacher in the 1940s

That young preacher was Billy Graham (1918– ). He first became prominent in the news media at about the same time a little Albanian nun named Agnes Bojaxhiu (1920–1997) was founding a new Roman Catholic order called the Missionaries of Charity to serve the poorest of the poor in the streets of Calcutta. The world remembers her today as Mother Teresa.

# KEY EVENTS

## 1900 TO 1950

Christ's People enter a new century with high optimism.

As prime minister of the Netherlands, the devoutly Christian Abraham Kuyper urges many reforms.

The social gospel movement works to improve human society.

The Azusa Street revival in Los Angeles marks the beginning of the Pentecostal movement.

A worldwide meeting of Christians in Edinburgh marks the beginning of the ecumenical movement.

The Manchu empire is overthrown in China; some of the new Chinese leaders are Christian.

William Wadé Harris evangelizes in western Africa, Jonathan Goforth in eastern Asia; Albert Schweitzer goes as a medical missionary to equatorial Africa.

World War I brings much suffering: Turkish Muslims massacre Armenian Christians; the tsar is overthrown as Communists take over Russia and nearby areas; a worldwide epidemic of influenza kills 20 million.

In opposition to liberalism and modernism, Karl Barth launches the Neo-Orthodox movement; G. K. Chesterton writes in defense of the faith; American Fundamentalists arouse controversy, causing divisions in several denominations.

Several denominations merge to form the United Church of Canada; other churches also unite.

Pentecostalism spreads worldwide; "prophets" start independent churches in Africa and elsewhere.

A financial depression causes worldwide suffering.

Communists and totalitarian dictators persecute Christ's People, many of whom oppose such tyranny.

Christians fight for peace; they spread the Good News through new ministries such as radio.

W. Cameron Townsend founds Wycliffe Bible Translators; this and other agencies seek to reach tribes that have not yet heard the Good News.

World War II brings massive death and destruction; Hitler leads Nazi Germany to kill 6 million Jews.

Christ's People lead in doing more to help war victims than ever before.

Many war veterans seek new opportunities and new methods for spreading the Good News worldwide.

The newly-formed United Bible Societies reports that the number of language groups with part of the Scriptures has doubled in half a century.

The newly-formed World Council of Churches brings together many Protestants and Orthodox.

Many of Christ's People believe that the discovery of the Dead Sea Scrolls and the founding of the state of Israel help to prove the authority of the Bible.

A youth revival movement brings to prominence a young preacher named Billy Graham.

Mother Teresa founds a new Catholic order, the Missionaries of Charity, for ministry to the poor.

Communists invade South Korea; Christians such as Sohn Yang-Won are martyred; Communists seem poised to conquer many other areas, as the Cold War continues with no end in sight.

Worldwide, the total of Christ's People has doubled in half a century, in spite of countless deaths caused by war, plague, and persecution.

## MARTIN LUTHER KING, JR. (1929–1968)

As a Baptist pastor he led the non-violent struggle against racism
in America and yet he was killed by an assassin's bullet.

# 15. TWENTY CENTURIES AND COUNTING: CHANGES
## (1950-2000+)

Historians try to take a clear look at the past. Yet historians sometimes seem to be blinded by the past when they look at the present and the future.

The conventional wisdom among many historical scholars of today paints a dark picture for the future of Christ's People: *Christianity is in decline. Islam is growing faster than Christianity. Europe will soon be a Muslim-majority continent. Asian religions will soon be as strong as Christianity in North America.*

Hogwash. That impolite word is a good description of such thoughts.

Such thinking is dead wrong. Some historical scholars have made the mistake of paying too much attention to people of European descent while failing to consider the wealth of data pouring in from other continents.

Yes, it is true that Christianity has declined disastrously in Europe. It is also true that Europe may become a Muslim-majority continent. But what about Asia, Africa, and Latin America, where growth rates among Christians are very rapid? What about North America, where Christian newcomers from Asia, Africa, and Latin America number more than those of non-Christian religions?

At the beginning of the new millennium Christ's People numbered nearly 2 billion worldwide. Islam was the second largest faith community with less than 1.2 billion people. The box on the following page shows totals for all of the world's major religions as of 2000.

| Christ's People and Others[1] | |
|---|---|
| Christ's People | 1.99 billion |
| Muslims | 1.19 billion |
| Hindus | 811 million |
| No Religion | 768 million |
| Buddhists | 360 million |
| Primal/Tribal Religions | 228 million |
| Atheists | 150 million |
| Newer Religions | 102 million |
| Sikhs | 21 million |
| Judaism | 14 million |

Christianity has become the first true *world* religion. At 20 centuries and counting, Christ's People are experiencing worldwide expansion on a scale never before seen for any other way of worshiping.

Historians who hold to a contrary opinion are experiencing something common to everyone: It is hard to take an accurate view of the present, much less the future. We are too close to it. How can we tell which people, movements, or events of our own time will be considered most important by future historians?

Yet as we explore church history since 1950, two themes emerge: changes and challenges.

Changes (covered in this chapter):

• In the recent past Christ's People have helped to bring about change in three aspects of human society that seemed utterly unchangeable not too many years ago.

• At the present time there are worldwide changes among Christ's People both in older and newer centers of Christianity.

Challenges (covered in chapter 16):

• Christians are facing major challenges from inside and outside.

• The greatest challenge of all is, *what lies ahead for Christ's People after 20 centuries?*

# CHANGING THE UNCHANGEABLE

Many older readers will remember a time not too long ago when Roman Catholicism, Communism, and legal, institutionalized racism seemed to be unchangeable forces in our world. Yet all three of these have experienced profound change since the 1950s.

## Catholicism

In 1950 the Roman Catholic Church seemed to be a closed system that related to the world around it only on its own terms. All worship services were held in the long-dead Latin language. All priests and nuns wore quaintly old-fashioned garments. All popes were Italians; most bishops and cardinals in America were Irish. Ordinary men and women were discouraged from studying the Bible; it was enough for the priest to tell them what the Scriptures said. In fact, Catholics were not supposed to read anything outside the approved list.

Things began to change in 1958 when an elderly Italian cardinal became Pope John XXIII (1881–1963). Born into a family so poor that they shared their house with six cows, he never lost his directness in looking at things. At age 77 Pope John was not expected to do anything unusual. He was thought to be a "caretaker" pope, a non-controversial old man who would "keep the throne warm" until a more likely candidate turned up. Yet Pope John surprised everybody by being a vigorous, forward-looking leader who brought new life and light into the fortress mentality that had long surrounded the Roman Catholic Church.

Pope John called Christians who were not Catholics "separated brethren." He asked Christ's People to think of him not as a powerful religious ruler but as a "good shepherd defending truth and goodness." He ruled out any use of force, insisting instead on "the medicine of mercy." He spoke out against "prophets of doom" in troubled times: "The habit of thinking ill of everything and everyone is tiresome to ourselves and to all around us," he declared.[2]

Most importantly, Pope John called for the first general council of the Roman Catholic Church in many years. It was also the first council with truly worldwide representation: Of its 2,500 participants, fewer than half came from Europe; more than 500 came from Asia and Africa. Pope John only lived to see the first of the council's four sessions, but he had already blazed a new path. The whole world mourned his death in 1963.

Since this was the second time such a meeting had been centered in the Vatican, the pope's Roman headquarters, it became known as the Second Vatican Council, or Vatican II for short. What did Vatican II accomplish? Two words from foreign languages make a good summary: *aggiornamento,* Italian for "to bring things up to date," and *ressourcement,* French for "to go back to the sources." The heart of the Catholic faith remained unchanged, but it needed to be brought into touch with the times. The way to do this was to return to the sources—to the Bible and to Jesus the Christ.

Overall, Vatican II brought about more far-reaching changes than Roman Catholics had seen since the Council of Trent in the mid-1500s. Here are a few of the many revolutionary results of the Second Vatican Council:

• The mass, or basic Roman Catholic worship service including the Lord's Supper, began to be conducted in local languages.

- The priest conducting the mass, instead of praying quietly with his back turned to the congregation, faced the people and spoke clearly, inviting their responses.

- Ordinary Roman Catholics were encouraged to read and study the Bible for themselves; newer Bible translations were approved for general use.

- Catholics were encouraged to take a different attitude toward non-Catholics among Christ's People, no longer considering them as infidels or enemies. There also was a call for complete religious liberty.

- Many mistakes of the past began to be corrected: In 1965 the heads of the Roman Catholic Church and the Eastern Orthodox Church withdrew their mutual excommunication that had been issued bitterly centuries before. In 1992 came an admission that the astronomer Galileo had been mistreated in the 1600s when the Inquisition forced him to deny his discoveries. In 1997 came an apology for failing to speak out strongly enough against anti-Jewish words and deeds.

Most Roman Catholics welcomed these and other changes. Yet some of them still yearned for the mystical certainties of earlier times. Protest movements to keep the mass in Latin sprang up in several places. A recording of monks singing ancient Gregorian chants hit the top of the charts in the 1990s. Passion plays, a staging of the last days in Jesus' earthly life, grew out of miracle plays from the Middle Ages. The best-known of these has been performed every ten years since the 1600s at Oberammergau, a village in the Alps of southern Germany. Many pious tourists are drawn to this and other Passion plays all over the world. In 2004 a popular movie followed the same theme.

The most serious reactions to Vatican II came in regard to the things it did not change: Still no married priests, no women as priests, no abortion, and no divorce. Everything was still under the control of bishops and archbishops and cardinals all the way up to the pope himself. During the 1960s and 1970s, thousands of men left the priesthood. Attendance at mass declined. Many Catholic theologians and university professors openly disagreed with official positions on certain issues.

Yet the Roman Catholic Church has proved it can still weather storms. Pope John Paul II (1920–2005), the first non-Italian pope in four and a half centuries, proved to be one of the strongest and most widely respected Roman Catholic leaders of all time. Born Karol Wojtyla in Poland, he became a strong athlete, an avid reader of St. John of the Cross (see chapter 9), and a secret seminary student during World War II. When Communists replaced Nazis as rulers of Poland, he continued to pastor his people. He took an active and positive part in the great council called by Pope John XXIII. In 1978 he was elected pope.

As leader of the world's Roman Catholics, Pope John Paul traveled more than all of the other popes before him put together—farther than a round trip to the moon. He wrote tirelessly and spoke eloquently for truth and peace and justice. While standing firm for Catholic tradition, he brought new vigor to Catholicism as a living faith. Some observers expect history books of the future to copy Christ's People of past centuries by adding "the Great" to the name of John Paul. John Paul II was succeeded by Pope Benedict XVI.

Another noted Catholic leader is Cardinal Sin (1928–  ), archbishop of Manila, who has been a major figure in two bloodless revolutions that have brought down corrupt regimes in the Philippines. Powerful new movements have arisen among Catholic lay people, such as Opus Dei that started in Spain and has since spread to more than 80 countries. The charismatic movement (see page 257) has also brought new vitality to Catholics in many countries.

## Communism

In 1950 Communism seemed to be unchangeable. Communist countries were isolated behind the Iron Curtain and the Bamboo Curtain; only bits and pieces of information filtered out about Christians living under such regimes. Sometimes Communist leaders would allow a slight thaw in the Cold War; then icy blasts would blow again from Moscow and Beijing, from Pyongyang and Hanoi. Russian Communists claimed that a time would come when the last living Christian in the Soviet Union would be paraded on government-owned television.

What changed the unchangeable? There were many factors including the faithful prayers of Christ's People. In 1984 Brother Andrew (see chapter 14) and other Christian leaders called for a seven-year campaign of prayer with the specific goal of complete religious liberty for all who lived behind the Iron Curtain.[3] This goal was reached early as Communism crumbled throughout eastern Europe and central Asia during the tumultuous years of 1989–1991.

In 1986 a nuclear accident at Chernobyl, Ukraine, revealed great weaknesses in the Communist system. Not only had there been carelessness and neglect in monitoring radioactive materials, but also the government initially refused to admit what had happened, leaving millions in Ukraine and Belarus to suffer the consequences. Many Christians turned to Revelation 8:10–11; these verses prophesy that a great star named Wormwood would fall to the earth and turn its waters into deadly poison. Christ's People noticed that the Ukrainian word for Wormwood is Chernobyl.[4]

Courageous Russian Christians played their part in changing the unchangeable:

- Alexander Men (1935–1990) was an outspoken Orthodox priest and theologian who challenged the thinking of intellectual Russians; he was bludgeoned to death on his way to church.

- Georgi Vins (1928–1998), a Baptist evangelist, was repeatedly jailed by Russian authorities until President Jimmy Carter's influence enabled him to find refuge in America.

- Alexander Solzhenitsyn (1918–    ), like many Russians living under Communism, was an atheist at first. For criticizing the dictator Stalin in a private letter to a friend, he was thrown into a prison camp. There he was deeply influenced by Anatoly Vasilyevich Silin, who had become a Christian while a prisoner of the Germans during World War II. The world might never have known about the brave witness of Silin and others like him if Solzhenitsyn had not survived his imprisonment to become a celebrated writer of the past century.

The election of a Polish pope in 1978 had a strong influence on the fall of Communism throughout eastern Europe and central Asia. When Pope John Paul II made a pilgrimage to his native country in 1979, he prayed: "Holy Spirit, renew this land."[5] Fully one-third of the nation turned out to see him. Protests by a Catholic labor movement began the very next year and eventually brought an end to Polish Communism in 1989.

Christ's People outside of Europe also played a part in changing the unchangeable. Chapter 14 tells about brave Korean Christians under Communist oppression. Later in this chapter the breathtaking growth rate among Christ's People in China is highlighted. Although Communists still dominate their homeland, Chinese Christians are now experiencing exactly what pastor and evangelist Nee Tosheng (or Watchman Nee as he is known elsewhere) predicted (see chapter 14).

By 1950 Nee could no longer speak freely because of Communist spies. Once he used gestures to show his congregation that a crystal vase on the pulpit symbolized Christ's People in China, while he himself symbolized the Communist government. Flinging the vase to the floor, he stomped on the broken glass. Then with a sudden expression of bewilderment he began trying in vain to pick up the many scattered pieces.

Since the time when Watchman Nee pantomimed his parable, the number of Christians in China has grown to nearly 100 million. For centuries European and American missionaries had tried to root Christianity in Chinese soil. What the missionaries never quite accomplished, the Communist government unwittingly did for them "by smashing the institutional church and grinding believers into underground home fellowships."[6]

# Racism

In 1950 legal, institutionalized racism seemed to be an immutable part of human society. Throughout much of the United States dark-skinned people were required by law to take an inferior position. Black Americans could not drink at the same water fountains, eat at the same restaurants, stay at the same hotels, ride in the same train coaches, or sit in the same bus sections as whites. Black children had to go to separate, but supposedly equal, schools. Black citizens were often barred from voting. Black workers faced harsh discrimination when they looked for jobs.

Many of Christ's People in America had a vague feeling of uneasiness about this situation. *Surely it isn't right, . . . but what can we do about it? That's just the way things are.*

As bad as racism was in America, it was worse in South Africa where the government set up an elaborate system of racial separation known as *apartheid,* or "apartness." Not only were dark-skinned people denied basic civil rights; they were also forcibly removed to certain sections of city and countryside, well away from white inhabitants. Any time they left these black "homelands," they had to carry passports to be shown whenever challenged—as if they were foreigners in their own land of birth.

Many men and women worked to change the unchangeable—in America, Africa, and elsewhere. A large number of these campaigners for civil rights were Christians. None among them became better known in the struggle against racism than the Rev. Martin Luther King, Jr., in America and Archbishop Desmond Tutu in Africa.

Martin Luther King, Jr., (1929–1968), was a big-city Baptist pastor, like his father and grandfather before him, and like Walter Rauschenbusch (see chapter 13), whose example greatly inspired him. King was also strongly influenced by Mahatma Gandhi, who followed the path of non-violent resistance in leading India to freedom. During the 13 brief years that King spearheaded the campaign for civil rights in the United States, he steadfastly refused to fight force with force. "Let us be Christian in all our actions," he urged.[7] In 1963 King made his most famous "I Have a Dream" speech before a quarter of a million people in Washington, D.C. In 1964 he became the youngest person ever to win the Nobel Peace Prize. Four years later he was shot to death.

Desmond Tutu (1931–    ) grew up in South Africa with the most rigid separation between races the world has ever seen. First a teacher, then an Anglican priest, he became a bishop and then the first black

CEO of the South African Council of Churches. His campaign for racial justice brought him a Nobel Peace Prize in 1984. More importantly, it helped bring about the dismantling of the apartheid system in the 1990s. Tutu served as Anglican archbishop of South Africa from 1986 to 1996. After retirement he chaired a Truth and Reconciliation Commission, trying to put to rest bitter past memories.

Today in the United States a national holiday honors King's birthday; many cities have streets bearing his name; many schoolchildren recite the most famous passage from his most famous speech. The younger generation finds it hard to realize how much hatred and opposition King had to face because he was trying to change the unchangeable. Yet in the strength of Jesus the Christ, Martin Luther King, Jr., and Archbishop Desmond Tutu and other brave Christians accomplished just that.


# WORLDWIDE CHANGES AMONG CHRIST'S PEOPLE

Chapters 12, 13, and 14 outline the remarkable worldwide growth and spread of the gospel between 1800 and 1950. Chapter 14 also traces the development of two new Christian movements of the early 1900s: Fundamentalism and Pentecostalism. All three of these aspects of world Christianity continued up to 2000 and beyond, while experiencing great change and gaining in strength.

## Worldwide Growth and Spread

Take a good look at the box on the facing page. These statistics are not the result of wishful thinking or pious hopes: They are based on careful, ongoing research. Even though too many Americans and Europeans are unaware, Christianity is growing and spreading in an unprecedented way. Highly educated guesses indicate that this trend will continue.

This spectacular growth and spread has been fueled by many factors including prayer, church growth among people groups, Bible translations, the JESUS Video Project ®, the end of colonial empires, the impact of world events, and missionaries from Third World or developing nations.

Prayer continues to have major impact in the worldwide increase of Christianity. For many years the majority of Protestant churches in South Korea have had well-attended early-morning prayer meetings. Brazilian Christians gather on Fridays to pray all night. Believers in Thailand fast and pray regularly.

Donald McGavran (1897–1990), a missionary and son of missionaries, stressed that no matter how many schools and hospitals missionaries may start or how much humanitarian good they may do, the real

### Christ's People—Past, Present, and Future[8]
(in millions unless noted)

| Continents | 1900 | 2000 | 2025 |
|---|---|---|---|
| Africa | 9 | 360 | 633 |
| Asia | 21 | 313 | 460 |
| Europe | 368 | 560 | 555 |
| North America | 60 | 260 | 312 |
| Latin America | 60 | 480 | 640 |
| Oceania | 4 | 21 | 28 |
| TOTALS | 522 | 1.9 billion | 2.6 billion |

measure of missions is church growth. McGavran's disciple Ralph Winter (1924–   ) helped move the focus of missions away from cities and countries to *people groups*—men, women, and children bound together by a common culture and language. Sometimes the same people group may spread across several political boundaries; sometimes the same nation may contain several different people groups.

Major emphases in missions over the past half-century have been:

• Finding unreached people groups.

• Fostering church planting among people groups.

• Encouraging church growth.

Another factor in accelerating the growth and spread of Christ's People has been a great increase in the number of languages with Bible translations. Speakers of nearly a thousand different language groups, or 94 percent of the earth's total population, now have access to a New Testament in their own language. At the dawn of the new millennium, the number of complete translations of the Scriptures was nearing 400; the number of other languages with at least one book of the Bible was approaching 1,000.[9]

A film based on the Gospel of Luke, entitled simply JESUS, has been viewed at least 4.3 billion times over a span of 20 years. It has been translated into more than 650 languages, with more than 139 million viewers indicating a decision to become one of Christ's People.[10]

The end of colonial empires has helped change some perceptions of Christianity. As long as Asian and African nations were ruled by foreign powers, foreign missionaries were associated with colonialism in people's minds in these countries. One of many possible examples: Indonesians used to speak scornfully of Christianity as "the Dutch religion."

Some shallow-minded observers thought Christ's People would dwindle in Asia and Africa after most of the missionaries were gone. Yet just the opposite has happened: The end of colonial empires after World War II has brought new strength to Asian and African Christianity.

Besides the end of colonialism, other events in world history have also had a positive effect on the growth and spread of Christ's People. On page 268 you can read about the rather contradictory results of Communist China's crackdown on organized churches. Another unexpected outcome of the Communist takeover of China was that many missionaries and Christian agencies who had clustered together were forced to move into other areas. One of many possible examples: The old China Inland Mission (CIM) founded by J. Hudson Taylor (see chapter 13) became Overseas Missionary Fellowship (OMF) with work in several different countries.

You could probably guess that more Christian missionaries are being sent from the United States than any other country. However, can you guess which country comes in second? It is South Korea, with more than 10,000 cross-cultural evangelists serving outside their native land.

More than 40,000 home missionaries serve in India, not counting missionaries sent there from other countries. Thousands of Christian missionaries have also been sent from Nigeria, Brazil, Myanmar, and the Philippines. Worthy of special note are Christ's People in Singapore, who support on the average more than one foreign missionary per church.[11]

Indeed, Third World missionaries have become a major force in the worldwide growth and spread of Christianity. Often their status as non-Europeans is an advantage: Indonesian missionaries from Java are witnessing to descendants of former Javanese plantation workers in Surinam, South America. Korean missionaries have found the languages of Kazakhstan and Uzbekistan relatively easy to learn as they are distantly related to their own. In general, missionaries with darker skin or Asian features do not remind people of colonial rulers in bygone days.

Not all Third World missionaries go to people similar to themselves; for example, Japanese and Korean missionaries serve in Indonesia. A Canadian of Chilean descent evangelizes in Egypt. An Aymara Indian pastor has been sent from Bolivia to India.

The beginning of the new millennium found large numbers of Christ's People in unexpected places: throughout Mongolia and Cambodia and Nepal; in Albania, which used to pride itself on being the world's first officially atheist nation; among the Masai tribes of Kenya and the Berber tribes of Algeria. Consider these facts:

- Last Sunday more believers probably attended church in China than in all of so-called Christian Europe combined.

- Last Sunday more Presbyterians went to church in Ghana than in Scotland, and more in South Africa than in the United States.

- Last Sunday more members of the Assemblies of God were at church in Brazil than the combined total of the two largest Pentecostal denominations in the United States: the Assemblies of God and the Church of God in Christ.

- Last Sunday more people attended a single church in South Korea than attended either all USA congregations combined of the Presbyterian Church in America, or all combined of the Evangelical Free Church, or all combined of the Christian Reformed Church.[12]

Yes, Christianity has become the first world religion in human history. In 1900, 82 percent of Christ's People lived in Europe and North America. In 2000, more than 50 percent of Christ's People worldwide lived outside those two continents.

## Fundamentalists, a.k.a. Evangelicals

The Fundamentalist movement of the early 1900s played a major role in the remarkable worldwide growth of Christ's People during the later 1900s . . . but not under that name.

Over the past half-century many Fundamentalists have pulled back from emphasizing differences or hard-line positions on certain social issues. These kinder, gentler Fundamentalists have mostly preferred to call themselves *evangelicals.* They are still as strong as ever in insisting that the Bible is true and that salvation comes only through faith in Jesus the Christ; yet they have found that in spreading the Good News they can work together with many different kinds of believers.

No one has better symbolized this new spirit in evangelicalism than Billy Graham (1918–    ). Beginning with youth revivals in the mid-1900s, Graham has led evangelistic campaigns all over the world. In 1973 he preached before the largest single crowd in human history: 1.1 million people in South Korea. Overall, he has spoken to more than 200 million people in 185 countries, not counting hundreds of millions more who have heard him on radio or seen him on television. A Baptist himself, he willingly works with any true believers among Christ's People.

As an advisor to American presidents and an encourager of world-changers such as Martin Luther King, Jr., Dr. Graham has used his great influence for good. Several times near the end of the 1900s he and his colleagues gathered thousands of evangelists from all over the world for on-the-job training in Amsterdam. Age and illness slowed but did not stop Graham's multi-form ministry.

It was Graham who first envisioned a new magazine as a forum of dialogue for evangelicals; as a result, *Christianity Today* has become the flagship for a whole family of publications. He also led in organizing the International Congress on World Evangelization held at Lausanne, Switzerland in 1974. (Chapter 16 tells more about this important movement toward unity among Christ's People.)

Yet Billy Graham is only one among many notable evangelicals of the past half-century:

- C. S. Lewis (1898–1963), native of Northern Ireland and lecturer/tutor at Oxford University (and later professor at Cambridge), was an atheist in his youth. Among those who influenced him toward Christianity were G. K. Chesterton (see chapter 14) and J. R. R. Tolkien (1892–1973), a staunch Roman Catholic who authored the popular *Lord of the Rings* series. Starting in 1950, Lewis wrote a series of seven children's books, *The Chronicles of Narnia,* and many other works aimed at adult readers (such as *Mere Christianity* and *The Problem of Pain*) that are still best sellers today. Perhaps no one of his time was more successful in communicating the truth and beauty of the Christian faith. The adjacent box showcases a few choice quotations.

> ### C. S. Lewis, Everyone's Theologian
>
> God whispers to us in our pleasures, speaks in our conscience, but shouts in our pains: It is his megaphone to rouse a deaf world.[13]
>
> A man can't always be defending the truth: There must be a time to feed on it.[14]
>
> Joy is the serious business of heaven.[15]
>
>

- In the later 1900s John R. W. Stott (1921–   ) brought a scholarly Anglican voice to evangelicalism, somewhat like C. S. Lewis in earlier years.

- Francis Schaeffer (1912–1984) wrote critiques of the moral decline in society as well as clearly-worded books of biblical theology. He and his wife Edith also worked together to found *L'Abri,* meaning "The Refuge," a Christian retreat center in the Swiss Alps.

- Bill Bright (1922–2003) and his wife Vonette began the college ministry of Campus Crusade for Christ on the campus of UCLA in 1950. Since that time this ministry has expanded around the world and has reached millions with the claims of Jesus the Christ through one-on-one evangelism, small group Bible studies, the JESUS film, and large group meetings.

New initiatives among evangelicals have added to the strength of Christ's People. Promise Keepers has helped many men to become better husbands and fathers. "See You at the Pole" has encouraged Christian teenagers to take a bold stand in front of their peer group, while "True Love Waits" has bolstered their resolve to stay sexually pure. Bible Study Fellowship (BSF) brings together believers across denominational lines for disciplined study of the Scriptures. Other specialized ministries have been developed—for mothers of preschoolers and school-age children, athletes, prisoners, college students, and more.

## Pentecostals, a.k.a. Charismatics

The Pentecostal movement of the early 1900s has also played a major role in the remarkable worldwide growth of Christ's People during the later 1900s, but—like Fundamentalism—it has also experienced significant change.

An old expression that took on a new meaning about half a century ago is *charismatic.* This term refers to being "annointed," seen as a fresh touch of the Holy Spirit, often resulting in spiritual gifts such as speaking in tongues, divine healing, and *power encounters* with the aim of driving out demonic forces.

In its earliest forms Pentecostalism was considered by many to be a religion of the lower social classes; respectable people went to more respectable churches. The charismatic movement, however, got its start during the 1960s from within those same respectable groups: Presbyterians, Lutherans, Episcopalians, even Roman Catholics. The "Jesus People," a youth movement spreading from California to other parts of the world, did much to publicize charismatics.

At first the old-style Pentecostals did not know what to make of the new-style charismatics. Gradually the two realized how much they had in common, until today it is sometimes hard to distinguish one from the other. Many new charismatic denominations have sprung up, such as The Vineyard in the United States and the Universal Church of the Kingdom of God in Brazil. Many charismatic congregations are independent, stressing that they are not affiliated with any denomination. Yet these independent churches often work together in ways that resemble new denominations; one such example is the Fullness/Praise Network with 6,000 churches and 3.5 million members in the United States.

Charismatics also form significant minorities in many non-charismatic churches. El Shaddai, a charismatic Catholic group, began in the Philippines and is now a global evangelistic network in over 25 countries including the United States and Canada.

Pentecostalism has triggered an unusually powerful response in parts of Asia, Africa, and Latin America where belief in spirits is widespread. Spiritual gifts and power encounters carry a lot of weight in such animistic societies. Along with the power of the Holy Spirit, Pentecostal Christianity offers a whole new way of life. Many new believers see great improvement in their standard of living as they turn away from gambling, alcohol abuse, and sexual immorality.

The oral nature of the Pentecostal/charismatic movement also becomes important in cultures where people learn more by what they hear and say than by what they read and study. The Christian faith is not so much an abstract list of doctrines to be understood and believed, as it is a new story to be told, a new song to be sung.

The first Pentecostals paid little attention to formal education. They relied on the Holy Spirit, sometimes scoffing at those who felt they must go to university or seminary before they could properly serve the Lord. This has changed through the past century as large numbers of Pentecostals/charismatics have become respected scholars in their various fields of expertise.

The early Pentecostals also paid little attention to needs in society around them; their job was to save as many people as possible, because the Lord would be returning soon. As the Pentecostal/charismatic movement has spread to all continents, many of its churches have become leaders in social betterment. Countless local congregations are working to root out anything and everything that causes men, women, and children to suffer or fall into sin.

Worldwide, the Pentecostal/charismatic movement looks very much like the wave of the future. In a time often described as the postmodern age, it appeals to body and spirit as well as mind; it relies more on personal experience than intellectual understanding; it acknowledges that there may be more than one psychological approach to how we come to know God through Jesus the Christ.

Looking at the total world population, the largest single group among Christ's People today is the one that has been the largest for many centuries: the Roman Catholic Church, with 950 million members. But the second largest group did not even exist until the 1900s: All Pentecostal and charismatic Christians put together have now reached a combined total of some 460 million. Some scholarly observers predict as many as a billion Pentecostals/charismatics by the year 2040. If so, then they would far exceed the total of Buddhists and would almost equal the total of Hindus![16]

# CHANGES IN OLDER CENTERS OF CHRISTIANITY

Look again at the box of statistics appearing on page 253, where four older centers of Christianity are listed as the bottom four entries. Generally speaking, these figures are in striking contrast to those for the two newer centers of Christianity listed at the top of the chart.

## Europe

The decline of Christianity in Europe is actually much worse than the statistics seem to show. Many millions listed as "Christians" are in fact baptized at birth and then never go near a church again except to be married or buried. In the United Kingdom, 98 percent of all university students are unchurched, non-Christian, or both.[17] In France, less than one person in ten attends a church of any kind.[18]

Of course there are still Christ's People in Europe, as there have been ever since the days of Peter and Paul. Remember such outstanding present-day European believers as Pope John Paul II, Alexander Solzhenitsyn, or John R. W. Stott. European composers have continued to add choral and instrumental works to the treasury of Christian music—composers such as Arvo Pärt (1935–    ) of Estonia, Krzysztof Penderecki (1933–    ) of Poland, Maurice Duruflé (1902–1986) and Olivier Messiaen (1908–1992) of France, John Tavener (1944–    ) and John Rutter (1945–    ) of England.

It is true that a flood of immigration from Muslim-majority countries has changed the face of Europe. Many historic churches have become museums, stores, garages, and even mosques. London is now the Islamic capital of Europe; more than a million of its 11.8 million residents are Muslims. Yet this same migration from the South has also brought many of Christ's People into Europe: The churches with the largest attendance in England and France today have mostly dark-skinned congregations.

The fall of Communism in eastern Europe has had mixed results for Christians living there:

- While under Communist control, many Polish people clung to Roman Catholicism as a national symbol of pride. After Communism fell, there seemed to be little reason to stand up and be counted: Between 1989 and 1999, church attendance fell from 58 percent to 23 percent.[19]

- A Communist dictator once boasted that Albania was the first officially atheistic country. Radio Tirana was built specifically to promote atheism. Today 74 percent of Albanians say they believe in God; of that number, well over half are Christians. And Radio Tirana broadcasts the Good News to eastern Europe and central Asia 80 hours a week.[20]

- The long-despised Roma (Gypsy) people of Romania and Bulgaria are turning to Jesus the Christ in significant numbers (like others of similar ethnic groups in France, Spain, and the United Kingdom).

- The Lord's Army is the name of an unofficial renewal movement within the Romanian Orthodox Church whose 300,000 members look and act remarkably like evangelical Protestants. Initially Orthodox leaders opposed this movement but now have wisely welcomed it.[21]

- Nearly 90 percent of the people of Ukraine claim to be Christ's People—Catholic, Orthodox, Pentecostal, evangelical.

- The situation is more complex in Russia. More than half of all Russians say they are Christians, even after 70 years of brutal Communist repression. Originally built for Communist propaganda, powerful transmitters of Radio Moscow and Radio Siberia are now being used by Christ's People. When Communism fell, Russia was flooded with missionaries from all kinds of Christianity, as well as Christian look-alikes and non-Christian groups. At the same time Russia was also being bombarded by consumerism, pornography, and everything else previously forbidden. Spooked by this sudden influx of new ideas and lifestyles, many Russian Orthodox leaders are being rather slow to grant others the new religious liberty they themselves now enjoy.

- A similarly mixed situation exists in many parts of the former Soviet Union. For instance, since the fall of Communism in Georgia, where Christianity dates back to the year 300, there has been an increased interest in religion. Although the former Department of Atheism at the national university has become a theological faculty, non-Orthodox Christians still face persecution. Pastors have been beaten, church buildings have been attacked, and a Bible warehouse has been burned to the ground.[22]

One hopeful sign is that many of Christ's People worldwide now recognize the fact that Europe is a mission field. Portuguese-speaking Christians from Brazil are spreading the Good News in Portugal; Spanish-speaking Christians from Mexico are doing the same thing in Spain. At least 1,500 foreign missionaries, mostly sent by Christ's People in Africa and Asia, are presently at work in Great Britain.[23]

## North America

Certain opinion-molders seem to think that the religious situation in North America today is not much different from what it is in Europe. Many of those who teach in American universities, write scholarly books, and produce popular films have a mind-set in which Christianity is a mere relic of the past.

Such ivory-tower intellectuals ought to drive across the countryside. They would notice how many current building projects are Christian churches, schools, and centers for assisted living. Many of these new structures are not mere imitations of older churches where darkened interiors emphasize the mystery of worship: Instead, contemporary places of Christian worship use light, space, stark simplicity, and state-of-the-art building materials to symbolize that God comes near and meets us as we worship.

Indeed, Christ's People are alive and well in North America. Both Canada and the United States have elected born-again Baptists as their leaders: John Diefenbaker (1895–1979), prime minister from 1957 till 1963, and Jimmy Carter (1924–    ), President from 1977 till 1981. Carter has also had a distinguished career since his presidency in providing housing for the homeless, monitoring elections for fairness, and seeking to improve international relations. In 2002 he was awarded the Nobel Peace Prize. George W. Bush (1946–    ), the American president elected in 2000 and reelected in 2004, has spoken openly of his personal relationship with Christ, as well as stressing biblical values for marriage and the family.

Canada used to have a higher rate of church membership and church attendance than the United States; this situation has now been reversed. Yet recent opinion polls indicate that many Canadians who stay home on Sundays might still be called "residual Christians"; they tend to view things from the standpoint of Christ's People.[24]

Generally speaking, older Christian denominations in North America have seen their membership drop in recent years. (One notable exception is the Southern Baptist Convention, which has continued to grow.) This decline has been more than made up for, however, by newer American denominations—most of them evangelical and many of them charismatic.

The United States has recently been blessed with an outstanding group of Christian writers. Worthy of mention is Carl F. H. Henry (1913–    ), co-founder of Fuller Theological Seminary, first editor of *Christianity Today* magazine, and author of weighty books on evangelical theology. Other notables are Frederick Buechner (1926–    ), Larry Woiwode (1941–    ), Walter Wangerin, Jr. (1944–    ), and Madeleine L'Engle (1918–    ), who (like C. S. Lewis) has done some of her best writing for young readers. Even Broadway musicals such as *Godspell* and *Jesus Christ Superstar* have told the Good News in a new form.

In an interesting turn of events the United States has become more strongly Christian as a result of the Immigration Reform Act of 1965. Many people thought that this relaxed policy would bring in a flood of new Americans who follow other ways of worshiping. The balance, however, has tipped the other way: So many newcomers are Christ's People that America is more strongly Christian now than it was half a century ago.

Here are a few examples:

- A cluster of strong, growing Nigerian churches has sprung up in Houston, Texas; many of them are from the Church of the Lord, or Aladura movement.

- Among Korean-Americans, Christians outnumber Buddhists more than ten to one.

- Many believers in North Carolina have heard the fervent sounds of the "Crazies for Jesus," a young vocal and instrumental ensemble that moved as a group from their native Congo.

- The great majority of Hispanic immigrants come from either Pentecostal or Roman Catholic backgrounds, whether or not they are strong Christians individually.

## Latin America

As mentioned earlier, during the 1800s the Roman Catholics of Latin America were dubbed "A Church Asleep." [25] That could certainly no longer be said.

Through the centuries a top-heavy society has developed in many parts of Latin America with a few of the rich and powerful controlling the economy, the government, and the Catholic Church. The rest of the people have been kept relatively poor, with little hope of ever doing anything about it. Certain Catholics have become convicted about the unfairness of this situation. In 1971 Peruvian university professor Gustavo Gutiérrez (1928–   ) published *A Theology of Liberation* in which he referred to Bartolomé de Las Casas (see chapter 9), who stood up for human rights in Latin America five centuries ago. Another leader of the new "liberation theology" movement was Dom Helder Camara (1909–1999), an archbishop in impoverished northern Brazil. Said Camara, "When I feed the poor, they call me a saint. When I ask why the poor have no food, they call me a Communist." [26]

Father Camilo Torres (1929–1966) even took up arms alongside anti-government guerillas in Colombia. Between battles he taught the poorest of the poor how to read. After his death in combat, Torres became a martyr-figure to many.

Even more of a martyr was Oscar Romero (1917–1980), archbishop of El Salvador. From the pulpit he thundered against those who oppressed the poor. His last sermon was based on John 12:24: "A single grain doesn't produce anything unless it is planted in the ground and dies. If it dies, it will produce a lot of grain". While leading a funeral mass moments later, he was shot by a right-wing death squad. Early in the new millennium a new statue of Archbishop Romero was placed on the west front of London's Westminster Abbey.

Many Latin American Catholics have a new vision of what it means to be a Christian. Some of them have stayed within the Catholic tradition; for instance, there are now twice as many Catholics of Japanese descent in Brazil as in Japan itself. Other Latin Americans have left the church of their ancestors in great numbers. There are now 32 million Pentecostals in Latin America, making up more than one-fourth of all Pentecostal Christians worldwide. Some Pentecostal churches in Latin America seat as many as 20,000 to 25,000 people.

Another noted mass evangelist of recent times is Luis Palau (1934–   ), who has shared the Gospel face-to-face with over 21 million people in 70 countries on five continents. Equally at home in Spanish and in English, he has found his strongest response among Hispanics.

In 1956 a major event in mission history occurred in Latin America. Five young North American missionaries who were trying to contact an isolated tribe deep in the jungles of Ecuador were martyred. Their story became a media sensation worldwide. More importantly, Elisabeth Elliot (1926–   ), widow of one of the martyrs, and Rachel Saint, sister of another one, continued their ministries as missionaries, Bible translators, writers, and speakers. Today that tribe, like many other jungle tribes in Latin America, is strongly Christian.

Luis Palau (1934–   ),
mass evangelist with strongest response
among Hispanics

## Oceania

Chapter 12 tells how quickly the Good News spread in Oceania, or the islands of the Pacific. Today it is a sad fact that Christ's People in Oceania have continued to follow the path of Christ's People in Europe. In country after country of the South Pacific, a strong majority still claim to be church members, yet there are many signs that the spirit of Christ no longer rules in their lives. Alcohol abuse, breakdown of families, and spiritual indifference are all too common. Christian look-alikes have pulled many away from biblical truth.

One of the strangest new movements in the Pacific has been the rise of so-called *cargo cults*. During and after World War II, simple islanders saw great cargoes of goods arriving for foreigners who seemed to have done little to earn such wealth. Out of this seeming contradiction arose the idea that if you performed certain religious ceremonies, then your ship might come in, too!

Christ's People in New Zealand are apparently putting up a stronger defense against spiritual erosion than Christ's People in Australia. Yet the most strongly Christian country in Oceania today is probably Papua New Guinea, where cannibals lived not too many years ago!

# CHANGES IN NEWER CENTERS OF CHRISTIANITY

As shown on page 253, during just one century Christ's People have increased forty-fold in Africa (from 9 million to 360 million) and fifteen-fold in Asia (from 21 million to 313 million). Projections for coming years indicate a slight slowing in the growth rate, but slight only in comparison to the almost unbelievable explosion in numbers already recorded. (See the map on page 270.)

## Africa

We used to call Africa "the Dark Continent"; nowadays we ought to call it "the Bright Continent."[27] Strangely enough, many people are still unaware that there has been a massive turning to Christ in Africa over the past few years. Consider the following facts:

- In 1999 one in six Roman Catholic baptisms worldwide was in Africa; among those three million new African Catholics, 37 percent of them were adults.

- The percentage of Christ's People is higher among the populations of both Zambia and Uganda than among residents of the United States.

- An estimated 16 thousand Africans become Christian believers every day or almost 6 million every year.

One knowledgeable observer has made an interesting comparison between the situation in Africa today and the situation in England two and a half centuries ago.[28] It is no secret that much of the African continent has been a disaster area since the end of colonial rule.

Country after country has suffered under a succession of greedy and bumbling rulers who have set up what some have called a "lootocracy." War and disease have broken down societies and infrastructures, creating huge numbers of penniless refugees.

But thanks be to God, the great spread of Christianity—especially Pentecostal Christianity—has been doing for Africa what the early Methodists did for England in the 1700s. Christ's People are providing hope and meaning; they are offering a way to reorganize shattered lives in a time of great distress.

There continues to be growth among the great African independent denominations that arose in the first half of the 1900s, but not as rapidly as Pentecostal/charismatic groups. Earlier sections of chapter 15 have briefly mentioned strong Christian movements that have swept out of Africa into other continents.

For a relatively unspectacular example of African church growth, take a fairly staid denomination like the Mennonites. This group has been in existence for five centuries and has done a lot of good for a lot of people but has rarely experienced wildfire expansion.

*Meserete Kristos* is the name used by Mennonites in Ethiopia. Beginning in 1952, it took them 20 years to reach a total of 1,000 baptized adults. Between 1972 and 1982 that number increased a commendable, but not sensational, five times. Then came a ten-year period of persecution when a harsh Communist government closed every one of their churches. Did these Ethiopian Mennonites survive a decade underground? More than that, they prospered and increased from 5,000 to 50,000! By February 2002, when they celebrated their fiftieth anniversary as a denomination, the number of baptized adults in Meserete Kristos had climbed to 90,000.[29]

The countries that form the top tier across Africa are strongly Islamic. Even counting those North African nations, the total population of the continent is now 48 percent Christian, compared to 41 percent Muslim. South of the Sahara, Africa is 60 percent Christian.

Archbishop Desmond Tutu is only one of several well-known leaders among Christ's People in Africa over the past century. Another noted Anglican archbishop in Africa was Festo Kivengere (1919–1988), who barely escaped with his life when the murderous dictator Idi Amin was ruling Uganda. Kivengere later explained why he wrote a book entitled *I Love Idi Amin:* "On the cross Jesus said, 'Father, forgive them, for they don't know what they are doing.' As evil as Idi Amin is, how can I do less toward him?"[30] Archbishop Kivengere is the co-founder of African Enterprise, a distinctively African effort "to evangelize the cities of Africa by word and deed."[31]

# Asia

The recent growth of Christ's People in Asia is perhaps even more remarkable than in Africa, considering that: Asia is the home of many great religions that have more strongly opposed the Christian faith than the more primitive belief systems of Africa. Furthermore, Asia was and is the home of China, the largest Communist country in the world.

Note these facts:

- In 1991 there were 12 known Christians in Kyrgyzstan. Today? 2,000+.

- In 1989 there were 4 known Christians in Mongolia. Today? 18,000.

- In 1959 there were 29 known Christians in Nepal. Today? 500,000.

And these:

- Of the world's 11 largest churches, 10 are in Seoul, the capital of South Korea—including the world's largest Methodist, Presbyterian, and Pentecostal congregations.

- In 1987 there were 2 churches in Istanbul, capital of Turkey. Ten years later? 16 churches. More Turkish New Testaments were sold in 1997 than during the entire prior decade.

- There are more Roman Catholics in the Philippines than in any single European country including Italy, Spain, and Poland.

- By 1999 the largest chapter of the Jesuit order was in India.

- In 2001 the leaders of 300 million Dalits (low-caste "untouchables") in India made a dramatic announcement: "The only way for our people to find freedom from 3,000 years of slavery is to quit Hinduism and . . . embrace another faith." Some have become Buddhists; others are seriously considering Christianity.[32]

In South Korea David Paul Yonggi Cho (1936–   ), pastor of the largest church in the world, has emerged as a key Christian leader. Each Sunday some 250,000 Koreans attend worship services at Yoido Full Gospel Church in Seoul. Yet humanly speaking all of this almost never happened, for in his teens Cho seemed near death from tuberculosis when a young Christian girl led him to become one of Christ's People. After recovering from his illness and graduating from a small Assemblies of God Bible school, he started a church in his own home. When it outgrew the house, he put up a tent in the yard. Even during Korea's harsh winters, church members often prayed all night. After six years the congregation had grown to 2,000, but then the young pastor collapsed during a worship service; he was almost literally tired to death.

David Paul Yonggi Cho (1936–    ),
pastor of the largest church in the world,
Yoido Full Gospel Church,
Seoul, South Korea

As he recovered once more, Pastor Cho felt God directing him to Exodus 18:13–26, where Moses' wise father-in-law advised him to share responsibility. Cho then set up a system of many small cell groups with hundreds of home cell leaders. By 1982 his congregation had planted nearly a hundred branch churches, sometimes spinning off as many as 5,000 people at a time. Yet the mother church itself could count over 600,000 members by the end of the century.

Throughout Asia traumatic events in secular history have helped to mold Christianity. Several examples follow.

In Cambodia from 1975 to 1979, the cruel Khmer Rouge dictatorship slaughtered a fifth of the population—nearly two million Cambodians, including most educated people and most Christians. By the year 1990 there were fewer than 600 Protestant believers left in Cambodia; yet by the year 2000 their number had increased to 60,000 or a hundred times!

After China and the Soviet Union, Indonesia once had the third largest Communist party. When Communism failed to take over Indonesia in the mid-1960s, a fierce backlash caused the deaths of hundreds of thousands of Communist sympathizers. This left a void in many people's lives—a void that only Jesus the Christ could fill. Muslim harshness, both in reprisals against leftists and in enforcing social issues, caused many Muslims-in-name-only to become Christ's People. At least 16 percent of the fourth most populous nation in the world are now Christians; among Indonesians of Chinese descent, the number exceeds 50 percent.

In 1979 the shah of Iran was overthrown by the Ayatollah Khomeini (1902–1989), an Islamic leader who became even more of a dictator than the shah. At that time there were only a few hundred Iranian believers from Muslim backgrounds. Since then, tens of thousands of Iranians have turned to Christ from the strictness of Islam. Perhaps half of these new Christians live in Iran itself; the rest are helping spread the Good News among Iranian refugees worldwide. An Iranian woman was heard to say, "I praise God for the Ayatollah. All I saw in that man was hatred, yet I was convinced that there must be a God of love."[33]

In 1978 the Soviet Union invaded Afghanistan, which had been closed to Christianity since Muslims killed or drove away the Nestorians a millennium before. Too many Communist soldiers from Muslim backgrounds started siding with the enemy, so Russian soldiers from Christian backgrounds were sent instead to become "cannon fodder." Many were evangelicals who shared the Good News with those around them. In Pakistan, war refugees from Afghanistan also met Christian aid workers who helped meet their needs. As a result of these two recent movements, there are now believers among the people of Afghanistan.

No other Asian country—in fact, no other country in the world—has seen a more dramatic turning to Christ than the People's Republic of China. In the mid-1900s when the Bamboo Curtain closed off Mainland China from the rest of the world, many people felt that Christianity had failed there. Indeed, the so-called Cultural Revolution of the 1960s and 1970s seemed bent on removing every trace of Christian influence. But then the Communist dictator Mao Zedong (or Tse-Tung) died in 1976 and his policies died with him. Since then Christ's People on the Chinese mainland have multiplied until there may well be close to 100 million Christians in China today.

What has fueled this explosive growth? A careful observer who has traveled widely in China suggests three reasons:

1. There is a vacuum in the minds and hearts of many Chinese people today; they no longer believe in Communism. Ideas and influences from the rest of the world are sweeping into China; along with much that is bad, the Christian faith is also attracting the attention of many Chinese.

2. Under the strict Communist rule of earlier years, Chinese people were afraid of their neighbors; they dared not say what they really felt or believed. In the loving, trusting atmosphere of Christian fellowships, Chinese people feel free to be themselves.

3. What is happening in China today proves that the age of miracles is not over. For example, there are far too many reports of divine healing among Chinese Christians for all of them to have arisen because of mistaken information or wishful thinking.[34]

The Chinese government has tried to get a handle on the wildfire growth of Christianity by promoting the official (and controllable) Three-Self Patriotic Movement. Yet the very term "three-self" indicates a form of Christianity that is at home on Chinese soil, since it stands for self-supporting, self-governing, and self-propagating (or self-spreading).

Most of Christ's People in China have been suspicious of government interference and so have preferred to gather in house churches or underground groups. Yet in some areas of China the difference between the two streams of Christianity may not be as great as some have thought: Certain Three-Self pastors also work with house churches, while certain former house churches have been given unofficial recognition.[35] At the same time Christians in other areas report ruthless crackdowns on unregistered groups.

Many stories are being told about Christ's People in China. Here are two examples:

In 1987 a man gave up his job in the city of Shanghai and went out into the countryside to preach. By 1988 he was pastoring churches in ten towns. By 1992 he was shepherding 90,000 believers in five provinces. By 1998 the movement he started had grown to half a million people in eight provinces, with an average of 548 new believers every day.[36]

Christianity first came to China via the silk routes across Asia (see the map on page 86). Some of Christ's People in China envision at least 100,000 Chinese missionaries taking the Good News back again from Beijing to Jerusalem, through the heartlands of Buddhism, Hinduism, and Islam.[37]

The spirit of Christ's People in China is reflected in the quotations in the adjacent box. With such a spirit, would it be too surprising if the greatest world leaders among Christ's People in this present century come from China?

## Voices of Christ's People in China

● Before 1949 we practiced Christianity in churches, and hardly anywhere else. After the persecution, we practiced it in our homes and therefore everywhere else.[38]
*–A pastor in Shanghai*

● It is true we cannot preach on the street; we have no broadcast or Christian newspaper. We live out our faith in our work, our families, and tell the truth to our neighbors. Everyone is a personal evangelist.[39]
*–Joseph Liu, an elder in Grace Church, Shanghai*

● We trust God to give us our land .... We must be patient. The power comes from God; ... nothing can stop God's power.[40]
*–Yu Xinli, a pastor/leader in the Beijing Christian Council and the Three-Self Patriotic Movement*

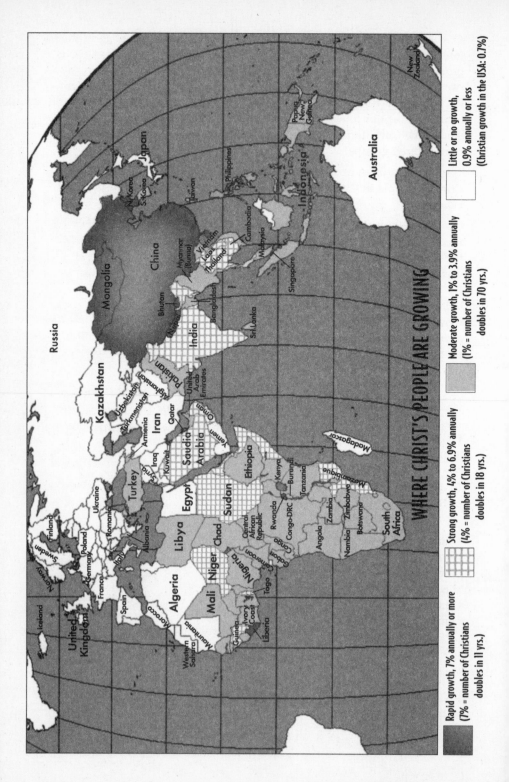

WHERE CHRIST'S PEOPLE ARE GROWING

Rapid growth, 7% annually or more
(7% = number of Christians
doubles in 11 yrs.)

Strong growth, 4% to 6.9% annually
(4% = number of Christians
doubles in 18 yrs.)

Moderate growth, 1% to 3.9% annually
(1% = number of Christians
doubles in 70 yrs.)

Little or no growth,
0.9% annually or less
(Christian growth in the USA: 0.7%)

EXPLORING CHURCH HISTORY

# KEY EVENTS

ᢒ

## 1950 TO 2000

Communists take over China; Christ's People there go underground.

C. S. Lewis writes popular books that set forth and strongly defend the Christian faith.

The end of colonial empires gives new strength to Christ's People in Asia and Africa.

Pope John XXIII calls for a new general council; Vatican II launches great changes among Catholics which are generally welcomed but also opposed.

Billy Graham leads great evangelistic campaigns.

Martin Luther King, Jr., and others lead the fight against racism in the USA.

A new charismatic movement arises in traditional churches; less controversial Fundamentalists become known as evangelicals.

In an anti-Communist backlash, many Indonesians become Christ's People; the writings of Alexander Solzhenitsyn expose the wrongs of Communism and include testimonies of Christian believers.

Leaders among Latin American Catholics fight for social justice; some of them become martyrs.

Billy Graham heads an International Congress on World Evangelization at Lausanne, Switzerland.

Communists commit genocide in Cambodia; 2 million people die, including most Cambodian Christians.

Pope John Paul II, the first non-Italian pope in 450 years, travels widely and exerts great influence.

Christ's People experience growth spurts in most of the world but disastrous decline in Europe and Oceania.

Fundamentalists and charismatics cause divisions in many churches and denominations; varying styles of worship also cause divisions among Christians.

In Seoul, South Korea, David Paul Yonggi Cho pastors the largest local church in the world.

Desmond Tutu and others lead the fight against racism in South Africa.

In North America, many older denominations decline, but growth among conservative churches more than matches this loss.

Communism crumbles in eastern Europe and central Asia; Orthodox Christians survive, but are slow to share religious liberty with others.

Christians in Communist China experience great growth, in both official and underground churches.

Immigration brings many Christians to North America but brings many Muslims to Europe.

Both Catholics and Protestants face shortages of ministers, but largely rule out women as pastors; Catholics also deny requests for married priests.

Genocide in "Christian" Rwanda wipes out 800,000.

Christians, especially Pentecostals/charismatics, grow in many previously unreached areas.

The number of short-term missionaries greatly increases, also the number of missionaries sent by Christ's People in Asia, Africa, and Latin America.

Fierce persecution of Christ's People continues in many parts of the world.

Christ's People are almost a majority of all Africans and a strong minority among Asians.

## Mother Teresa (1910–1997)

An Albanian nun, she ministered to the poorest in the streets of
Calcutta, India, and founded the Missionaries of Charity,
a new religious order.

# 16. TWENTY CENTURIES AND COUNTING: CHALLENGES
## (2000 AND BEYOND)

Change almost always brings challenge. This is especially true concerning Christ's People in recent years. As society in general and Christianity in particular have changed, Christ's People are faced with challenges unique to today. These challenges can be grouped into those from within and those from without.

## CHALLENGES FROM THE INSIDE

At 20 centuries and counting Christians are confronted with three internal realities: problems with leadership, divisions among themselves, and alternatives to these divisions.

### Leadership Problems

In recent years moral failures on the part of Catholic priests, Protestant youth pastors, and big-name television evangelists have been well publicized. Actually this is nothing new: There have always been Christian leaders who have proven unworthy of their calling. Yet today's leadership issue goes deeper than that.

Simply stated, here's the problem: Christians need many more leaders, both to shepherd believers and to spearhead mission advance into unreached areas. Yet many Christians are not ready to accept the kinds of leaders who may be available.

Catholics and Protestants are facing a shortage of ministers in many parts of the world. After the dramatic changes made by the Second Vatican Council, many men left the Catholic priesthood.

More recently, other priests have been removed from ministry because of scandals involving sexual abuse of children. Many Catholics believe the situation would be healthier if their ministers had the option of marriage, as is the case among most non-Catholic clergy. Many Catholics are also calling for acceptance of women priests. Yet thus far the Roman Catholic Church limits the priesthood to single males only.

The proportion of younger adults among Protestant pastors has dropped considerably in recent years. Seminaries are flourishing, but many of their students are either females or else older males looking toward a career change. Many younger male seminary students say they do not feel called to pastor local churches. Methodists started ordaining women as pastors in 1954, but relatively few other Protestant denominations have followed their lead; many Christians believe that the New Testament forbids female pastors. Thus the number of women educated for ministry is growing, but without a matching growth in leadership positions open to women. (The number of churches without pastors is growing too.)[1]

In many parts of the world, new churches are springing up faster than pastors can be trained to lead them. One obvious solution is accepting less-educated people as pastors while offering them on-the-job training. Newer initiatives such as theological education by extension have been effective in many places; yet older church leaders who receive their training at a regular seminary or Bible school have often opposed these non-traditional methods. These older ministers have been slow to give bi-vocational or part-time pastors equal status.

There are also differing opinions among Christians as to who should be a missionary. The number of Christian missionaries worldwide has greatly increased in recent years, yet these higher numbers may be misleading. Many groups count anyone who goes to another place and helps to spread the Good News there, even for such a brief time that the person never learns to speak the local language or honor the local culture. This tremendous growth in short-term missions has led to such negative expressions as "mission tourism" or "the amateurization of missions."[2]

Short-term missionaries no doubt do a great deal of good. They can take over certain tasks, thus freeing career missionaries to do other things they themselves cannot do. When short-term missionaries return home, they often become strong advocates for world outreach. Not a few Christians have gone first to do short-term projects, only later to seek a lifetime ministry in missions.

Despite all the pluses of short-term missions, the backbone of worldwide outreach still needs to be what it has always been: a dedicated corps of men and women who are willing to establish their lives in a place that is strange to them and to stay there long enough to make a difference. Even as God became incarnate on planet earth in Jesus the Christ, so missionaries need to become incarnate in foreign cultures.

A striking example of this kind of incarnational ministry is Agnes Bojaxhiu, a Roman Catholic nun from Albania who became known worldwide as Mother Teresa (1910–1997). Serving as a teenager in India, she first taught at a girls' high school but then started reaching out to the poorest in the streets of Calcutta. In 1950 she gained the pope's approval for a new religious order, the Missionaries of Charity. Mother Teresa and her coworkers ministered to throwaway children, leprosy (Hansen's disease) sufferers, and dying people with no one to care for them. Remembering Christ's words, she said that each of these unfortunates was "Jesus in disguise, . . . sometimes a most distressing disguise."[3]

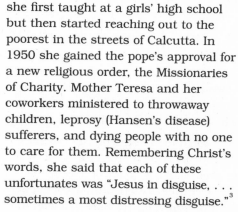

**Jesus of Nazareth**

Whatever you did for one of my brothers or sisters, no matter how unimportant they seemed, you did for me (Matthew 25:40).

Mother Teresa first became famous when a journalist interviewed her on British television in 1969. A book and film followed, both entitled *Something Beautiful for God.* When she died in 1997, the government of India ordered that she be given a state funeral. The quotation in the adjacent box captures something of the spirit of the little woman with the wrinkled face whose love and devotion touched people everywhere.

**Mother Theresa of Calcutta**

By blood and origin, I am Albanian. My citizenship is Indian. I am a Catholic nun. As to my calling, I belong to the whole world. As to my heart, I belong entirely to Jesus.[4]

Are enough women and men volunteering to serve as cross-cultural missionaries? Probably not. Too many church members tend to look at missionaries as holy oddballs. Not being fully convinced that followers of other religions are spiritually lost, such church members wonder why anyone needs to go and cause confusion by spreading the Good News.

Even among Christians who are convinced that Jesus the Christ is the only way to God, some are saying, in effect: *Why bother with going to other countries? Look at all the foreigners right here where we live! Look at all the needy people at our doorstep!* Certainly those who minister among internationals and meet human needs in their homeland are performing worthwhile and rewarding tasks; yet they are not the only kind of outreach leaders who are needed among Christ's People today.

# Divisions Among Christians

In one sentence Archbishop Desmond Tutu clearly stated a second major challenge facing Christians today: "The dividedness of the Churches makes it difficult for people to believe in the gospel of Jesus Christ." [5] For a quick example of what he meant, in North America alone there are 22 distinct branches of the Orthodox church, 36 kinds of Methodists, and 241 different Pentecostal groups. [6]

Can't Christians agree to disagree? Can't they diversify without causing divisions?

The answer to these questions seems to be: *Some Christians can; some Christians cannot.* Some of Christ's People seem to need the assurance that their understanding of Christianity is the only right way, for it is only with this kind of assurance that their faith can blossom and grow.

Chapter 15 tells how charismatic groups have arisen in traditional churches all over the world. Some of those churches have proved able to live with diversity; others have excluded the charismatics. Some of the charismatics themselves have become impatient with old-fashioned Christians; they feel that new wineskins are needed to contain their new wine (see the adjacent box). The result? Many new charismatic and Pentecostal denominations.

> ### Words of Warning
>
> Nor do people pour new wine into old wineskins. If they do, the skins burst, the wine runs out, and the skins are ruined. Rather, people pour new wine into fresh skins, and both are saved (Matthew 9:17).

In Chapter 15 we saw how Fundamentalists began to pull back from emphasizing their differences and by so doing, found they could work together; most Christians of this type prefer to be called evangelicals. Yet not everyone could go along with this movement away from divisiveness.

For example, when Billy Graham began working with all who claimed to be Christ's People, certain Fundamentalists refused to support him any longer. And during the second half of the 1900s, two of the more conservative American denominations were the Missouri Synod Lutherans and the Southern Baptists; yet certain Fundamentalists caused deep divisions within both of these already-conservative denominations.

What causes divisions among Christ's People?

### Divisions Within Society

Sometimes divisions among Christians are reflections of wider divisions within society as a whole. Starting in the 1960s there has been a revolution in thought and behavior among many North Americans. Lifestyles formerly frowned upon have moved into the mainstream.

Acts formerly condemned as sin are now commonplace. Many traditional Protestants have tried to adapt to this changed situation, but overall their well-meaning attempts have had two results: Mainline Protestant denominations have gradually shrunk in size, while more conservative churches—whether Fundamentalist, Evangelical, Pentecostal, or Charismatic—have grown.

The 1980s and 1990s were marked by a distinctly conservative swing in American politics. Adding strength to this change was a movement that came to be known as the Religious Right; among its leaders are:

- Jerry Falwell (1933–   ), pastor of a megachurch, who for a time headed an organization called the Moral Majority.

- Pat Robertson (1930–   ), who built up such a personal following with his Christian Broadcasting Network and his 700 Club that he even tried to run for president.

- James Dobson (1936–   ), a child psychologist and former university professor who founded Focus on the Family, rivaling the Billy Graham Evangelistic Association as an evangelical media giant.

Both Falwell and Robertson founded large Christian universities. All three of these leaders, along with others like them, have skillfully used television to promote their beliefs.

No one can fault high-profile Christians who stand up for truth and morality. Yet an unfortunate side-effect of this movement has been a tendency to seem to be saying: Unless you join the *right* political party, vote for the *right* candidates, and take the *right* position on certain social issues, you must not really be one of Christ's People.

### Divisions Over Worship Styles

Through the centuries Christians have come together for worship; yet worship itself has recently been causing divisions among Christ's People.

Starting in the 1960s the new charismatic movement tried to increase personal involvement in worship by creating many praise songs. These brief melodies, sometimes using words from the Bible, are usually repeated many times with much raising and clapping of hands. Many congregations have done away with hymnbooks, organs, choirs, and all other traditional aspects of church music. Instead, they project praise song lyrics on large screens; praise bands use guitars, drums, and other instruments, as praise teams lead the congregation in singing.

It is not surprising that this new approach to worship has little or no appeal to traditionally minded Christians. Strange as it seems, the movement away from hymns has arisen at the same moment when Christ's People are creating more hymns of better quality than they have done for a long time. Some churches have chosen to combine hymns and praise songs in what is known as blended worship. Other churches reject both the tradition of recent centuries and the changes of recent years: They have gone far back to Christian history and revived forms of liturgical worship.

Still other new streams of Christian music have recently been flowing. Each stream adds to the depth of worship resources available to Christ's People, . . . but at the same time differences may increase as to when and where it is appropriate to use which kind of music in worship.

Christians all over the world are writing both hymns and praise songs in their own distinctive styles; many of these are being translated and used in other countries as well. For example, the box on the facing page features a hymn text from Indonesia. Notice how in only three stanzas this hymn summarizes the whole story of humankind—our creation, fall into sin, redemption, and gathering in as Christ's People from every race and place. Notice also the hymn-writer's unusual name. This Indonesian pastor rejected the tradition of taking a new biblical name when he became a Christian out of an Islamic background. Instead, he stated: "Let it stand as a testimony that our Lord Jesus Christ can save and even call into the ministry a person with a name like Mohammed Syamsul Islam."[7]

Roger Schutz-Marsauche (1915– ), generally known as Brother Roger, is the son of a Swiss Protestant pastor who founded a joint Protestant-Catholic retreat center at Taizé in southeastern France. The Taizé community has produced a large number of biblically-based chants that repeat the same notes many times. These simple but hauntingly beautiful chants, along with quiet prayer and meditation, are now being used in worship services all over the world.

Commercialized Christian music has become big business. Many church choirs and soloists use taped accompaniments for their singing, with various kinds of orchestrations and electronic backgrounds. Some big-name Christian recording artists perform mainly for fellow believers; others are so-called crossovers, competing in the secular marketplace. Even during the economic downturn of 2001, sales of contemporary Christian music showed a strong increase.[8]

### Divisions Over Ethnic Conflict
Controversy over styles of worship, disagreements over doctrine and organization, and church splits, as bad as all of these are, cannot compare with the more serious kinds of divisions among Christians that keep turning up in the world news.

Why is it that places with large numbers of Christ's People also become places of war and ethnic cleansing? The world has watched in horror happenings in such places as Northern Ireland, Serbia and Croatia in Europe, Rwanda and Burundi in Africa, and Ambon and Timor in Indonesia. All of these places have had a strong Christian presence for many years, some even for centuries. If throughout those years Christ's People had lived and taught Christ's love for everyone—even for those who considered themselves Christ's enemies—would such bitterness and bloodshed have ever come to be?

Nearly three-fourths of all Rwandans claim to be Christ's People. Yet since 1994 when an intertribal genocide wiped out 800,000 people, the percentage of Muslims among Rwandans has doubled.

Of course Christ's People do not usually start the deadly cycle of killing, revenge, and then more killing. But they often do become victims. Statistics show that at least 160,000 Christians die for their faith every year. The correct figure may be twice that large, for many of Christ's People are attacked in out-of-the-way places that never make it into the evening news.[10]

## Alternatives to Divisions

Some of Christ's People have tried to opt out of divisions among Christians. What alternatives have they found? These include building megachurches, leaving churches, and ecumenical movements.

Some Christians have sought out megachurches, with sprawling buildings, multiple staff positions, and daily age-focused activities. Some of these huge congregations are completely independent; others claim some sort of denominational or associated relationship while developing and supporting their own programs. Many megachurches are led by a dynamic senior pastor who exercises a considerable degree of control.

No doubt these large fellowships have done much that is good and have brought many people to Jesus the Christ. *Yet thoughtful observers can't help wondering:* Are members of such churches echoing the rich young ruler in asking, "What must I do?" (See Mark 10:17.) Or are they asking, "What do I get out of this?"

Some Christians have tried to opt out of divisions among Christ's People by leaving churches entirely, yet without turning away from Christ. Books have been published in recent years with such titles as *A Churchless Faith, The Church and the Dechurched,* and *Exit Interviews: Revealing Stories of Why People Are Leaving the Church.* "Jesus worshipers" in many countries try to keep their roots in their own religious backgrounds, whether Hindu or Muslim, while avoiding any contact with organized churches.

Worldwide, researchers have classified more than 125 million people as "churchless Christians." *Yet thoughtful observers can't help wondering:* Are all of these believers really outside the church itself? Or are they only outside what is traditionally thought of as "the church"? [11]

Have Christ's People given up trying to overcome the many divisions among them? No, although the older ecumenical movement has weakened considerably after having reached a milestone with the founding of the World Council of Churches in 1948. Much of its support comes from mainline denominations, and as these have shrunk in numbers and financial resources, so has the movement itself suffered.

Many Christians also wonder whether this older ecumenical movement has gone too far in two directions: toward universalism, believing that everyone will eventually be saved whether Christ's People or not, and toward taking direct political action for social improvement rather than working together to spread the Good News.

The fact is, today there is not just one ecumenical movement, there are several. Throughout the past century many similar denominations have joined to form worldwide fellowships. For example, Baptists work together through the Baptist World Alliance, Lutherans through the Lutheran World Federation, and so on.

Dr. Billy Graham launched a broad ecumenical movement in 1974 with the gathering of the International Congress on World Evangelization at Lausanne, Switzerland. A covenant signed at this meeting states, "the church's visible unity in truth is God's purpose." [12] Since then many kinds of Christians—while making no move toward church union— have found that they can work together to carry out Christ's Great Commission.

There are many other examples of Christ's People from widely differing branches of Christianity working hard to lessen the divisions among them. Here are four:

David du Plessis (1905–1987), an Assemblies of God minister from South Africa, almost single-handedly brought Pentecostal Christians into contact with more than one form of the ecumenical movement. He was one of several Protestant observers who reached out to Roman Catholics by attending the Second Vatican Council in 1958–1963. He also made friends with the leaders of ecumenical councils of churches on various levels.

> ## Christ's Great Commission
>
> . . . All authority in heaven and on earth has been given to me. So wherever you go, make disciples of all nations: Baptize them in the name of the Father, and of the Son, and of the Holy Spirit. Teach them to do everything I have commanded you. And remember that I am always with you until the end of time (Matthew 28:18-20).

Since 1994 a small group of Roman Catholic and evangelical scholars have met occasionally and issued joint declarations, stating clearly where they agree and stating kindly where they disagree.

In 1996 Pope John Paul II stated that the office of pope itself ought to be re-examined, with the hope that it would become "more of a focus of unity, and less a stumbling block for other Christians." [13]

May 2005 has been set as a target date for the founding of Christian Churches Together in the USA, a new ecumenical fellowship "expected to encompass denominations from across the spectrum of Christianity." [14]

# CHALLENGES FROM THE OUTSIDE

At 20 centuries and counting, Christ's People are facing not only challenges from inside Christianity but from the world around them.

## Many Challenges

The following list of trends, perspectives, technologies, and world events summarizes an array of factors current-day Christians must confront:

- Secularism considers all religions irrelevant; the number of people who say they have no religion is on the rise. They hold a worldview devoid of God or gods.

- Materialism and consumerism are sweeping across many parts of the world; if making money and living the good life are most important, why do I need to think about spiritual matters?

- Relativism is driving the recent emphasis on tolerance. Since all truth is considered relative and nothing is thought to be absolute any more, if you try to tell someone what you believe about Jesus the Christ, you are not showing proper tolerance toward others.

- Globalization is offering Christ's People new ways to spread the Good News; at the same time it is breaking down cultural standards of behavior and traditional attachments to religious faith.

- Communication via Internet websites and chat rooms offer a new means of drawing Christians together and of connecting Christians with those who need Christ. (Do churches need new definitions of "attendance" and "participation"?) Yet at the same time the Internet is spilling out poisonous filth onto computer screens worldwide.

- Through genetic research, biotechnology offers the hope of a brave new world in fighting disease and prolonging life; yet many Christians are wondering just where they should take a stand, saying, "This you must not do."

- AIDS/HIV is already a global epidemic rivaling past plagues such as influenza and the Black Death; 20 million have already died, with 9,000 more dying daily. Furthermore, the illness has hit hardest in African countries where there are many Christians. Medical experts fear AIDS/HIV will get worse in such heavily-populated countries as Russia, China, India, and Indonesia.

- Communism, in its few remaining outposts (China, North Korea, Vietnam, Cuba), still stands as a bitter enemy of Christians— or indeed of anyone who believes in God.

- New Christian look-alikes have arisen to confuse many people; among them are Scientology, the Unification Church founded by the Korean leader Sun Myung Moon (1920–    ), and various destructive cults that subject their followers to brainwashing or worse.

- Hindu extremism shocked people worldwide in 1999 when it caused the martyrdoms of a missionary and his two young sons who were burned to death inside their car in India.

Each of these challenges could be explored in great detail in another text. In the scope of this book there is but room to mention them.

## Muslim Extremism

Probably the greatest of all outside challenges that Christ's People must face today is Muslim extremism. In many parts of the world Christians are under siege. The terrorist attacks of September 11, 2001 brought home to America the intensity and bitterness of Islamic hatred.

For many Muslims there can be no distinction between religion and politics, between private faith and public law and order. When movies and music videos show the slimy underside of American society, they tell their children, "This is what it's like in Christian America." When a Christian leader such as Jerry Falwell makes a statement critical of Islam, they start a riot, believing that the American government surely ought to have been able to muzzle him.

The conventional wisdom among many so-called scholars today is that Islam is growing much faster than Christianity, and that it is bound to become the world's largest religion sometime this century. Such predictions usually do not mention that Muslim growth in many areas is biological increase caused by an exploding population. Nor is anything said about the fact that Muslim men in many areas deliberately marry Christian girls (or get them pregnant before marriage); most such wives and almost all of their children then become Muslims.

Viewed on a worldwide scale, Christian growth is at least holding its own with Muslim growth. Despite scare-tactic headlines about the rapid increase of Islam in the United States, Muslims represent only a little over 1 percent of all Americans today.

Muslims like to present themselves as peaceful in places where they are in the minority, such as America. Things are quite different in places where Islam is in the majority. Consider:

Indonesia: Muslim officials can find countless ways to block building permits for new churches.

Saudi Arabia: Foreigners cannot legally conduct Bible study or Christian worship even in their own homes.

Sudan: The air force of the Islamic regime mounts bombing raids that deliberately target Christian hospitals, schools, and even churches during worship.

Northern provinces of Nigeria: There is a determined effort to force Islamic law on everybody, Muslim or not, including penalties such as stoning, beheading, or cutting off a hand.

Pakistan: A Christian's testimony counts half as much as a Muslim's testimony in a court of law. If the Christian is female, divide that by half again into fourths. Thus, if a Muslim man were accused of raping a Christian woman, it would take the eyewitness testimony of four Christian women to convict him. Also if a Muslim accuses any Christian of saying something bad about the Prophet Muhammad, the accusation is likely to stick.

The tension between Muslim extremism and Christianity is likely to increase. According to Philip Jenkins, a leading church historian, this increase will most likely occur in the following types of places where:[15]

1. Huge Muslim majorities exist, such as Pakistan, Bangladesh, and Saudi Arabia.

2. Large Muslim majorities exist but also strong Christian minorities that have a long history, such as Indonesia, Egypt, and Sudan.

3. Muslims and Christians are about equal in strength, such as Nigeria, Tanzania, and Ethiopia.

4. Large Christian majorities face growing Muslim minorities, such as the Philippines, Uganda, Germany, France, and Britain.

5. Most people are Christians (or secularists) but there are many small and prosperous Muslim communities, such as Brazil, Mexico, and the United States.

6. Places that used to be parts of the old Soviet Union, where Christian minorities may be asking the Russian Orthodox Church to help protect them against Muslim majorities.

If worst comes to worst, says Jenkins, future conflicts with Muslims could be greater than anything Christ's People have ever experienced in the past. He warns, "Imagine the world of the 13th century armed with nuclear warheads and anthrax." [16]

# WHAT'S AHEAD FOR CHRIST'S PEOPLE?

As we come to the end of our 20-century journey of exploring church history, we are faced with the greatest challenge of them all: What does the future hold for Christ's People?

Hopeful opinions from two trustworthy sources, one Roman Catholic and the other an evangelical Protestant, are expressed in the adjacent box. Even with such positive perspectives from Christian leaders, doubts may arise: Look at places where Christ's People used to be many and strong but later faded

## Two Views of the Future

Only love lasts forever. Alone, it constructs the shape of eternity in the earthly and short-lived dimensions of the history of man on the earth.

*-Pope John Paul II* [17]

Christians can hope because faith always reaches beyond earthly circumstances. Its confidence is in a person. And no other person in recorded history has influenced more people in as many conditions over so long a time as Jesus Christ.

*-Bruce L. Shelley, a leading church historian* [18]

away to virtually nothing—places such as Turkey and northern Africa many centuries ago, places such as Europe and Oceania in more recent years.

Such hard facts of history highlight a truth that all of us must heed:

### *Christ's People are always just one generation away from extinction.*

If those of us who are Christ's People today do not tell others the Good News of salvation, if we do not lead younger folks to follow Jesus the Christ, then after the passing of a single generation, the Christian faith will vanish like the dinosaurs.

This is a tough idea to face, but one that has been true all the way back to that first generation—to Peter and Andrew, James and John, Joanna and Susanna and all the rest who saw Jesus with their own eyes, heard him with their own ears. Every generation of human history carries with it the possibility that Christ's People will soon be no more.

Yet, let us remember what Jesus the Christ said to those first 12 followers: ". . . I will build my church. And the gates of hell shall not overpower it" (Matthew 16:18).

Christ's words have been proven true over and over again. Christ's way of worshiping is now 20 centuries old and still counting. Christ's People of every generation have succeeded in passing on their faith to the next generation.

Now it's our turn.

# KEY EVENTS

### 2000 AND COUNTING

Terrorist attacks in the USA emphasize the worldwide challenge posed by Muslim extremists.

Christ's People have spread faster and more widely than followers of any other religion in all of human history; they number nearly two billion world wide.

After the death of Pope John Paul II, Joseph Ratzinger of Germany is elected to be the 265th pope, taking the name Benedict XVI.

# ENDNOTES
~

## Chapter 2

1. Richard Lovelace, as paraphrased by George Marsden in "Christian History Today," *Christian History,* issue 72, p. 52.

2. Justin Long of the Global Evangelization Movement, as quoted by Craig Bird in "In Harm's Way," *FaithWorks,* vol. 2, #4 (July–August 1999), p. 19.

3. Adapted from *Christian History,* issue 27, pp. 12–15, taken from "The Passion of the Holy Martyrs Perpetua and Felicitas" in *The Acts of the Christian Martyrs,* tr. Herbert Musurillo (Oxford: Oxford University Press, 1972). Used by permission.

4. Ibid. "The Martyrdom of Polycarp" in *Documents of the Christian Church,* 2nd ed., Henry Bettenson, ed. (New York: Oxford University Press, 1963). Used by permission.

5. Quoted in E*erdmans' Handbook to the History of Christianity,* Tim Dowley, ed. (Grand Rapids MI: Eerdmans, 1977), p. 72.

6. Stephen Neill, *A History of Christian Missions,* 2nd ed., rev. Owen Chadwick (London: Penguin Books, 1964, 1986), pp. 46–47.

7. Patrick Johnstone and Jason Mandryk, *Operation World,* 21st Century Edition (Carlisle UK: Paternoster, 2001), p. 244.

8. T. R. Glover, indirectly quoted in Kenneth Scott Latourette, *Christianity Through the Ages* (New York: Harper & Row, 1965), p. 38.

9. *Christian History,* issue 64, p. 3; quoted from *Sayings of the Desert Fathers* as translated by Owen Chadwick in *Western Asceticism* (Philadelphia: Westminster Press, 1983).

10. Samuel Hugh Moffett, *Beginnings to 1500,* vol. 1 of *A History of Christianity in Asia* (Maryknoll, NY: Orbis Books, 1992, 1998, 2001), p. 54; quoted from J. H. Charlesworth, *The Odes of Solomon: The Syriac Texts Edited with Translation and Notes* (Oxford: Clarendon Press, 1973; reprint with corrections and added indices, Missoula MT: Scholars Press, 1977). Used by permission of J. H. Charlesworth.

11. Moffett, *Christianity in Asia,* p. 112; taken from S. P. Brock, tr., "The Martyrdom of Qndyr" in "A Martyr of the Sassanid Court," *Analectica Bollandiana* (Bruxelles, 1978), t. 96, fasc. 1–2, pp. 167–181.

## Chapter 3

1. Various translations of these famous words appear in many sources; see for instance Matthew A. Price and Michael Collins, *The Story of Christianity: 2,000 Years of Faith* (Wheaton IL: Tyndale House Publishers, Inc., 1999), pp. 68–69.

2. Adapted from the version of this ancient liturgy found in *Chalice Hymnal* (St. Louis MO: Chalice Press, 1995), number 31. Used by permission of Chalice Press and Christian Board of Publication.

3. Neill, *History of Christian Missions,* p. 51; Bruce L. Shelley, *Church History in Plain Language,* 2nd ed. (Dallas TX: Word Publishing, 1982, 1995), p. 157; B. K. Kuiper, *The Church in History* (Grand Rapids MI: Eerdmans, 1951, 1964, 1998), p. 55.

4. Quoted by Moffett, *Christianity in Asia*, from Nestorius, in a letter to John of Antioch, December 430, cited by F. Loofs in a collection of early fragments entitled *Nestorius and His Place in the History of Christian Doctrine* (Cambridge University Press, 1912), p. 29.

5. Paraphrased summary from Moffett, *Christianity in Asia*, p. 174.

6. Moffett, *Christianity in Asia*, p. 278, from *The Book of the Himyarites*, 9a, A. Moberg, ed. (London and Oxford, 1924), p. cvi.

7. *Ibid.*, 169.

8. Altered for clarity and modernity from *The Methodist Hymnal* (Nashville: The Methodist Book Concern, Whitmore & Smith, 1932, 1935, 1939); Neale's original translation is in the public domain.

9. *The Rule of St. Benedict in English*, ed. Timothy Fry, O. S. B. (Collegeville MN: Liturgical Press, 1981), pp. 69 and 73, as quoted in Mark A. Noll, *Turning Points: Decisive Moments in the History of Christianity*, (Grand Rapids MI: Baker Academic, 2nd edition, 1997, 2000), pp. 93–96. Used by permission.

10. Quoted by Moffett, *Christianity in Asia*, from A. R. Vine, *The Nestorian Churches: A Concise History of Christianity in Asia from the Persian Schism to the Assyrians* (London: Independent Press, 1937; Repr. AMS Press, 1980), p. 109f. Used by permission.

## Chapter 4

1. Of course these unworthy leaders among Christ's People had names, but in this work they will not be dignified by stating their names. The same thing applies to several other less-than-Christian characters in several parts of this book.

2. Reprinted here as it appeared (without further attribution) in *Christian History*, issue 63, p. 10.

3. Quoted (without further attribution) in *Christian History*, issue 54, p. 36.

4. From *The Primary Chronicle*, attributed to Nestor the Monk; reworded and abridged from the translation quoted in *Christian History*, issue 18, p. 11.

5. Altered for clarity and modernity from Neale's translation, which is in the public domain.

## Chapter 5

1. Adam of Bremen, *Bishops' Chronicle*, 1072–1076; quoted in Stephen Neill, *History of Christian Missions*, p. 92.

2. Paraphrased from Louis Bouvet, "The Rich Heritage of Eastern Slavic Christianity," in *Christian History*, issue 18, p. 27.

3. Nestor the Monk, "A Life of St. Theodosius," in *A Treasury of Russian Spirituality*, ed. G. P. Fedotov (New York: Sheed & Ward, 1948), p. 40.

4. Slightly altered from the *Admonition of Prince Vladimir Monomakh* as quoted by Bouvet, "The Rich Heritage of Eastern Slavic Christianity," in *Christian History*, issue 18, pp. 29–30.

5. Adapted from a paraphrase in Timothy Paul Jones, *Christian History Made Easy* (Torrance CA: Rose Publishing, 1999), p. 64.

6. Price and Collins, *The Story of Christianity*, p. 93.

7. As quoted in *Chalice Hymnal*, number 52. Used by permission of Chalice Press and Christian Board of Publication.

8. Paraphrased from Anselm's famous dictum as quoted in Jones, *Christian History Made Easy*, p. 67.

9. Ibid.

10. Paraphrased from the quotation in Bruce L. Shelley, *Church History in Plain Language*, p. 197.

11. Ibid., paraphrased.

12. Paraphrased from the quotation in Price and Collins, *The Story of Christianity*, p. 92.

13. Ibid.

14. Moffett, *Christianity in Asia*, pp. 504, 512, based on Kenneth Scott Latourette, *A History of the Expansion of Christianity*, vol. 1 (New York: Harper, 1937), p. 108 and on David Barrett, *World Christian Encyclopedia* (New York: Oxford University Press, 1980), pp. 3, 25.

15. John Mason Neale, *A History of the Holy Eastern Church* (London: Masters, 1847) 1:143, as quoted in Moffett, *Christianity in Asia*, p. 380.

## Chapter 6

1. Moffett, *Christianity in Asia*, pp. 401–402.

2. Kenneth Scott Latourette, *History of Christian Missions in China* (New York: Macmillan, 1929), p. 71.

3. Paraphrased from Moffett, *Christianity in Asia*, pp. 445–446, based on A. C. Moule, *Christians in China*, (London: SPCK, 1930), p. 129.

4. Bar Hebraeus entitled his book on church history *Chronography*, meaning the study of intervals of time.

5. Moule, *Christians in China*, p. 104, quoted by Moffett, *Christianity in Asia*, pp. 431–432.

6. Quoted (without further attribution) by Mark Galli, "When a Third of the World Died," in *Christian History*, issue 49, p. 37.

7. Quoted (without further attribution) by Caroline T. Marshall, "Catherine of Siena," in *Christian History*, issue 30, p. 9.

8. Price and Collins, *Story of Christianity*, p. 115.

9. These well-known words are paraphrased here from several different sources.

10. Paraphrased from Shelley, *Church History in Plain Language*, p. 200.

## Chapter 7

1. Quoted in *Christian History*, issue 30, p. 32, attributed to *Eerdmans' Book of Famous Prayers* (Grand Rapids MI: Eerdmans.)

2. Quoted (without further attribution) by Bruce L. Shelley, "A Pastor's Heart," in *Christian History*, issue 68, p. 32.

3. Altered from a quotation in Shelley, *Church History in Plain Language*, p. 232; attributed to Herbert B. Workman, *Dawn of the Reformation*, vol. 2 (London: ©1953, Epworth Press), p. 325. Used by permission of Methodist Publishing House.

4. Philotheus the Monk, quoted by Paul D. Steeves, "The Orthodox Church in Eastern Europe and Russia," in *Eerdmans' Handbook*, p. 313.

5. Written by Christopher Columbus in 1501 and quoted (without further attribution) by Kevin A. Miller, "Why Did Columbus Sail?" in *Christian History*, issue 35, p. 10.

6. From *Libro de las Profecias (Book of Prophecies)* by Christopher Columbus, first translated in 1991, quoted in *Christian History*, issue 35, p. 4; and by Miller, "Why Did Columbus Sail?" in *Christian History*, issue 35, p. 10.

7. Taken from Columbus' prologue to the official account of his first voyage, as quoted by Miller, "Why Did Columbus Sail?" in *Christian History,* issue 35, p. 12.

8. Readers who wish to explore further the complicated subject of what the Nestorians actually believed may want to read Moffett, *Christianity in Asia,* pp. 198–199, 248–250, 306–309, 507.

9. Quoted (without further attribution) in B. K. Kuiper, *The Church in History* (Grand Rapids MI: Eerdmans, 1951, 1964, 1998), p. 151.

10. Thomas à Kempis, *The Imitation of Christ,* Book 2, as quoted (without poetic lines) in *Eerdmans' Handbook,* p. 356.

11. Jones, *Christian History Made Easy,* p. 77.

12. Quoted (without further attribution, also without poetic lines) in *Eerdmans' Handbook,* p. 359.

## Chapter 8

1. Adapted from Philip McNair, "Seeds of Renewal," in *Eerdmans' Handbook,* p. 359.

2. Shelley, *Church History in Plain English,* pp. 238, 246.

3. Quoted words from Martin Luther and his contemporaries throughout this chapter appear with different wordings in many different places; among the sources most used are Shelley, *Church History in Plain English,* pp. 237–246; Noll, *Turning Points,* pp. 151–174; and *Christian History,* issues 34 and 39, passim.

4. There is considerable debate over exactly what Luther said at this climactic moment. The words recorded here are slightly altered from: Noll, *Turning Points,* p. 154; Shelley, *Church History in Plain English,* p. 242; and James M. Kittelson, "The Accidental Revolutionary," in *Christian History,* issue 34, p. 16.

5. Noll, *Turning Points,* p. 155.

6. *Christian History,* issue 39, p. 13.

7. *Eerdmans' Handbook,* p. 376.

8. All quotations in this box are found (without further attribution) in *Christian History,* issue 39, pp. 15 and 24.

9. Thielman J. Van Braght, *Martyr's Mirror* (Scottdale, PA: Mennonite Publishing House, 1951), pages 984–987; slightly altered from the quotation in Bruce H. Shelley, *Church History in Plain Language,* p. 251. Used by permission.

10. Frank A. James III, "It Was Both 'A Horrible Decree' and 'Very Sweet Fruit': Calvin on Predestination," in *Christian History,* issue 12, pp. 24–26.

11. Shelley, *Church History in Plain English,* pp. 256–257.

12. Ibid., p. 260.

13. Alister McGrath, "The Tradition Continues: The Distinctive Legacy of Thomas Cranmer, and the Anglican 'Middle Way' Today," in *Christian History,* issue 48, pp. 40–42.

14. Both quotations from *The Book of Common Prayer* in this box are taken from *Christian History,* issue 48, pp. 38–39.

# Chapter 9

1. Quoted (without further attribution) in Helen L. Kaufmann, *The Story of One Hundred Great Composers* (New York: Grosset and Dunlap, 1943), p. 2.

2. Quoted (without further attribution) by Caroline T. Marshall, "Teresa of Avila," in *Eerdmans' Handbook*, pp. 417–418.

3. Quoted (without further attribution) by Robert G. Clouse, "John of the Cross," in *Eerdmans' Handbook*, p. 420.

4. Quoted (without further attribution) by J. I. Packer, "Ignatius of Loyola," in *Eerdmans' Handbook*, p. 411.

5. Alessandro Valignano, quoted in Shelley, *Church History in Plain English*, p. 280; see also Neill, *History of Christian Missions*, pp. 134–135,139.

6. Abridged and reworded from two different translations of Montesinos' sermon, as quoted (respectively) in Neill, *History of Christian Missions*, p. 145, and Justo L. González, "Lights in the Darkness," in *Christian History*, issue 35, pp. 32–34.

7. Eugene A. Nida, *God's Word in Man's Language* (New York: Harper & Brothers, 1952), p. 94.

# Chapter 10

1. William N. McElrath, *Kinfolks* (self-published, 1999), pp. 143–144, based on *THE CLOUD OF WITNESSES for the Royal Prerogatives of Jesus Christ: Being the Last Speeches and Testimonies of Those Who Have Suffered for the Truth in Scotland Since the Year 1680* (1st ed., 1714; 15th ed., reprinted 1989). Used with permission.

2. George B. Woods, Homer A. Watt, and George K. Anderson, eds. *The Literature of England: An Anthology and a History*, (Chicago, Atlanta, Dallas, and New York: Scott, Foresman and Co., 1936, rev. ed. 1941) vol. 1, p. 647.

3. Shelley, *Church History in Plain English*, p. 307.

4. John Robinson, slightly modernized from the quotation in Shelley, *Church History in Plain Language*, p. 305.

5. Slightly altered from a translation by Jesse Edgar Middleton, 1926; © Frederick Harris Music Co Ltd., in *Chalice Hymnal* (St. Louis: Chalice Press, 1995), number 166. Used by permission.

6. Abridged and slightly modernized from the quotation in a leaflet published by Christian History Institute in 1991, *Glimpses* #20.

7. Abridged and slightly modernized from the quotation in a leaflet published by Christian History Institute in 1991, *Glimpses* #22.

8. Jones, *Christian History Made Easy*, p. 106; see also *Christian History*, issue 41, p. 34.

9. Slightly abridged, with modernized spelling and punctuation, from "An excerpt from the diary of Cotton Mather, February 1684," in *Christian History*, issue 41, p. 18.

10. The first three quotations from Pascal in this box appear (without further attribution) in *Eerdmans' Handbook*, p. 485.

11. Quoted (without further attribution) by Price and Collins, *The Story of Christianity*, p. 159.

12. Quoted (without further attribution) by William Bright, *Jesus and the Intellectual*, (Campus Crusade for Christ International: Arrowhead Springs, San Bernardino, CA, 1968).

## Chapter 11

1. Adelle Banks, Religion News Service, in *Western Recorder*, July 16, 2002, p. 15.

2. Quoted in Wallace Brockway and Herbert Weinstock, *Men of Music: Their Lives, Times, and Achievements* (New York: Simon and Schuster, 1939, 1950), p. 78.

3. See, for instance, *Christian History*, issue 31, passim.

4. Quoted (without further attribution) in Price and Collins, *The Story of Christianity*, p. 171.

5. See, for instance, Noll, *Turning Points*, p. 232; also *Christian History*, issue 10, p. 3.

6. *Christian History*, issue 1, pp. 7–9, 31–35.

7. J. Herbert Kane, *A Concise History of the Christian World Mission* (Grand Rapids MI: Baker Book House, 1978), p. 80.

8. Quoted (without further attribution) in *Christian History*, issue 2, p. 4.

9. Quoted (without further attribution) in *Christian History*, issue 69, p. 41.

10. Elsie G. Harrison, *Son to Susanna* (R. West, 1937).

11. Quoted (without further attribution) in Shelley, *Church History in Plain English*, p. 337.

12. Spelling and punctuation modernized from the quotation (without further attribution) in *Christian History*, issue 62, p. 38.

13. Quoted as Carey's spoken words "at Kettering" (the town in England where Carey and his fellow Baptists founded a new missionary society) in *Christian History*, issue 1, p. 13.

## Chapter 12

1. Submitted excerpt from p. 445, from *The Great Century: Northern Africa and Asia* (Vol VI of *A History of the Expansion of Christianity by Kenneth Scott Latourette*. Copyright 1944 by Harper & Row, renewed ©1972 by Hazen Y. Mathewson. Reprinted by permission of HarerCollins Publishers Inc.

2. Originally titled *The Lives of The Three Mrs. Judsons* by Arabella W. Stuart, first published 1851. Now reprinted as *The Three Mrs. Judsons*, ed. Gary W. Long (Springfield MO: Particular Baptist Press, 1999).

3. Genesis 8:22: "As long as the earth exists, planting and harvesting, cold and heat, summer and winter, day and night will never stop" *(God's Word)*.

4. Latourette, *A History of Christian Missions in China*, pp. 824–825.

5. Based on lists in J. Herbert Kane, *A Concise History of the Christian World Mission*, pp. 161–172.

6. Quoted (without further attribution) in Price and Collins, *The Story of Christianity*, p. 188.

## Chapter 13

1. Quoted in *Christian History*, issue 53, p. 32.

2. Quoted in *Christian History*, issue 26, p. 9, from Allan Satterlee, *Notable Quotables: A Compendium of Gems from Salvation Army Literature* (Atlanta GA: The Salvation Army). Used by permission.

3. Reworded from Timothy K. Beougher, "Did You Know?" in *Christian History*, issue 45, p. 3.

4. Quoted (without further attribution) by Ted Olsen, "By Any Means Necessary," in *Christian History*, issue 62, p. 21.

5. Quoted (without further attribution) in Arthur Huff Fauset, *Sojourner Truth: God's Faithful Pilgrim* (Chapel Hill NC: University of North Carolina Press, 1938), p. 123. Used by permission.

6. Quoted (without further attribution) by Jacqueline Bernard, *Journey Toward Freedom, the Story of Sojourner Truth* (New York: W. W. Norton and Co., 1967), pp. 251–252. Used by permission.

7. See Mark A. Noll, "The Puzzling Faith of Abraham Lincoln," in *Christian History*, issue 33, pp. 10–15; Preston Jones, "Whence the Evangelical Mind?" in *Touchstone*, May 2003, pp. 45–46; Richard Carwardine, "The Wisest Radical of Them All," in *Books & Culture*, July–August 2003, pp. 20–21, 36–37.

8. All three of these quotations from Charles Journeycake appear in William N. McElrath, *Bold Bearers of His Name: 40 World Mission Stories* (Nashville TN: Broadman Press,1987), pp. 87–88. Used by permission.

9. Price and Collins, *The Story of Christianity*, p. 196.

10. William J. Coleman, *Latin-American Catholicism: A Self Evaluation* (Maryknoll NY: Maryknoll Publications, 1958), p. 3.

11. William N. McElrath, *To Be the First: Adventures of Adoniram Judson, America's First Foreign Missionary* (Lewisville TX: Accelerated Christian Education, Inc.,1994), p. 79. Used by permission.

12. Ruth A. Tucker, *From Jerusalem to Irian Jaya: A Biographical History of Christian Missions* (Grand Rapids MI: Zondervan, 1983), p. 134.

13. "From Greenland's Icy Mountains" in *The Broadman Hymnal* (Nashville TN: Broadman Press, 1940), number 35; in the public domain.

14. Quoted (without further attribution) in Neill, *History of Christian Missions*, p. 266.

## Chapter 14

1. Ruth A. Tucker, *From Jerusalem to Irian Jaya, A Biographical History of Christian Missions* (Grand Rapids MI: Zondervan, 1983), p. 269.

2. Heinrich Himmler, quoted (without further attribution) in Price and Collins, *The Story of Christianity*, p. 211.

3. Quoted (without further attribution) in Price, p. 206.

4. Shelley, *Church History in Plain Language*, p. 419.

5. Kenneth Scott Latourette, *Christianity Through the Ages* (New York: Harper & Row, 1965), pp. 280–281.

6. Craig Bird, "In Harm's Way," *FaithWorks*, July–August 1999, p. 19.

7. Latourette, p. 266.

8. Quoted (without further attribution) in *Church History*, issue 32, p. 20.

9. Taken from differing translations of Bonhoeffer's words in Timothy Paul Jones, *Christian History Made Easy* (Torrance CA: Rose Publishing, 1999), p. 135, and *Christian History*, issue 32, pp. 12, 13, and 29.

10. William N. McElrath, *Bold Bearers of His Name: 40 World Mission Stories* (Nashville TN: Broadman, 1987), p. 243; used by permission.

11. *Songs from the Slums*, interpreted by Lois J. Erickson (New York and Nashville: Abingdon-Cokesbury, 1935), p. 81.

12. Both quotations from the Niebuhr brothers are available in many sources; they are quoted here from Jones, pp. 128–129.

13. Reworded from B. K. Kuiper, *The Church in History* (Grand Rapids MI: Eerdmans/CSI, 1952, 1964, 1998), p. 388.

14. *Christian History*, issue 65, p. 19.

15. McElrath, pp. 139–143. Used by permission.

16. John T. Seamands, *Pioneers of the Younger Churches* (New York and Nashville: Abingdon, 1967), p. 180.

17. McElrath, page 27; used by permission.

18. Jamie Buckingham, *Into the Glory* (Plainfield NJ: Logos, 1974), p. 21.

19. All of these quotations from G. K. Chesterton are found in *Christian History*, issue 75, pp. 12, 40, and 17, respectively; some of the quotations are attributed to specific writings and others are not.

20. Latourette, *A History of the Expansion of Christianity*, vol. 7 (New York: Harper & Brothers, 1945).

## Chapter 15

1. Statistics taken from Patrick Johnstone and Jason Mandryk, *Operation World, 21st Century Edition* (Carlisle UK: Paternoster, 2001), p. 2.

2. These brief quotations appear (without further attribution) in Bruce L. Shelley, *Church History in Plain Language* (Dallas TX: Word, second edition, 1995), pp. 452–453, and in *Christian History*, issue 65, pp. 30–31.

3. Johnstone and Mandryk, p. 540.

4. Patrick Johnstone, *The Church Is Bigger Than You Think* (Pasadena CA: William Carey Library, 1998), pp. 126–127.

5. Timothy Paul Jones, *Christian History Made Easy* (Torrance CA: Rose Publishing, 1999), p. 137.

6. *Operation Reveille Shofar* newsletter, March–April 2000, pp. 2–3.

7. Quoted (without further attribution) in *Christian History*, issue 65, p. 38.

8. Statistics and estimates from several sources, especially David Barrett in *World Christian Encyclopedia* and other publications, also Philip Jenkins, *The Next Christendom: The Coming of Global Christianity* (Oxford UK: Oxford University, 2002).

9. Johnstone and Mandryk p.7, and *World Pulse* newsletter, December 1, 2000, p. 7.

10. Judy Douglass, editor, and Ron Londen, senior writer, *Until Everyone Has Heard*, Campus Crusade for Christ, 2001, p. 96.

11. Johnstone and Mandryk, pp. 748–751.

12. Based on a quotation from Mark Noll in *First Things* magazine, April 2002, p. 81.

13. Quoted from *The Problem of Pain* in *Eerdmans' Handbook to the History of Christianity*, Tim Dowley, editor (Grand Rapids MI: Eerdmans, 1977), p. 605.

14. Quoted from *Reflections on the Psalms* by Dowley, p. 605.

15. Quoted (without further attribution) in Price and Collins, *The Story of Christianity*, p. 209.

16. Philip Jenkins, reviewing David Martin, *Pentecostalism: The World Their Parish* (Blackwell, 2002), in *Books & Culture*, March–April 2002, p. 33.

17. *Missions Mosaic*, August 2002, p. 37.

18. Johnstone and Mandryk, p. 256.

19. Ibid., p. 527.

20. Ibid., p. 64.

21. Ibid., p. 537.

22. Ibid., p. 268; *Baptist World*, April–June 2002; *World Pulse* newsletter, September 20, 2002, p. 2.

23. From Philip Jenkins, *The Next Christendom: The Coming of Global Christianity* (Oxford UK: Oxford University, 2002) in a book review by Mark A. Noll, *Books & Culture*, March–April 2002, p. 32.

24. John G. Stackhouse, Jr., reviewing Reginald W. Bibby, *Restless Gods: The Renaissance of Religion in Canada* (Stoddart, 2002), in *Books and Culture*, November–December 2002, pp. 20–21.

25. Price and Collins, *The Story of Christianity: 2,000 Years of Faith* (Wheaton IL: Tyndale, 1999), p. 196.

26. From an *Agence France Presse* news release on the Internet announcing Camara's death, August 29, 1999.

27. Shelley, p. 465.

28. David Martin, in a multiple book review article entitled "Africa: A Mission Accomplished?" in *Books & Culture*, November–December 2002, p. 15.

29. Donald R. Jacobs, who attended the February 2002 celebration, in *World Pulse* newsletter, May 24, 2002, p. 6.

30. Quoted from "Festo Kivengere, Africa's Apostle of Love," an Internet press release.

31. Price and Collins, p. 223.

32. Quoted from an Internet news release dated October 1, 2001, sent by the All India Christian Council, the largest evangelical network in India.

33. Johnstone, *The Church Is Bigger Than You Think*, p. 123.

34. Chan Kim–Kwong, co-author (with Alan Hunter) of *Protestantism in Contemporary China* (Cambridge, 1994), in *Christian History,* issue 53, pp. 42–44.

35. Ibid., pp. 42–44

36. Credited to Alex Buchan in *Operation Reveille Shofar* newsletter, December 1, 1999, p. 6.

37. *World Pulse* newsletter, August 6, 2004, p. 6; also www.backtojerusalem.com.

38. Quoted in *Operation Reveille Shofar* newsletter, December 1, 1999, p. 6.

39. Quoted in *CBF Fellowship* newsletter, September 2002, p. 7.

40. Ibid., p. 7.

## Chapter 16

1. Andrew Black, "The Pastor Gap" (and related articles) on the website of *FaithWorks* (www.faithworks.com); Cindy George, "Woman's Place: The Pulpit," *The News & Observer*, Raleigh NC, November 11, 2002, page B-1.

2. Marshall Allen, "Mission Tourism?" (and related articles) on the website of *FaithWorks* magazine (loc. cit.); "amateurization of missions" is a term used by (and perhaps coined by) Dr. Ralph Winter.

3. Quoted (without further attribution) in Philip Yancey, *Soul Survivor* (New York, Toronto, Sydney, Auckland: Doubleday, 2001), p. 157.

4. Quoted (without further attribution) in *Christian History*, issue 65, p. 21.

5. Quoted (without further attribution) in Price and Collins, *The Story of Christianity*, p. 226.

6. Philip Gleason's review of Mark A. Noll, *The Old Religion in a New World: The History of North American Christianity* (Grand Rapids MI: Eerdmans, 2002), in *First Things*, June–July 2002, p. 59.

7. Based on the author's personal first-hand knowledge.

8. Lou Carlozo of the *Chicago Tribune*, reprinted in *The News & Observer*, Raleigh NC, November 1, 2002, p. 6-E.

9. Mohammed Syamsul Islam, 1977; translation by William N. McElrath; all rights reserved; used by permission.

10. Craig Bird quoting David Barrett, "In Harm's Way," FaithWorks, July–August 1999, p. 19.

11. Craig Bird, "A Churchless Faith," in *FaithWorks*, September–October 2002, pp. 4–8; Stanley Grenz, "Post-Congregational but Not Post-Communal," *loc. cit.;* David Barrett, *World Christian Encyclopedia* (Oxford UK: Oxford University Press, 2001).

12. Bruce L. Shelley, *Church History in Plain Language*, p. 449.

13. Price and Collins, p. 228.

14. *Baptists Today*, August 2004, p. 3.

15. Summarized from Philip Jenkins, *The Next Christendom*, in a book review by Mark A. Noll, *Books & Culture*, March–April 2002, p. 33.

16. Quoted by William Bole, Religion News Service, in *Baptists Today*, July 2002, p. 26.

17. Quoted (without further attribution) in Price and Collins, p. 229.

18. Shelley, p. 494.

# GLOSSARY OF TERMS

## A

**Abbess:** Director of a convent or spiritual retreat center for women.

**Abbot:** Director of a monastery or spiritual retreat center for men.

**Albigenses:** See Cathars.

**Ancient Church of the East:** Name preferred by Nestorian Christians.

**Apostles:** "Sent-out ones," a name Jesus gave to his 12 closest disciples. The name has since been given to others who go out sharing the gospel, such as Paul, Apostle to the Gentiles or Anskar, Apostle of the North.

**Apostles' Creed:** A simple statement of what Christ's People believe; it dates from early Christian history but does not actually go back to the time of the first 12 apostles.

## B

**Byzantine:** Referring to the eastern half of the Roman Empire, which continued for a thousand years after the western half came to an end.

## C

**cardinals:** "Hinges," a name given to certain important bishops of the Roman Catholic Church as decisions turn upon them like a door on its hinges. Cardinals elect each new pope.

**Cathars:** Literally, "Pure ones"; Christian look-alikes in Europe during the 1100s and 1200s who believed in two gods and considered Jesus a phantom, not God in human form; also called Albigenses (after the French city of Albi).

**catholic church:** "General" or "universal" church including all who profess Jesus the Christ.

**Catholic Church:** See Roman Catholic Church. A name used for Christ's People early in their history to distinguish them from Christian splinter groups.

**Catholic Reformation:** A movement of major changes in the Roman Catholic Church beginning in the mid-1500s, mainly in response to the Protestant Reformation.

**Charismatic:** Term describing Christ's People who emphasize the "charisma," or anointing by the Holy Spirit.

**Coptic Church:** The most ancient group among Christ's People in Egypt, named after an old form of the word "Egyptic"; similar in beliefs and practices to the Eastern Orthodox Church.

**Councils:** Policy conferences called by the pope. Decisions made by Councils in the first few centuries of Christianity are recognized by most Christians—Catholic, Orthodox, and Protestant. Actions taken by later Councils apply only to the Roman Catholic Church.

**Crusades:** European military campaigns mounted to seize control of the Middle East from Muslims.

**Cyrillic script:** A system of writing Slavonic languages that was developed during the 800s by Cyril, a Christian missionary; Cyrillic script is still used today for Russian and other languages.

## D

**Dominicans:** Members of a monastic order of Roman Catholic friars founded by Dominic in the early 1200s.

## E

**Eastern Orthodox Church:** General term for several groups of Christ's People, mostly in eastern Europe and Russia, who gradually broke away from Roman Catholics between the 300s and the 1200s.

**ecumenical:** Term describing various movements among Christians to bring Christ's People closer together.

**evangelical:** Term describing Christ's People who emphasize spreading the Good News ("evangel") to those who have not yet heard it or responded to it.

**excommunicate:** To state that a certain person is no longer considered to be one of Christ's People, to be shunned by all Christians and losing all privileges of church membership.

## F

**Franciscans:** Members of a monastic order of Roman Catholic friars founded by Francis of Assisi in the early 1200s.

**friars:** "Brothers," a term for monks (such as Dominicans or Franciscans) who wandered from place to place serving human needs rather than staying in a monastery.

**Fundamentalist:** Term describing Christ's People who emphasize certain "fundamental" beliefs such as inerrancy of the Bible.

## H

**heresy:** "Choice"; a belief which is different from that held by the majority.

**heretic:** One who chooses to follow a belief that is different from that held by the majority; those judged to be heretics have often been excommunicated, harassed, or even condemned to death.

**Hussites:** Followers of the martyred Czech Christian leader Jan Hus; they (and others) helped form the Moravians.

**Hvita Kristr:** "The White Christ," a Viking term used to distinguish Jesus from their old gods.

## I

**icons:** Images of Jesus, his mother, other Bible characters, and Christians of later times; after centuries of controversy Eastern Orthodox Christians finally decided to use icons in worship as "windows to heaven."

**indulgences:** Permission to be free from punishment for certain sins; some Roman Catholics sold indulgences for money, an act which helped trigger the Protestant Reformation.

**Inquisition:** System of Roman Catholic courts beginning in the 1200s, especially to root out so-called heretics; those leading the Inquisition became judge, prosecutor, and jury all in one.

**interdict:** To ban Roman Catholic worship throughout an entire area.

**Islam:** "Submission," the name used for a religion proclaimed by the Prophet Muhammad in the early 600s.

## J

**Jacobites:** Nickname for one of several ancient groups of Christ's People in the Middle East.

**Jesuits:** Members of the Society of Jesus, a monastic order founded by Ignatius of Loyola in the mid-1500s.

## L

**Lollards:** "Mumblers," a nickname for those John Wyclif sent out in the 1300s to explain the Bible to English-speaking people.

**martyr:** "Faithful witness," a name given to one who dies for the sake of Jesus the Christ.

**mass:** Roman Catholic worship service that centers around the Lord's Supper; derived from the Latin "*Missa est*" meaning "Go forth."

**Messiah:** "Anointed One," a Hebrew title corresponding to "Christ" in Greek.

**Missionaries of Charity:** Members of an order of Roman Catholic nuns founded by Mother Teresa in the mid-1900s, especially to serve the poor, sick, and dying.

**monastic order:** Monks, friars, or nuns who follow the same set of rules and are obedient to the same spiritual superior.

**monk:** A man who makes a lifetime commitment to sexual purity, obedience to his spiritual superior, and communal sharing of property; some monks live in monasteries (Christian retreat centers) while others serve in the everyday world.

**Moravians:** Protestant Christians from Germany and the Czech Republic who arose as spiritual successors of the Hussites.

**Muslims:** "Those who submit": followers of Islam, a religion proclaimed by the Prophet Muhammad in the early 600s.

# N

**Nameless Ones, the:** Nickname for the many unknown Christians who spread the Good News about Jesus throughout the Roman Empire before the year 300.

**Nestorians:** Nickname for several groups of Christ's People in the Middle East who for a thousand years were the most active missionaries among Christians. In smaller numbers today, they prefer to be known as the Ancient Church of the East.

**Nicene Creed:** A statement of what Christians believe, formulated in its earliest version by the Council of Nicea in 325.

**nun:** A woman who makes a lifetime commitment to sexual purity, obedience to her spiritual superior, and communal sharing of property; some nuns live in convents (Christian retreat centers) while others serve in the everyday world.

# P

**Pentecostal:** Term describing Christ's People who emphasize gifts of the Holy Spirit, especially as shown on the first Day of Pentecost after the resurrection of Jesus.

**Pietists:** Protestant Christians who began during the 1600s to emphasize a closer relationship with God and other marks of spirituality.

**Poor Clares:** Members of an order of Roman Catholic nuns founded by Clare of Assisi in the early 1200s as a female counterpart to the Franciscans.

**pope:** "Father," a title once given to any bishop but later only to the bishop of Rome as the leader of all Roman Catholics worldwide.

**priest:** One who makes contact with God on behalf of others; a term that gradually came to be used for ministers among Roman Catholics, Eastern Orthodox, and other Christian groups.

**Protestant:** One who protests, a term given to Christ's People who came out of the Roman Catholic Church during or after the Protestant Reformation of the 1500s. Many Christian groups are included among Protestants, such as Anglicans (Episcopalians), Baptists, Lutherans, Methodists, Presbyterians, and Reformed (to name only a few). Pentecostals, charismatics, Fundamentalists, and evangelicals are groups of Christians that may be considered subsets of Protestants.

**Protestant Reformation:** A movement beginning in the early 1500s in reaction against certain beliefs and practices of the Roman Catholic Church.

# R

**Reformation:** See "Catholic Reformation" and "Protestant Reformation."

**relics**: Body parts or other objects believed to be connected with a dead Christian considered a saint; some Roman Catholics treated relics almost as objects of worship, and this practice helped to trigger the Protestant Reformation.

**Roman Catholic Church:** Those who claim to be direct spiritual descendants of the first Christians and who give supreme earthly allegiance to the pope as bishop of Rome; the largest group among Christ's People in the world today.

# S

**sacraments:** Baptism, the Lord's Supper, and certain other religious acts (a total of seven), believed by many Christians (especially Roman Catholics) to be ways of receiving God's grace.

**saints:** In the Bible, this term means those who are set apart as God's people. Among certain groups of Christians (especially Roman Catholics and Eastern Orthodox), "saints" refers to certain men and women who have been specially designated because of their goodness, godliness, or great achievement for the cause of Christ.

**Sleepless Ones, the:** Monks of the Studium (an Eastern Orthodox monastery near Constantinople), so called because they took turns praying and singing praises to God continuously.

## T

**Thomas Christians:** Several groups of Christians in India who claim origin from the ministry of the Apostle Thomas.

**transubstantiation:** Belief held by Roman Catholics that the bread and wine used in the Lord's Supper really become the body and blood of Christ.

## V

**Vulgate:** Translation of the entire Bible into the common or "vulgar" language (Latin) by Jerome in the early 400s.

## W

**Waldenses/Waldensians:** A Christian group founded by Pierre Valdes (Peter Waldo); sometimes nicknamed "Protestants before the Protestant Reformation" because they held certain Protestant beliefs as early as the 1200s.

**White Fathers:** Monastic order that sent many Roman Catholic missionaries to the African continent beginning in the 1800s.